VOICE OVER IP

ISBN 0-13-022463-4

90000

9 780130 224637

Prentice Hall Series In
Advanced Communications Technologies

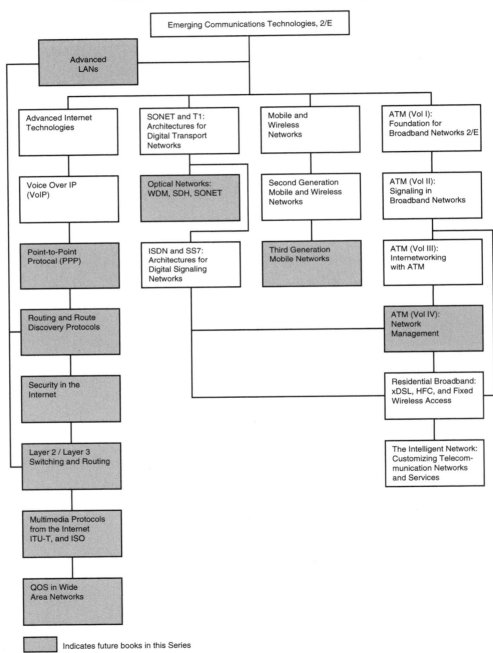

Emerging Communications Technologies, 2/E

Advanced LANs

Advanced Internet Technologies

SONET and T1: Architectures for Digital Transport Networks

Mobile and Wireless Networks

ATM (Vol I): Foundation for Broadband Networks 2/E

Voice Over IP (VoIP)

Optical Networks: WDM, SDH, SONET

Second Generation Mobile and Wireless Networks

ATM (Vol II): Signaling in Broadband Networks

Point-to-Point Protocol (PPP)

ISDN and SS7: Architectures for Digital Signaling Networks

Third Generation Mobile Networks

ATM (Vol III): Internetworking with ATM

Routing and Route Discovery Protocols

ATM (Vol IV): Network Management

Security in the Internet

Residential Broadband: xDSL, HFC, and Fixed Wireless Access

Layer 2 / Layer 3 Switching and Routing

The Intelligent Network: Customizing Telecommunication Networks and Services

Multimedia Protocols from the Internet ITU-T, and ISO

QOS in Wide Area Networks

Indicates future books in this Series

Voice Over IP

UYLESS BLACK

Prentice Hall PTR
Upper Saddle River, New Jersey 07458
http://www.phptr.com

Library of Congress Cataloging-in-Publication Data

Black, Uyless D.
    Voice over IP / Uyless Black ; editor, Mary Franz.
        p.   cm.
    Includes bibliographical references.
    ISBN 0–13–022463–4
    1. Internet telephony. 2. TCP/IP (Computer network protocol)
    I. Title.
    TK5105.8865.B53   1999
    004.6—dc21   99–31326
                                                                 CIP

Acquisitions editor: Mary Franz
Editorial assistant: Noreen Regine
Cover designer: Talar Agasyan
Cover design director: Jerry Votta
Manufacturing manager: Alexis R. Heydt
Marketing manager: Lisa Konzelmann
Project coordinator: Anne Trowbridge
Compositor/Production services: Pine Tree Composition, Inc.

© 2000 by Prentice Hall PTR
Prentice-Hall, Inc.
Upper Saddle River, New Jersey 07458

Prentice Hall books are widely used by corporations and government agencies for training, marketing, and resale.

The publisher offers discounts on this book when ordered in bulk quantities. For more information contact:

Corporate Sales Department
Phone: 800–382–3419
Fax: 201–236–7141
E-mail: corpsales@prenhall.com

Or write:

Prentice Hall PTR
Corp. Sales Dept.
One Lake Street
Upper Saddle River, New Jersey 07458

Printed in the United States of America
10 9 8 7 6 5 4 3 2 1

ISBN: 0–13–022463–4

Prentice-Hall International (UK) Limited, *London*
Prentice-Hall of Australia Pty. Limited, *Sydney*
Prentice-Hall Canada Inc., *Toronto*
Prentice-Hall Hispanoamericana, S.A., *Mexico*
Prentice-Hall of India Private Limited, *New Delhi*
Prentice-Hall of Japan, Inc., *Tokyo*
Prentice-Hall (Singapore) Pte. Ltd., *Singapore*
Editora Prentice-Hall do Brasil, Ltda., *Rio de Janeiro*

In memory of John and Katherine Schwartz,
and especially Bill Waters

I have chosen the parrot for the cover of this book because of its ability (at least as told in many stories) to be able to speak parts of a human language.

On several occasions, I have had an opportunity to listen to some of the utterances of a parrot, and on the whole, I found this bird's speech about equal in audio quality to that of a human's conversations over the public Internet during periods when the Internet is busy. I am being a bit harsh, because speech quality on the Internet varies. Sometimes it is acceptable, but some of the time it is not very good, and it is not "toll" quality.

Why is it difficult to understand the parrot's "speech"? And why is it sometimes difficult to understand speech over the Internet? The problem with the parrot is the bird's lack of a vocabulary, its inability to form phonemes, and of course its inability to know what it is uttering. The problem with the Internet is its long delay in delivering speech packets, its tendency to lose or discard traffic, as well as the variable delay in the delivery of the traffic to the receiving end user.

Then why is voice over IP (VoIP) a topic of widespread interest? The excitement is not because of the ability of IP to carry voice traffic, but rather because of the more general ability to carry voice traffic over data networks. IP just happens to be part of the picture because it is the prevalent forwarding protocol used in data networks.

The parrot will never improve its human speech capabilities unless DNA manipulation reaches new heights. The Internet will refine its ability to support speech traffic and is improving its "speech capabilities" almost weekly.

As you read this sentence, the Internet is being re-wired and reworked to support voice traffic. Eventually, the Internet and the telephone network will be one and the same. It is only a matter of time.

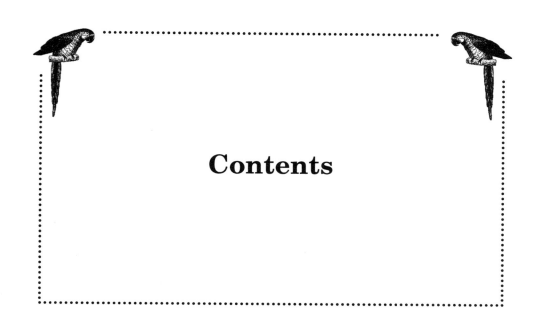

Contents

CHAPTER 2   **Characteristics of the Internet and IP**   **31**

CHAPTER 3   **Digital Signal Processors (DSPs)**   **52**

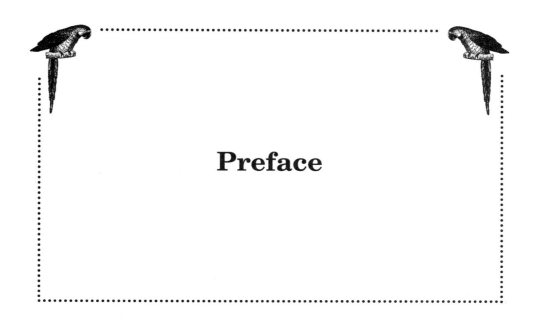

Preface

This book is one in a series of books called, "Emerging Communications Technologies." As the name of the book implies, the focus is on the Internet and private internets in relation to the support of voice traffic. The book is an expansion of *Advanced Features of the Internet,* also part of this series.

The subject matter of this book is vast and my approach is to provide an introduction to the topic. But in consonance with the intent of this series, this survey also has considerable detail but not to the level of detail needed to design a system. For that, I leave you to your project team and the various specifications that establish the standards for Internet telephony.

This book is an intermediate-to-advanced level text. As such, it assumes the reader has a background in voice and data communications and the Internet protocol suite. Notwithstanding, for the new reader, I have provided several tutorials, and I guide you to them in the appropriate parts of the book. I guide the more experienced reader away from them.

I hope you find this book a valuable addition to your library.

NOTES TO THE READER

In writing multiple books about data and voice communications systems, the author is faced with a question: How much overlap (redundancy of material) should there be among the books in the series? If the overlap is too little, the reader must buy other books in the series to fill the gaps. If the overlap is too great, the reader who has purchased other books in the series may feel cheated by spending additional money to obtain the same information.

My approach is to try to strike a compromise between the two extremes. If another book in the series contains information on a topic that is relevant to the topic of the current book, yet is not an impelling subject to know in order to read the current book, I make reference to the book. However, that is not always possible. In a few cases, it is necessary to include material from other books in the series. Otherwise, the book in question becomes a fragmented reference to other books. I have taken this approach with this book. I trust you find this an efficient and useful way to deal with this matter.

To help strike this compromise, I have included four appendices that are extracted from some of my other books. A basic knowledge of telephony signaling, the V.34 modem, ISDN, and SS7 will be very helpful as you read some of these chapters about voice over IP, and I have included tutorials on these subjects in the Appendices at the back of this book. I also have a tutorial on the V.34 and V.90 modems.

EXPLANATIONS OF MESSAGES AND PROTOCOL FLOWS

This book is a survey (albeit a detailed one) of the emerging VoIP technology. A wide variety of VoIP control messages and protocols are used to support VoIP, and the standards bodies and the Internet tasks forces are defining hundreds of messages and scores of protocol flows between VoIP gateways, call agents, and user machines. It is not the intent of this book to explain the contents of each message and each protocol flow, which would simply duplicate the VoIP specifications. Instead, I provide tutorial explanations of these messages and flows, as well as selected examples of each. In each case, I provide you references to the original specifications. In this manner, the book should provide you with a handy tutorial and reference tool, as well as a pointer toward more information if you so desire.

INTERNET DRAFTS: WORK IN PROGRESS

A considerable portion this book is devoted to explaining many Internet-based specifications pertaining to packet telephony. I had planned on waiting a year or so before writing about these specifications, but requests from my clients and publishers dictated otherwise. Indeed, some vendors are already writing code based on the specifications, even though they are not yet finished.

Keep in mind that the Internet Drafts are works in progress, and should be viewed as such. You should use the drafts with the expectation that they may change. Notwithstanding, if used as general tutorials, the Drafts discussed in this book are "final enough" to warrant their explanations.

For all the Internet standards and draft standards the following applies:

THANKS TO

I would like to thank four organizations for their contributions to this book.

First, Mier Communications provided two studies on VoIP products, and this information can be found in Chapter 8. I thank Mier for their excellent work. Second, Nortel provided me with valuable information on Nortel's One Meg Modem, as well as some of their emerging IP connect technologies, found in several chapters. Third, British Telecom (BT) has been a great help in their contributions on codecs. Fourth, the various Internet Task Forces have provided much of the information on the emerging VoIP protocols.

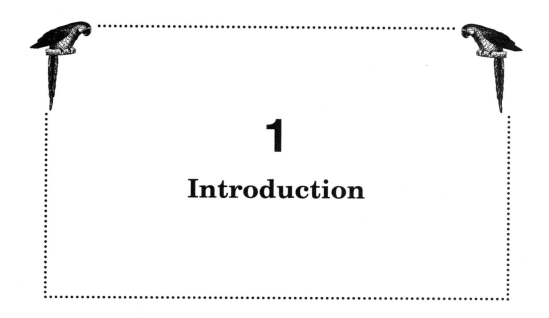

1

Introduction

This chapter introduces the reader to the Internet Protocol (IP), voice over IP (VoIP), packetized voice, and internet telephony. The chapter includes several sections. The first section explains why VoIP is of such keen interest to the industry. The next section explains the prevalent configurations for VoIP. The third section provides a brief introduction to the basic terms and concepts associated with IP-based packet networks, such as the Internet and internets. Following this overview, several key factors for the support of packetized voice in an internet are evaluated.

INTERNET TELEPHONY AND PACKETIZED VOICE

Voice over IP (VoIP) means the transmission of voice traffic in packets.[1] Several terms are used to describe this process. Unless otherwise noted, I will use these terms synonymously: Internet telephony, IP telephony, packet-voice, packetized voice, and voice over IP (VoIP).

---

[1] For the uninitiated reader, a packet is a small unit of data appended to a routing field. The packet may be variable in length, it can vary in its duration, and it is usually a few bytes in length. This approach is in contrast to telephony-based circuit switched data, which is always of fixed length and fixed in time (duration).

WHY INTERNET TELEPHONY?

IP telephony is viewed by some people to be an effective technology, and by others as nothing more than an irritant. The irritating aspect stems from those people who have used the public Internet to make telephone calls. In most cases, they are not happy with the quality of the speech and the overall ability of the Internet to support voice traffic.

Why then is VoIP of such keen interest to the communications industry, in view of its relatively poor performance in the support of voice traffic?

There are four major reasons for this interest, and for the deployment of IP telephony. The next part of this chapter discusses these reasons in this order:

1. The business case
   (a) Integration of voice and data
   (b) Bandwidth consolidation
   (c) Tariff arbitrage
2. Universal presence of IP
3. Maturation of technologies
4. The shift to data networks

The Business Case

The first reason is a compelling business case for the deployment of the IP protocol suite and associated equipment to support telephony services. This case can be summarized with three suppositions.

Integration of Voice and Data. First, clearly the *integration* of voice and data traffic will be demanded by multiapplication software resulting in the inevitable evolution to Web servers capable of interacting with the customer with data, voice, and video images. Text-only images with still-life photos will be a thing-of-the-past.

Bandwidth Consolidation. The next two suppositions stem from the first. The second supposition is that the integration of voice and data allows for *bandwidth consolidation*, which effectively fills up the data communications channels more efficiently. The telephony legacy of channelized voice slots, with the expensive associated equipment [channel banks, and data service units (DSUs)] are inefficient tools for the support of data applications.

The commonsense idea is to migrate away from the rigid telephony-based time division multiplexing (TDM) scheme wherein a telephony user is given bandwidth continuously, even when the user is not talking. Since voice conversations entail a lot of silence (pauses in thinking out an idea, taking turns talking during the conversation, etc.), using the data communications scheme of statistical TDM (STDM) yields a much more efficacious use of precious bandwidth. STDM simply uses the bandwidth when it needs it; otherwise, the bandwidth is made available to other talkers who need it at that instant.

To give you an idea of how wasteful the telephony TDM approach is, consider that about 50 percent of a normal speech pattern is silence (at least in most conversations). Voice networks that are built on TDM use bandwidth to carry those silent periods. Data networks do not. Furthermore, another 20 percent of speech consists of repetitive patterns that can be eliminated through compression algorithms. The conventional TDM operations do not exploit this situation.

Moreover, by using modern analog-to-digital operations, a high-quality speech channel can operate at about 4.8 to 8 kbit/s, in contrast to current TDM telephony channels that operate at 64 kbit/s. In the future, it is expected that the packet voice rate will be reduced further. Let's assume a 6 kbit/s rate for purposes of comparison. The bandwidth consumption ratio is 8:1 in favor of the packet-based method.

Other factors come into play that widen the gap even farther, and they are discussed shortly.

Tariff Arbitrage and Beyond. The third supposition regarding the business case is based on the concept called "tariff arbitrage." This term means bypassing the public switched telephone networks' toll services and utilizing an internet backbone. This approach avoids the costly long distance charges incurred in the tariffed telephone network in contrast to lower costs of the untarrifed Internet.

Some people believe that VoIP will not be attractive if or when the Federal Communications Commission (FCC) removes the Enhanced Service Provider (ESP) status granted to Internet Service Providers (ISPs). The effect of this status is that ISPs are not required to pay local access fees to use the telephone company (telco) local access facilities. There is no question that this status gives ISPs huge advantages in competing for voice customers, because access fees are the most expensive part of a long distance call. Table 1–1 reflects a study conducted by Merrill Lynch and available in [STUC98].[2] Access charges make up almost 50 percent

---

[2][STUC98] Stuck, Bart and Weingarten, Michael, "Can Carriers Make Money on IP Telephony?", *Business Communications Review*, August, 1998.

Table 1–1   Long Distance Cost and Profit Structure [STUC98]

	Cost per Minute (in $)	Percentage of Revenues	Percentage of Cost
Average rate	.140	100.0%	—
Access	(.050)	(35.75)	45.5%
Network operations	(.015)	(10.7%)	13.6%
Depreciation	(.010)	(7.1%)	9.1%
Sales, General & Administrative	(.035)	(25.0%)	31.8%
Total Cost	(.110)	(78.6%)	100.0%
Net Profit	.030	21.45	

of an interchange carrier's (IXC) costs for a switched long distance call. The other major costs are sales, general and administrative (SG&A), and network expenses (equipment, personnel, software, etc.)

Studies indicate (and common sense dictates) that the removal of the ESP status will certainly level the playing field to a great extent, and indeed, if this does occur, there will surely be less hype about VoIP. But the fact remains that even without this special status, conventional circuit-switched telephony cannot compete with packet-switched telephony on a cost basis. This fact stems partly from the concept of bandwidth consolidation and speech compression, discussed earlier.

Some studies that favor packet voice over circuit voice cite a 3:1 or 4:1 cost ratio advantage of packet voice over circuit voice. And that ratio is considered conservative by some people. James Crowe, CEO of Level 3, has stated that VoIP calls cost 1/27 of circuit switched calls.

Figure 1–1 illustrates a few facts and predictions from a study that compares the cost performance of telephony-based TDM circuit switches and data-based STDM packet switches [SCHM98].[3] The figure compares the rate of improvement in throughput of these switches, measured in bits per second (bit/s) per dollar. The study holds that packet-switching is a more cost-effective approach, and the gap between the two switching approaches will widen. The circuit switch vendors understand this fact, and all are going to migrate their TDM circuit switch architectures to STDM packet switch technologies. Asynchronous Transfer Mode (ATM) is the leading technology in this migration.

---

[3][SCHM98]. Schmelling, Sarah and Vittore, Vince. "Evolution or Revolution," *Telephony*, November 16, 1998.

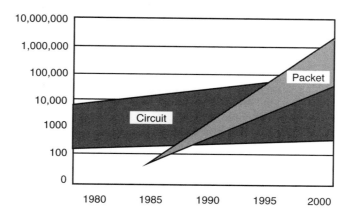

Figure 1–1   Cost Performance: Bit/s per dollar [SCHM98]

Those Who Disagree.   Not all people in the industry agree with the studies just cited. One of the most visible and vocal critics is Jerry Lucus [LUCA98].[4] Dr. Lucas sets out what he states to be ten myths about the issues (and blames these myths on the trade press). His first myth is the issue of cost that we have just discussed, and we know that the favored status accorded to ISPs certainly is an issue. But most of his other "myths" are straw dogs. A few of his straw dogs include: Myth 2: IP networks are more robust and reliable. Myth 3: IP telephony switch standards are now in place. Myth 4: IP over x Digital Subscriber Line (xDSL) is ready for mass deployment. I know of no knowledgeable person who makes these claims, nor do most of the trade journals!

Universal Presence of IP

The second major reason for IP telephony is the universal presence of IP and associated protocols in user and network equipment. Of key importance is the fact that IP resides in the end-user workstation (in contrast to potentially competitive technologies such as ATM and Frame Relay that operate as user network interfaces [UNI]). Figure 1–2 shows where these technologies are placed (the term packet switch in this figure is used generically, it could be a Frame Relay or ATM switch).

Make no mistake; the existence of IP in user personal computers and workstations gives IP a decided advantage over other existing tech-

---

[4][LUCA98]. Lucas, Jerry, "IP Myth vs. Reality," *Telestrategies*, September/October, 1998.

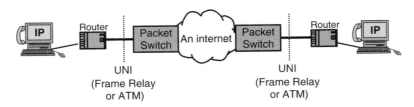

Figure 1–2   Location of IP vs. ATM and Frame Relay

nologies that are not resident in the user appliance. This "location" of IP makes it a very convenient platform from which to launch voice traffic.

Many people already use the PC to assist them in making telephone calls. Before long, computer-based telephony will be common, and will be a natural extension to the telephony system. Moreover, IP operates in both wide area and local area networks (LANs), whereas Frame Relay operates only in wide area networks. The issues surrounding VoIP, Frame Relay, and ATM are covered in Chapter 12.

Maturation of Technologies

The third major reason for the deployment of internet telephony is the maturation of technologies that now make IP telephony feasible. Much of this technology is supported by the wide-scale deployment of digital signal processors (DSPs), discussed in Chapter 3. The DSPs are found in codecs (voice coders and decoders) and high-speed modems. Their tailored operations and high-speed performance have opened the way for the support of applications that were unthinkable just a few short years ago. DSPs are now mass-produced, relatively inexpensive, and they are finding their way into many consumer appliances, even the new mouse you use with your PC.

Applications: The Next Revolution.   Another aspect of the maturation of technologies (or perhaps the maturation of expectations and demand) is the increased sophistication of user applications. The days are passing that end-users will be satisfied with browsers that retrieve and display text-only images. Increasingly, we will use applications supporting three-dimensional, real-time, voice, full-motion video, and data displays.

Indeed, whatever the skeptics say, we are witnessing the maturation of three key technologies that will foster a revolution in information technology. They are (a) the increased capacity of communications links, (b) the increased capacity of computers (CPUs), and (c) the advent of reuseable plug-and-play software code with artificial intelligence (AT) capabilities. The convergence of these maturing technologies will at last lay the groundwork for a new generation of user-friendly applications. And you will see the results of this remarkable revolution in a few short years in your browser package.[5]

The real challenge of today is not providing bandwidth and computer capacity. The real challenge is in managing, retrieving, and displaying (in milliseconds) information stored in databases throughout the world—information in thousands of places, consisting of billions of bytes, much of which is fragmented and not correlated to each other. I said during a recent lecture: "In today's society, knowledge is power, if you know where the bytes are stored." I would also add "if you know how to retrieve and display them to the consumer."

The Shift to Data Networks

Finally, the fourth major reason for the assured success of VoIP and other data networks is the fact that the world is experiencing a shift away from circuit-based networks to packet-based networks (data networks). Some market forecasts place the ratio of data networks-to-circuit networks at 80 to 20 percent by 2005.

WHY USE IP FOR TELEPHONY TRAFFIC?

But why use IP for telephony traffic? Why not use Appletalk, IBM's Systems Network Architecture (SNA), or some other protocol? IP is the chosen protocol for internet telephony because, as the mountain climber says, "It is there." IP is not a particularly attractive protocol for telephony, because it was designed to transport data traffic. However, its universal presence in PCs, servers, and workstations makes it a logical and convenient platform for the support of telephony traffic.

However, IP is only one part of the overall technology. When someone says, "I am using voice over IP," the sentence means much more than just placing voice signals into the IP packets. (A more suitable term for an IP packet is IP datagram, but I use both terms in this book in accordance with industry practice.) The VoIP platform encompasses a vast ensemble of technologies and protocols. As you read this book, I will intro-

---

[5]This prediction is based on the assumption that this capacity will be pushed out to the local loop to the consumer, and not just reside inside the network.

duce them to you. As a brief precusor, VoIP cannot deliver effective speech images by itself. It needs the Real Time Protocol (RTP), the Media Gateway Control Protocol (MGCP), the Resource Reservation Protocol (RSVP), H.323, and many others to provide a "VoIP Platform" to the user. And it cannot be deployed on a mass scale until it incorporates telephony call features, such as caller ID, call forwarding, etc.

BARRIERS TO SUCCESSFUL DEPLOYMENT OF IP TELEPHONY

It is the view of many that IP telephony (and voice over other data networks) is a given because of the reasons just cited. However, the deployment of VoIP is not a trivial matter. The principal reason for this statement is that the Internet protocol suite (and other data networks) is not designed to accommodate synchronous, real-time traffic, such as voice. In addition, the traffic loss experienced in IP networks as well as the amount and variability of delay militates against effective support of voice and video traffic.

Variable delay is onerous to speech. It complicates the receiver's job of playing out the speech image to the listener. Furthermore, the delay of the speech signal between the talker and the listener can be excessively long, resulting in the loss of information (the late-arriving samples cannot be used by the digital-to-analog converter).

Another factor to be considered in the public Internet is its "noncooperative nature." The Internet is a amalgamation of disparate networks and service providers who have formed associations in an evolutionary and somewhat fragmented manner. Unlike most telephone networks, the Internet never had a "Ma Bell" or a PTT (Postal, Telephone, and Telegraph Ministry) to define the behavior of the network, such as guaranteed bandwidth for the telephone call. Indeed, the Internet makes no such guarantees. It need not grant the user's bandwidth needs. Sometime you get the service you need and sometime you do not (after all, you get what you pay for . . .).

Some people believe the connectionless nature of the Internet also militates against the effective support of voice traffic. These critics point to the connection-oriented operations of telephony networks and cite how its architecture imposes more predictability and discipline in the networks' support of the users' traffic. I agree with this point to some extent, and there is no question that connectionless networks provide a much bigger challenge in supporting synchronous, voice traffic. But the configuration of an internet to use priority scheduling, upper-layer resource reservations, and source (fixed) routing can effectively simulate many aspects of a connection-oriented technology. So, I do not think the connectionless argument has much merit.

VoIP IN THE INTERNET AND IN PRIVATE INTERNETS

From a technical standpoint, the deployment of synchronous traffic over a private internet offers the same challenges as just described for the public Internet.

However, there is one big difference between IP telephony in a public Internet and a private intranet: An internet can be made to be much more "cooperative" than the Internet. Private networks can be more readily tuned than the public Internet. Therefore, they provide much better support of VoIP than the public Internet, at least for the time being. Eventually, I believe the public Internet will perform well enough to support toll-quality (telephone quality) traffic.

THE QUESTION: NOT IF, BUT HOW?

Even with the uncooperative nature of the public Internet, and data networks in general, the question is not if IP telephony will be implemented; the question is how. Many issues surround this question. Let me cite four examples that are explained later in more detail.

First, what happens to the current telephone network? This is not a trivial issue, and VoIP systems must be able to internetwork with the current telephone company (telco) network. Is the lynchpin of the telephone network, Signaling System Number 7 (SS7), going to be eliminated? No, it will interwork with IP in order for a user to have all the features in VoIP that are taken for granted today in telco-based SS7 networks, such as call hold, calling party id and so on.

Second, what happens to telephone key sets and PBXs? They will remain in the inventory, but they will surely evolve away from the circuit switched technology to one that is packet-based. Today, over ten vendors offer IP-based PBXs, but their features are limited.

Third, which bearer services will be used to support VoIP? Shortly, we will see that IP operates in layer 3 of the classical layered model. What is to be in the lower layers? Will it be Frame Relay, Ethernet, or ATM, at layer 2, and SONET, or wave division multiplexing (WDM) at layer 1? In all likelihood, it will be combinations of all of these technologies.

Fourth, what supporting upper-layer protocols will be used? Will it be the Real Time Protocol (RTP), Differentiated Services (DiffServ), the

Resource Reservation Protocol (RSVP), the Media Gateway Control Protocol (MGCP), or others? No one knows yet, and once again, it will likely be all of these protocols, and many more.

These four questions are examples of the many issues surrounding VoIP. A great deal remains to be worked out in order to migrate to a cohesive, cost-effective, and efficient VoIP infrastructure. But that infrastructure is being built this very moment. And things are changing so quickly that these questions may already be answered by the time this book is published.

Let there be no doubt about VoIPs future. It is here, it will continue to grow, but until it is integrated into the telephone services, it will remain a niche technology in the industry.

CONFIGURATION OPTIONS

We have discussed the issues surrounding VoIP. Let us now look at some VoIP configurations and topologies. Several configuration options are available to support VoIP operations. Figure 1–3 shows five examples. In Figure 1–3(a), conventional telephones are employed as well as the telephone network (you may have noticed that the term telco is used in this book as a shorthand notation for the telephone network). The VoIP gateway provides the translation functions for the voice/data conversions. On the transmit side, the gateway uses a low-bit rate voice coder and other special hardware and software to code, compress, and encapsulate the voice traffic into data packets (IP datagrams). It accepts conventional telco traffic (usually encoded by the telco central office into digital 64 kbit/s DS0 signals), and uses the voice coder to convert these signals into highly compressed samples of the telco signal, usually about 6–8 kbit/s. At the receiving VoIP gateway, the process is reversed. The gateway converts the low-bit rate speech back to the telco DS0 signals. These signals are converted to conventional analog signals before they are passed to the user's telephone.

This gateway is an n:1 machine, because it accepts n telephone connections and multiplexes them into IP datagrams onto one link to the Internet or an intranet.[6] Chapter 9 examines these machines in more de-

---

[6]The convention in this book is to use the term Internet (with an upper case I) to identify the public network. The terms internet (lower case i), and intranet identify private networks that use the IP suite of protocols.

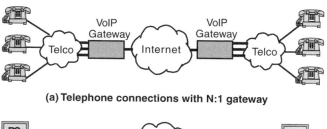

(a) Telephone connections with N:1 gateway

(b) PC connection with router

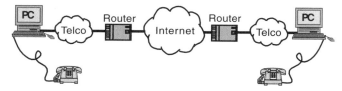

(c) Telephone to PC connection

(d) Connection with 1:1 gateway

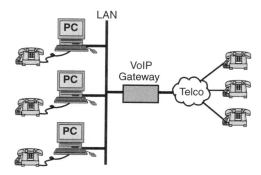

(e) PC-to-phone calls

Figure 1–3 VoIP Configurations

tail, and we will see that they are capable of delivering high-quality voice traffic. The limitation of this configuration is not within the gateways, but how efficiently (or inefficiently) the Internet transports the traffic to the receiver gateway.

Figure 1–3(b) shows the use of a personal computers (PC) and the employment of a router. With this operation, the encoding, compression, and encapsulation operations are performed at the personal computers. The router's job is to examine the destination IP address in the datagram and route the traffic accordingly. The router treats the traffic just like any other datagram, and is not aware that the bits in the datagram are voice traffic.

This configuration will eventually be one that delivers high-quality voice traffic. But for the present, it is not an optimal approach. First, the generalized processors in PCs are not designed to code (analog-to-digital [A/D]) and decode (digital-to-analog [A/D]) voice signals as efficiently as VoIP gateways. Second, the configuration depends on the use of the PC's microphone to accept the speech signal, and consequently, background noise is picked up as part of the speech. Of course, this noise can be dealt with (today's voice coders are capable of handling background noise), but the current PCs are not designed to support this level of sophistication. In due course, a common PC will have the capability to support this configuration quite effectively, a subject that is treated in Chapter 3. And the newer PC-based voice cards are moving in this direction.

The VoIP layout depicted in Figure 1–3(c) eliminates background noise problems found in Figure 1–3(b) by using a telephone instead of an open microphone. Like the configuration in Figure 1–3(b), the PC is tasked with A/D and D/A operations.

A simple and low-cost approach to VoIP is the 1:1 VoIP gateway, shown in Figure 1–3(d). The 1:1 ratio means that only one voice connection is supported by the gateway. The 1:1 gateway sets beside the telephone. It is about one-half the size of the telephone. It accepts the speech analog signals and performs A/D operations (at this time, typically G.723.1 or G.729, explained in Chapter 4) on the signals. At the receiver, the reverse operation takes place.

There are a wide array of 1:1 gateways in the industry, and they are relatively easy to use. The configuration can be a bit of a hassle, since you must use the telephone dial-pad to enter the configuration parameters, such as IP addresses, ISP phone numbers, etc. In addition, both parties must have the same 1:1 gateway device in order to use this configuration.

Another configuration option is shown in Figure 1–3(e). It is a variation of the configurations in Figures 1–3(c) and 1–3(d) with these special attributes. First, the configuration does not require a gateway at each end of the connection. Second, the users are attached to a local area network (LAN) at one site, and local calls on the LAN are managed by the gateway. Inside the gateway (or inside another machine on the LAN) a call manager performs the management functions. The PCs and workstations run VoIP, and thus execute the low-bit rate voice coder. If the telephone call must go outside the LAN the gateway performs the necessary conversion of the signals to meet the telco's requirements. Once the traffic is given to the telco, it is handled like any other call.

This configuration is one that is gaining considerable attention in the industry, because the local LANs (such as Ethernet) can be used for both voice and data traffic. Also, for simple telephone calls, there is no expensive key system or private branch exchange (PBX) in the system.

Problems with the Configurations

The configurations shown in Figure 1–3 represent low-function systems. These are bare-bones operations when compared to the services taken for granted by most telco users. The configurations shown in Figure 1–3 do not include the equipment to support call forwarding, call holding, caller id, or other telco services voice users expect. These services are provided by machines (such as key sets, PBX, centrex, etc.) absent from the Figure 1–3 configurations.

Additionally, configurations In Figures 1–3(a) through (d) utilize the public Internet, which is not set up to deliver toll-quality voice traffic.

PRIVATE VoIP NETWORKS

There is a better way. It incorporates the attractive features of the IP platform with those of the PBX. The five configurations just described use the public Internet and/or the public telco to convey the voice signals between the two users. Another configuration, shown in Figure 1–4, uses a private intranet and/or leased lines instead of the Internet. This configuration also includes the PBX and key sets.

It is this configuration that can offer substantial cost benefits to the IP telephony user. First, the long-distance toll network is avoided. Second, the integration of voice and data can occur with servers and routers for bandwidth consolidation. Third, the use of these components obviates the installation of potentially expensive voice components such as channel banks. Fourth, the approach provides high-quality voice signals, just as good as the plain old telephone service (POTS).

Companies that have opted for this approach are saving money and finding that the careful selection of a VoIP gateway vendor can result in toll-quality voice traffic in the network. These enterprises are also deploying company call centers, using the VoIP technology. For example, in Figure 1–4, the top part of the configuration might be a remote office that is connected to the call center, shown at the bottom part of the figure.

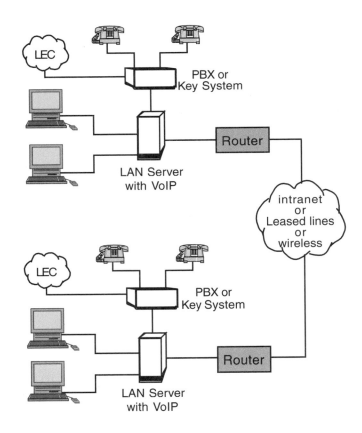

Where:
   LEC   Local Exchange Carrier
   PBX   Private branch exchange

Figure 1–4   VoIP configurations through a private network

THE NEXT STEP

VoIP is proving to be effective in private enterprises. While the technology is still in its infancy, as it grows, it will require rethinking the traditional role of channel banks, PBXs, key systems, data service units (DSUs) and even Centrex. As you are reading this paragraph, several Internet task forces are developing standards that provide the interworking of the traditional telco technology with the IP platform, and vendors are already writing the code and building the hardware for these systems. A general view of these systems is provided in Figure 1–5, and they are described in more detail in later chapters.

The key components to this operation are the VoIP Gateway and the VoIP Call Agent, also called a Gatekeeper. We use the initials (CAG) to identify both terms, since both are used extensively. As explained earlier, the Gateway is responsible for connecting the physical links of the various systems. Therefore, telephone network trunks may be terminated with user local loops, and LANs might be connected with SONET links, and so on.

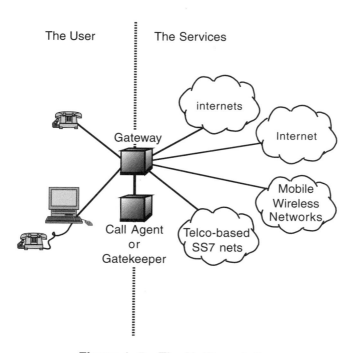

Figure 1–5   The VoIP evolution

The Gateway is also responsible for signal conversions between the systems. For example, a 64 kbit/s digital voice image coming from the telephone network might be translated into a low-bit 8 kbit/s voice image for transfer to a personal computer on a LAN, and vice versa.

The overall controller of the system is the CAG. Indeed, the Gateway is a slave to the master CAG, and does not do much until the CAG gives the orders. For example, the CAG might direct the Gateway to monitor a particular line for offhook, and then instruct the Gateway how to collect the dialed digits, and then how to forward the call to the next node.

Although not shown in this general figure, the CAG usually connects to the telco-based SS7 networks or the mobile wireless networks with signaling links, whereas the Gateway's connections to these networks and the internets in the figure are with user links. These user links are called bearer channels.

If you wish to follow up immediately and examine more information on this subject, refer to Chapter 5. For now, we must leave the subject of configuration options to later discussions, and turn our attention to an emerging phenomenon called electronic commerce (E-com), and how VoIP with IP-based call centers are being deployed to support E-com.

E-COM AND IP-BASED CALL CENTERS

E-com is the use of computer networks to support financial transactions. Common examples are on-line shopping, electronic funds transfer (EFT), commercial video-conferencing, and airline/car rental reservations. Companies like Amazon.com and e*Trade are examples of E-com enterprises.

Many companies are experiencing very large increases in their Web site enquiries. Even though the enquiry may not result in a specific financial transaction at that time, it is known to enhance the company's marketing position. Figure 1–6 reflects a study conducted by the International Data Corporation (IDC) of the growth of software implementations for email and Web response applications [POLE98].[7]

But we should make clear that setting up E-com in a company is a big job. It requires all the resources of a conventional commercial en-

---

[7][POLE98]. Poleretsky, Zoltan. "Customer Interaction in an Electronic Commerce World," *Business Communications Review* (BCR), Nortel Supplement, January, 1999.

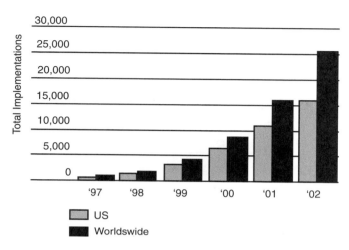

Figure 1–6   E-mail and web response software implementations [POLE99]

deavor (such as catalog shopping), plus the ability to integrate on-line, real-time interfaces with the customer. Those industries that do it routinely (the airlines, for example) are exceptions. Most companies will require major changes to their culture and infrastructure in order to move to E-com. Moreover, many companies using E-com are not yet turning a profit.

We learned earlier that some companies have already migrated to IP-based call centers. The call centers are not using the public Internet; it is too slow and unreliable. Their approach is to use private intranets and/or leased lines to support VoIP. Private VoIP networks are proving to be cost-effective. At the same time, they provide high-quality voice signals.

In addition to IP-based call centers, many companies are betting that online shopping will be as big a success as catalog shopping. If so, the revenue for online shopping will be very high. Without question, the potential market for online shoppers is big and still growing. Prudential Securities has published a study of the number of households in the U.S. that are, and will be, shopping online [RAPP98].[8] Figure 1–7 summarizes some of the findings of Prudential Securities, which indicates a substantial growth in the online shopping industry.

---

[8][RAPP98]. Rappaport, David M. "The Next Wave in Do-It-Yourself Customer Service." *Business Communications Review* (BCR), June, 1998.

(a) Online Households in U.S.

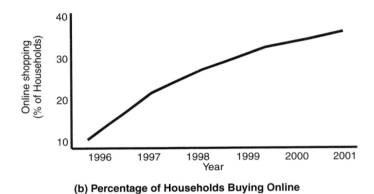

(b) Percentage of Households Buying Online

Figure 1–7   Online Shopping [RAPP98]

At this point in this evolving marketplace, no one really knows how big the market will be for E-com and online shopping. Most agree that it will be a big market. There is less ambiguity about the role of VoIP-based call centers. As I stated, it is already proving to be a big success. We discussed this system earlier in this chapter (see Figure 1–4).

CONFIGURATION AND TOPOLOGY CHOICES

Let us return to the subject of the supporting technologies for VoIP. We stated earlier that the issue of IP telephony is not if, but how. Figure 1–8 shows some of the technology choices to answer the how question.

It is very unlikely that IP telephony will operate over a single bearer service. Moreover, as the Internet task forces continue to refine multiser-

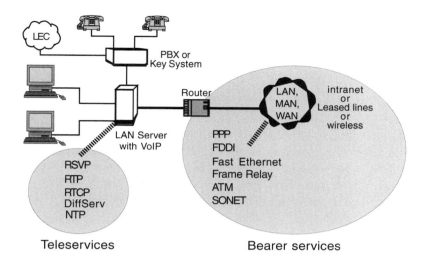

Figure 1–8   Technology choices to support VoIP

Where:

ATM	Asynchronous transfer mode
Diffserv	Differentiated services
FDDI	Fiber distributed data interface
LAN	Local area network
LEC	Local exchange carrier
MAN	Metropolitan area network
NTP	Network time protocol
PBX	Private branch exchange
PPP	Point to point protocol
RSVP	Resource reservation protocol
RTCP	Real time control protocol
RTP	Real time protocol
SONET	Synchronous optical network
VoIP	Voice over IP
WAN	Wide area network

vice Request for Comments (RFCs), it is also unlikely that only one tele-services protocol stack will be used.[9] A more likely scenario is the existence of a multiplicity of support options. Here are some examples:

- VoIP over PPP over twisted pair
- VoIP over PPP over SONET wave division multiplexing

---

[9]For the uninitiated reader, the term *bearer service* refers to the lower three layers of the OSI Model, and the term *teleservices* refers to the upper four layers of the Model. Bearer channels refer to user channels (in contrast to signaling channels).

- VoIP over Fast or Gigabit Ethernet
- VoIP over AAL 1/AAL 2/AAL 5 over ATM over SONET
- VoIP over Frame Relay
- VoIP over FDDI
- VoIP over RTP over UDP, then over IP, and layers 2 and 1

We could go on, for there are other choices and combinations. The purpose of this discussion is to emphasize that different bearer and tele-services products will be available to meet diverse customer requirements. Later chapters will provide overviews of some of these technologies, but the main emphasis in this book is VoIP itself. Other books in this series are dedicated to the detailed discussion of these supporting technologies.

BASIC TERMS AND CONCEPTS

Some of the readers of this book are familiar with the Internet, and others are not. I use the next part of this chapter to provide a tutorial on some basic Internet terms and concepts. The experienced reader can skip to the section titled, Evaluation the Factors in Packetized Voice (page 25).

The Internet is an association of thousands of user computers that communicate with each other through networks. These user computers are called "hosts." The networks are connected together through another machine that relays the host computer traffic between user applications (such as e-mail and file transfer) that are running on the hosts. The Internet uses the term *Gateway* or *router* to describe the machine that performs the relaying functions between networks. Figure 1–9 shows a Gateway/router placed between networks A, B, and C. Routers A, B, and C are said to be internetworking machines, since they connect networks together.

Networks are often grouped together, and the individual networks are called subnetworks. They are full networks unto themselves, but the idea allows a set of subnetworks (subnets) to be associated with one organization, or some type of administrative domain, such as an Internet Service Provider (ISP). The organization can identify each network with a subnet identifier (ID) and can group these IDs (networks) together (or treat them separately). The grouping concept is called address aggregation. In Figure 1–9, Subnets A.1 and A.2 can be collectively identified with address A.

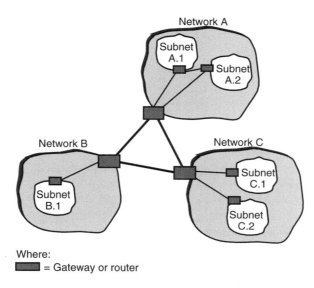

Where:
▬ = Gateway or router

Figure 1–9   Internetworking and Internets

This approach is useful because, like the telephone system, it allows the Internet components to be identified with a hierarchical address. For example, in a telephone system, a person can be reached by dialing first an area code, then an exchange number, and then a subscriber number. In the Internet, addresses are managed by a form of hierarchical aggregation called address prefixes.[10]

An internetworking router is designed to remain transparent to the end-user application. Since the end-user application resides in the host computer, the router need not burden itself with application protocols, and can dedicate itself to fewer tasks, such as managing the traffic between networks.

ATTRIBUTES OF THE INTERNET

The Internet was developed to support the transfer of data traffic (packets) between computers and workstations with the use of adaptive routing features, see Table 1–2. Adaptive routing means the traffic may

---

[10]The concept of a network address in the Internet is based on the use of class-based IP addresses. With prefixing, address classes are no longer important. For more information see [BLAC98] Black, Uyless. *Advanced Features of the Internet*, Prentice Hall, 1998.

Table 1–2   Attributes of the Internet

Attribute	Consequence(s)
Data applications	Not "tuned" for voice, or video
Adaptive routing:	Path may vary during traffic transfer, and packets may arrive out-of-order
Connectionless:	Circuits are not set up between users
"Best effort" delivery service:	Traffic discarded if problems occur

take different routes through the Internet depending on network conditions at a specific time, such as congestion, a failed link, etc. The possible result of adaptive routing is that the destination user may receive the packets out-of-order. An Internet protocol (the Transmission Control Protocol, TCP) at the receiver can be used to reorder the packets into the proper sequence. The other possible result of adaptive routing is that the arrival rate of the packets at the receiver may vary; some packets may arrive with little delay while others take longer.

The Internet is designed as a connectionless system. This means that there are no "affiliations" established between the machines in the Internet. As a result, the Internet does not maintain ongoing knowledge of the user's traffic, and does not build a fixed path between the switches from the source and to destination host machines. In effect, Internet Protocol (IP) traffic routing is stateless; that is to say, it does not build tables to maintain information about a connection, because there is no connection.

The connectionless aspect of the Internet goes hand-in-hand with the adaptive routing concept. But in the telephone network, the opposite architecture is employed: connection-oriented fixed paths between the calling and called parties. The telephony approach is needed to support the real time, non-varying delay requirements of speech. Whereas, the Internet is a data network, and most data applications do not require the real-time transport service.

The Internet is a "best effort" delivery network. The term best effort means that the Internet will attempt to deliver the traffic, but if problems occur (damaged bits due to noise, congestion at a router, etc.), or the destination host cannot be found, the traffic is discarded. In most instances, TCP in the originating host machine can resend the lost or damaged packets.

Internet Attributes vis-à-vis Voice Traffic

It is evident from this brief examination of the Internet, and our previous discussions about the requirements for toll-quality voice, that the Internet is not a particularly good choice for the transport of voice traffic. However, this is a moot point, since it is the anointed technology for packetized voice. And as stated before, the Internet will evolve to support toll quality voice.

THE INTERNET LAYERED ARCHITECTURE

Many of the concepts in this book are explained with the layered protocol concept. This section provides a brief review of the Internet layers and Chapter 2 gives more detailed information.

Figure 1–10 a reviews the Internet protocol suite layers. With some exceptions, the Open Systems Interconnection (OSI) Model layer 6 is not used. Layer 5 is not used at all.

The physical and data link layers are (as a general rule) also not defined. The philosophy is to rely on existing physical and data link systems. One notable exception to this practice is at the data link layer, where the Internet task forces have defined the Point-to-Point Protocol (PPP).

For the newcomer, here is a summary of the functions of the layers:

- *Physical layer:* Defines the media, and physical aspects of the signals (voltages, etc.). Defines clocking and synchronization operations. Defines physical connectors. Also identified as layer 1 or L_1. Examples are T1, E1, SONET, and L_1 of Ethernet.

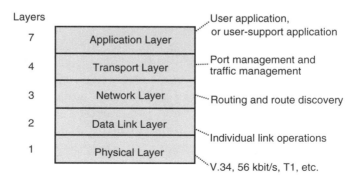

Figure 1–10   The Internet Protocol suite layers

- *Data link layer:* Supports the transfer of traffic over one link. May perform error detection and retransmission, depending on the specific link layer protocol. Also identified as layer 2 or L_2. Examples are PPP, LAPD, and L_2 of Ethernet.
- *Network layer:* Performs forwarding operations and route discovery. Supports some limited diagnostic functions, such as status reports. Also identified as network level, layer 3, or L_3. An example of forwarding is IP. An example of route discovery is Open Shortest Path First (OSPF).
- *Transport layer:* Supports end-to-end acknowledgment of traffic, as an option. At a receiving host, supports the identification (with a port number) of the layer_7 protocol to be invoked to support incoming traffic. Also identified as layer 4 or L_4. Examples are TCP and UDP.
- *Application layer:* Contains the end user application, or another application that directly supports the end user application, such as a file transfer or an email operation. Also identified as layer 7 or L_7.

EVALUATING THE FACTORS IN PACKETIZED VOICE

Now that we have a general understanding of the Internet attributes, as well as the Internet protocol suite, it is appropriate to evaluate how to place speech traffic on an internet. The VoIP designer must evaluate three key factors: (a) packet delay, (b) bandwidth requirements, and (c) computational effort.

Packet delay describes how long it takes to send the packet from the sender to the receiver. Two aspects of packet delay should be known. The first aspect is how long it takes to send the traffic from the sender to the receiver. The second aspect is the variation in time of the arrival of the packets at the receiver. The variation in delay is called jitter.

The second factor deals with how much bandwidth is required to support the voice or video transmission. The bandwidth calculation must factor in the bits required to represent the speech signal as well as the overhead headers (protocol control information) that are used to support the signals. At a minimum this includes the L_2 header, the IP header, the UDP header, the L_7 header, and the headers created by the voice coder. All totaled, they add significant overhead to the voice packet, and until we have all the bandwidth we need, this protocol control information is a big drain on the bandwidth bucket.[11]

The third factor is the computational effort needed to support the coding, transport, and decoding of the speech images in each machine in the network. The term computational effort refers to the expense and complexity involved in supporting services to the audio application. In simple terms, it refers to the millions of instructions per second (MIPS) required to support the operation, as well as the amount of memory needed; that is, the complexity and expense of the voice coder/decoder (codec).

As examples of computational efficiency, a conventional 64-kbit/s voice signal can be produced in a high-quality manner by the use of a 2-MIPS machine. If a 8-to-10 MIBS machine is employed, the signal can be reduced to 16 kbit/s. Furthermore, a 15–20 MIBS machine can produce a high-quality signal of 8 kbit/s. Currently, the ITU-T is examining a standard for a 4-kbit/s machine which is expected to require 40–45 MIPS.

ACCOMMODATING TO THE VOICE AND DATA REQUIREMENTS IN A NETWORK

In a previous section in the chapter (see "Barriers to Successful Deployment of IP Telephony"), I made some general comments on the difficulty of supporting speech traffic in the Internet. This section provides more information in the context of how the requirements for voice and video traffic differ.

Tolerance for Errors

Voice transmissions exhibit a high tolerance for errors. If an occasional packet is distorted, the fidelity of the voice reproduction is not severely affected. In contrast, data packets have a low tolerance for errors. One bit corrupted likely changes the meaning of the data. Furthermore, voice packets can afford (on occasion) to be lost or discarded. In the event

---

[11]Unlimited bandwidth? The reader must think the author is Pollyannaish. I am not, but I do believe the eventual placement of xDSL and coax modems in the local loop, as well as wave division multiplexing (WDM) in the network will go a long way toward giving us that bandwidth rainbow.

of excessive delays in the network, the packets may be discarded because they are of no use if they arrive at the receiver too late. Again, the loss does not severely affect voice fidelity if the lost packets are less than 10 percent of the total packets transmitted. As discussed before, data packets can ill-afford to be lost or discarded.

Tolerance for Delay

Yet another difference between voice and data transmissions deals with network delay. For packetized voice to be translated back to an analog signal in a real-time mode, the two-way delay for voice packets must be constant and generally must be low—usually less than 300 ms. Why is low delay important? If it takes a long time for the voice packets to be sent from the speaker (person A) to the listener (person B), when speaker A stops talking, receiver B is still receiving the speech packets. Person B cannot start talking until all the speech signals have arrived. In the meantime, person A hears nothing for a while.

The two-way delay measures how long it takes: (a) for A's speech to reach B, (b) for B to hear the speech, (c) for B to talk back, and (d) for A to hear B's response. If the delay becomes long (say, over 400 or 500 ms), the conversation appears phony, almost like a half-duplex connection where the two people are taking turns talking, but waiting a while before taking the turn. All-in-all, it can be quite annoying.

For data packets, the network delay can vary considerably. Indeed, the packets can be transmitted asynchronously through the network, without regard to timing arrangements between the sender and the receiver.

Tolerance for Delay and the Effects on Queues.   Voice packets require a short queue length at the network nodes in order to reduce delay, or at least to make the delay more predictable. The short voice packet queue lengths can experience overflow occasionally, with resulting packet loss. However, data packets require longer queue lengths to be longer to prevent packet loss in overflow conditions.

Tolerance for Variable Bit Rates (VBRs) and Constant Bit Rates (CBRs)

A useful method to describe the nature of applications traffic is through two concepts known as variable bit rate (VBR) and constant bit rate (CBR). An application using VBR schemes does not require a constant and continuous allocation of bandwidth. These applications are said to be bursty, which means that they transmit and receive traffic asynchronously (at any time with periods in which nothing is sent or received). VBR applications are most any type of data communications process.

These applications permit the queuing of traffic in a variable manner from the standpoint of time, and they do not require a fixed timing relationship between the sender and the receiver. Therefore, if traffic is sent from the sender and is buffered (queued) for variable periods of time, the receiver is not disturbed. Typical applications using VBR techniques are interactive terminal-to-terminal dialogues, inquiry/response operations, client-server systems, and bulk data transfer operations.

It should be emphasized that while VBR permits loose timing and asynchronous operations between the sender and the receiver, most VBR applications do require some type of timing constraint.

In contrast, an application using CBR schemes requires constant and continuous (or nearly so) allocation of bandwidth. These applications are said to be non-bursty. The term non-bursty has to be used carefully with these applications because some of the applications will tolerate a certain amount of burstyness.

Typical CBR-based applications are voice transmissions. These applications require guaranteed bandwidth and a constant and continuous timing relationship between the sending and receiving devices. They also require a predictable delay between the sender and the receiver.

Packetized Voice: Its VBR traffic!   However, packetized voice is classified as VBR traffic, because it is transported over a VBR-based data network, and not a CBR-based telephony network. So, the challenge is to receive the data network's bursty voice packets at the receiver and smooth the VBR behavior to that of CBR, thus permitting conventional CBR digital-to-analog operations to take place.

Examples of Voice, Video, and Data Applications Requirements

The need to support multiapplication traffic requires the Internet to extend its capabilities far beyond what it can do now. It must support the diverse needs of different types of traffic. As examples, Tables 1–3, 1–4, and 1–5 show the performance requirements for several audio, video, and data applications [RADI94].[12] Several of the tables show the Mean Opinion Scores (MOS) for the technologies. A MOS of 3.5 is considered to be fair-to-good.

---

[12][RADI94] Radhika R. Roy. "Networking constraints in Multimedia Conferencing and the Role of ATM Networks," *AT&T Technical Journal*, July/August, 1994.

Table 1–3   Audio bandwidth and MOS performance applications [RADI94]

Coders	Uncompressed bit rates in kbit/s	Transmission mode	Expected bit rates in kbits/s**		MOS
			Peak	Average	
CD audio	1411.4–1536	CBR	192	192	*
(proprietary algorithm)		VBR	384	192	*
FM stereo audio	1024–1536	CBR	128	128	*
Wideband audio (G.722)	128	CBR	64/ 56/ 48	64/ 56/ 48	*
PCM audio (µ-law, G.711)	64	CBR	64	64	4.3
		VBR	64	32–21	*
ADPCM audio (G.721)	64	CBR	32	32	4.1
LD-CELP audio (G.728)	64	CBR	16	16	4.1

*Expected MOS may be between 4 and 4.5, but is yet to be supported by published results
**Some of the bit rates are compressed
where:

ADPCM	Adaptive differential pulse code modulation
CBR	Constant bit rate
CD	Compact disc
CELP	Code excited predictive linear coding
FM	Frequency modulation
LD-CELP	Low delay CELP
MOS	Mean opinion score
PCM	Pulse code modulation
VBR	Variable bit rate

Table 1–4   Video bandwidth and performance for VBR codecs [RADI94]

Video quality, coding resolution, and format	Transmission mode	Encoder-decoder delay in frames**	Compressed video bit rate/s kbit/s*		MOS*
			Peak	Mean	
Low rate videoconferencing quality	VBR with negligible buffer	0	2562	239.6	4.5–5.0
360 × 288 pixels non-interlaced 4:1:1, 8 bits/ sample 30 Hz, p × 64 or MPEG-1 standards	VBR with buffer	1	1400	239.6	4.0–4.5
		2	934	239.6	3.5–4.5
		3	847	239.6	3.5–4.5
		4	822	239.6	3.5–4.5

*Estimated
**Delay increases with the increase in buffer size (one frame delay = 33 milliseconds)
where:

MOS	Mean opinion score
MPEG	Motion Pictures Expert Group
VBR	Variable bit rate

Table 1–5 Bit rates required for data [RADI94]

Data (text, still images, graphics) object size	Uncompressed object size in Mbit/s	Typical compression ratio	Retrieval & transfer of object*	Document browsing*	Retrieval and transfer**		Document browsing**	
					Uncompressed	Compressed	Uncompressed	Compressed
ASCII text, 8.5″ × 11″ page, (88 char/line × 55 lines × 8 bits/char)	0.029	2–4	2	0.5	0.015	0.008–0.004	0.059	0.029–0.015
8.5″ × 11″ color page (200 pixels/inch, × 24 bits/pixel)	90	10–20	2	0.5	45	4.5–2.3	180	18–9
Medium resolution, 8.5″ × 11″ color page (400 pixels/inch, × 24 bits/pixel)	359	10–20	2	0.5	180	18–9	700	70–35
High resolution, 8.5″ × 11″ color page (400 pixels/inch, × 24 bits/pixel)	1436	10–20	2	0.5	718	72–36	2,872	287–144
Graphics quality, (1600 pixels/inch, × 24 bits/pixel)	5744	10–20	2	0.5	2872	287–144	11,488	1152–575

*Typical response time in seconds
**Peak bandwidth requirements in Mbit/s

Table 1–3 shows several audio applications and the ITU-T G Series Recommendations that use devices to code/decode the analog signals to-from digital images. These devices are called coders, vocoders, or codecs. The MOS ratings are acceptable, but there is one significant problem: the bit rates are high. The G.722, G.711, G.721, and G.728 coders are not efficient in this regard, and Chapter 3 describes other coders that are more efficient.

Table 1–4 shows some MOSs for video systems. Notice the requirements for large bandwidth (kbit/s) needed to obtain an acceptable MOS.

Finally, Table 1–5 shows the response time and bandwidth requirements for several data applications. Once again, it is obvious that the support of high-quality images requires considerable capacity. Moreover, for interactive browsing, the network must provide fast response times.

MAKING THE INTERNET LOOK LIKE THE TELEPHONE NETWORK

It is clear from the AT&T study that applications' requirements vary, and these variances occur not just between voice, video and data applications, but within these applications as well.

One cannot simply say, "The Internet should change to support voice, video, and data." Instead, we must say, "The Internet should change to support different types of voice systems, different types of video systems, and different types of data systems."

In other words, the challenge is to make the Internet behave more like a telephone network and a CATV system, yet retain its characteristics to support data. And that is precisely what we will turn our attention to for the remainder of this book with regards to voice support.

SUMMARY

The Internet was designed as a network to support data traffic. Its success stems from its (now) ease-of-use and its low-cost to access and transport traffic. As the need for multiservice networks grows, the need to "upgrade" the Internet becomes compelling, and much of the multiservice architecture is being put in place today. The ultimate challenge is to change the Internet (and other data networks) from a data-only service to a multiservice (multiapplication) architecture.

2

Characteristics of the Internet and IP

This chapter is divided into three sections. The first section explains the Internet architecture and the characteristics of the Internet; that is, how it "behaves" (or misbehaves) in the handling of user traffic. This section is a more detailed explanation than the generalized discussion in Chapter 1. The next section provides a brief overview of IP. The last section provides a brief overview of Internet ports and sockets and the major features of Transmission Control Protocol (TCP) and User Datagram Protocol (UDP).

The reader who is experienced with the Internet can skip the last two sections, but I recommend all read this first section.

ARCHITECTURE OF AN INTERNET

Today, the Internet is a complex collage of regional and national networks that are interconnected together with routers. The communications links used by the ISPs are leased lines from the telephone system, usually DS1 or DS3 lines, and increasingly SONET lines. Other lines are provided by competitive access providers (CAPs), and still others are provided by private carriers, such as private microwave, and satellite operators.

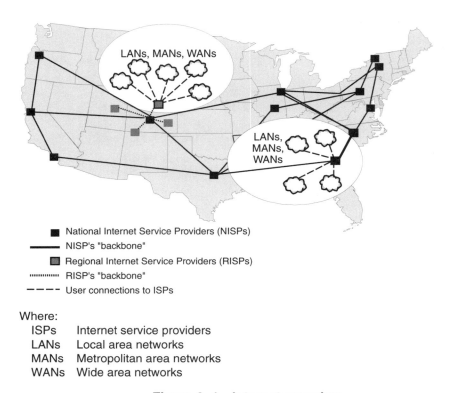

Figure 2–1   Internet overview

The Internet connections and the many ISPs are impossible to depict in one illustration, but Figure 2–1 provides an accurate view of the basic structure of the Internet topology.

ISPs AND THE TELEPHONE NETWORK

The Internet Service Providers (ISPs) provide the access into the Internet. They provide this access through the telephone network, and the Internet user (say from the home) uses a dial-up modem to connect to the ISP through the telco local exchange carrier (LEC), and the LEC central office (CO), see Figure 2–2.

The telephone companies are required to provide the ISPs with connections to the telephone company's customers. The connections are provided at the telco's plant. These connections from the customer to the CO's main distribution frame (MDF, a physical "patch panel") may be

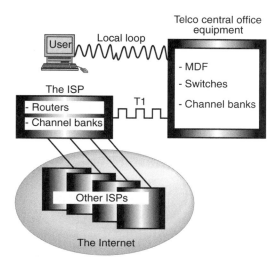

Figure 2–2   Typical telco and Internet service provider (ISP) set-up

patched to the local switch (a conventional circuit switch, for example). Alternately, the line from the customer may be patched to a digital cross connect (DCS) machine, which is a software-based component that can support leased lines—in this example, leased lines to the ISP.

The basic idea of Figure 2–2 is to emphasize that the Internet user gains access to the Internet and the user's ISP through the telco's local loop and CO's equipment. At the CO, the connection to the ISP is attained through the DCS.

The trunk connections from the CO to the ISP are at an agreed upon point of presence (POP), say at the CO's site. On the trunk side, the signals are now either of the T1 family or the SONET STS/OC family (Synchronous Optical Network, Synchronous Transport Signal, Optical Carrier).

ATTRIBUTES OF THE INTERNET

Before we begin analyzing the Internet operations, it will prove helpful to examine in more detail the major attributes of the Internet, introduced in Chapter 1.

As we learned, the Internet was developed to transfer data traffic by using adaptive routing features. By adaptive routing, we mean that the traffic may take different routes through the Internet depending on the conditions at a specific time. In addition, the Internet is designed as a connectionless system which means that there are no "affiliations" established between the machines in the Internet. As a result, the Internet does not maintain an ongoing knowledge of the user's traffic. In effect, the Internet Protocol (IP) is stateless; that is to say, it does not build tables to maintain information about a connection because there is no connection.

The Internet is a "best effort" delivery network. The term best effort means that the Internet will attempt to deliver the traffic, but if problems occur, the traffic is discarded.

Finally, the Internet supports either unicasting (one-to-one) or multicasting (one-to-many) operations. The multicasting feature has proved to be a very useful tool for conference calling as well as for the downline loading of software or data to multiple sites.

Round-Trip Time (RTT)

Round-trip time (RTT) is a measure of the time it takes to send a packet to a destination node and receive a reply from that node. RTT includes the transmission time in both directions and the processing time at the destination node.

Most RTTs in the Internet are within the range of 70–160 ms, although large variations to RTT do occur. Due to the asynchronous nature of the Internet, RTT is not consistent. During periods where Internet traffic is heavy, the RTT may exceed 300 ms.

The ITU-T G.114 recommendation limits RTT to 300 ms or less for telephone traffic. This performance factor is based on many studies and observations; they conclude that longer delays in a telephone-based conversation gives the impression to the conversationalists that they are using a half-duplex circuit. (Interestingly, other surveys show some people tolerate large RTTs of up to 800 ms. But this tolerant population is in the minority.)

PACKET LOSS

Another Internet characteristic that is important to voice and video applications is packet loss. Two factors are involved: (a) how often packet loss occurs and (b) how many successive (contiguous) packets are affected. Packet loss is masked in a data application by using TCP to resend the lost TCP segments. Certainly, the loss of many segments and their retransmissions will affect the application's performance, but on the whole, the end-user data application is not concerned (or aware) of packet loss.

Packet loss is quite important in voice and video applications, since the loss may affect the outcome of the decoding process at the receiver, and may also be detected by the end-user's ears or eyes. Notwithstanding, today's voice coders can produce high-quality voice signals in the face of about 10 percent loss of the voice packets (G.723.1 as the example, see Chapter 4), *if* the packet losses are random and independent. G.723.1 compensates for this loss by using the previous packet to simulate the characteristics of the vocal signal that was in the lost packet.

Traffic loss in the Internet is bursty: large packet losses occur in a small number of bursts. This characteristic of internet behavior complicates the support of telephony, because packetized voice works best if the packet loss is random and independent.

The effect of packet loss can be alleviated somewhat by the use of forward error correction (FEC) schemes, and methods have been devised to compensate for loss bursts [BORE97].[1] These schemes add extra delay to the process, and may result in the loss of the packet because it is made available to the user in a time domain that is too late to be useful.

One FEC approach borrows from the tried-and-true mobile wireless technology: repeat the signal more than once. With mobile wireless systems, this operation interleaves successive copies of the coded voice image across multiple packets (slots in the mobile wireless terminology). With Internet telephony, experiments are underway to send copies of the packet 1 to n times. If one copy is lost, say copy n, it can be recovered from the other copies. However, this operation is only effective if a copy arrives safely, and therefore implies that one of the copies survives the burst error. If the copies are spaced-out too far in time to survive the error, they may arrive too late to be useful.

Order of Arrival of Packets

The subject of the order of the arrival of packets at the receiver is not of keen interest to the data application if it is supported by TCP, because TCP can re-order the TCP segments and present the traffic to the application in the correct order. TCP is not used for voice and video, so

---

[1][BORE97]. Borella, M. S. "Analysis of End-to-End Internet Packet Loss: Dependence and Asymmetry," *IEEE Network,* Reprint, 1997).

the order of packet arrival is an important subject to these applications. As of this writing, studies are underway to capture statistics and discover the incidences of misordered packet arrival. Several studies show that out-of-sequence arrival is not unusual.

Another factor is to note that Internet delays follow a diurnal cycle. During the hours of 8:00 A.M. to 6:00 P.M., delays are greater. For example, in the middle of the business day, delays are about 20 ms greater than in the evenings.

Hop Distance

Hop distance is a term used to describe the number of hops between a sender and a receiver. It is a critical aspect in internet telephony because more hops means more delay, and more variable delay. Hop distance must consider round-trip time (RTT), because of the interactive, real-time nature of telephone conversations. Figure 2–3 shows several aspects of hop distance and RTT, and its deleterious effect on the quality of voice applications.

The traffic is to be sent from a host on subnet 1 to a host on subnet 2. The IP datagrams must be processed by both hosts as well as all the routers on the path between the hosts. Let us assume the traffic traverses through the fewest number of hops (a common approach), which means the datagrams are processed by seven routers, numbered router 1 through router 7 in the figure. Thus, the datagrams are sent through nine hops. If the routers are not heavily loaded with traffic, then queuing delay will be short, and the delay at each router, while variable, will not create a major problem when the traffic arrives at the receiver. However, if traffic is heavy and/or if the routers are not performing their datagram forwarding operations efficiently, the accumulated and variable delay will result in the inability of the receiver to reconstitute the real-time voice signal into a high quality speech pattern.

We learned earlier that round-trip delay in the Internet rarely exceeds 200 ms. But we also know that the delay is highly variable. For example, a delay going through the same number of nodes might be 100 ms on one occasion; on another it may be 200 ms.

However, these studies focus only on the RTT in the network. Keep in mind that this RTT figure does not include analog-to-digital conversion, codec operations, or other factors that would increase the RTT.

Several studies also reveal that it is clear that geographical distance cannot be correlated to round-trip delay. Indeed in one study, a short distance of only 477 miles, but with a hop count of 21 resulted in a 500-ms

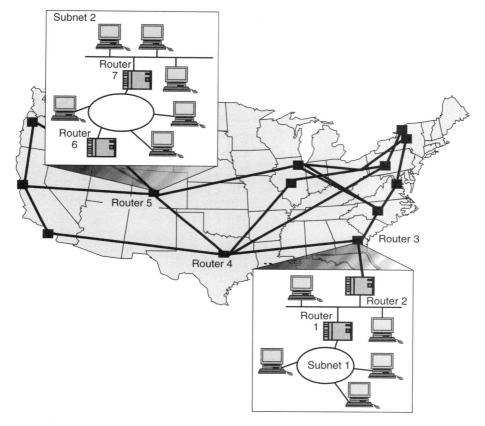

Figure 2–3   Hop distance and round-trip delay (RTT)

round-trip delay. Therefore to emphasize, hop distance is a key factor in delay and geographical distance is less a factor.

The telephone network does not have these problems. First, the path between the talker and listener is fixed during the call set-up. Second, the circuit switches do not queue the traffic. Rather, the voice channels are time division multiplexed into DS0 channels (TDM slots) and sent directly from the input interface on the switch to a corresponding DS0 slot on a preconfigured output interface. The delay through the voice switch is miniscule (it is not even a factor), and fixed.

Thus, circuit switches provide fixed paths, as well as very low, fixed delay. In contrast, packet switches, such as routers, provide variable paths, and variable delay, which is sometimes a low delay and sometimes a lengthy delay.

Table 2–1   Routing persistence [PAXS97]

Time	% of Total	Comments
Seconds	NA	Used in load balancing
Minutes	NA	In tightly-coupled routers
10's of minutes	9	Changes usually through different cities or autonomous systems
Hours	4	Usually intranetwork changes
6+ hours	19	Usually intranetwork changes
Days	68	(a)50% of these routes persist for < 7 days
		(b) Other 50% persist for > 7 days

NEED FOR FIXED ROUTING?

Given that fixed routing is a desirable feature for real-time, delay-sensitive traffic, one can ask: is it needed? That is, does an internet (or more precisely, the Internet) shuffle traffic around frequently, with the routers altering routes often? If so, routing headers are important for real-time traffic.

Studies conducted on the routing behavior of the Internet reveal that most of the traffic between two or more communicating parties remains on the same physical path during the session. In fact, route alteration is more an exception than the rule.

One study on Internet "routing persistence" is summarized in Table 2–1. This information represents a small part of the study that is available from: [PAXS97][2] and conducted by Vern Paxson.

Paxson defines routing persistence as how long a route endures before changing. Even though routing changes occur over a wide range of time, most of the routes in the Internet do not change much.

A point should be emphasized in Paxson's study. The not applicable (NA) entries in Table 2–1 represent situations in which frequent routing fluctuations do occur in parts of the Internet. While they are not a factor in the "big picture," if your traffic flows through that part of the Internet, it will be affected by these changes.

---

[2][PAXS97]. Paxson, Vern. IEEE/ACM Transactions on Communications, "End-to-End Routing Behavior in the Internet." Vol. 5, No. 5, October 1997.

SIZE OF PACKETS AND KINDS OF TRAFFIC IP SUPPORTS

We continue analyzing the attributes of the Internet by examining the traffic characteristics relating to average size of the protocol data unit (packet), see Figure 2–4(a). The most common packet size is 40 bytes, which accounts for TCP acknowledgements (ACKs), finish messages (FINs), and reset messages (RSTs). Overall, the average packet sizes vary from 175 to about 400 bytes, and 90 percent of the packets are 576 or smaller. Ten percent of the traffic is sent in 1500-byte sizes, which reflects traffic from Ethernet-attached hosts.

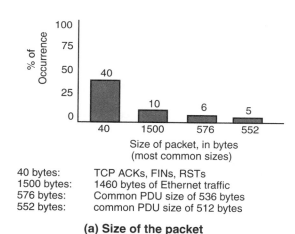

40 bytes:	TCP ACKs, FINs, RSTs
1500 bytes:	1460 bytes of Ethernet traffic
576 bytes:	Common PDU size of 536 bytes
552 bytes:	common PDU size of 512 bytes

(a) Size of the packet

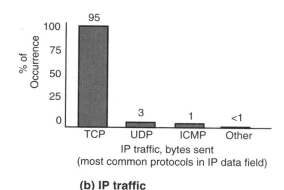

(b) IP traffic

Figure 2–4   Traffic characteristics of the Internet

The other common occurrences are packet sizes of 576 bytes (6 percent of the traffic), and 552 bytes (5 percent of the traffic). These sizes reflect common protocol data unit sizes used in the Internet protocols.

In Figure 2–4(b), the type of traffic carried by IP is shown. Almost all the traffic is TCP, followed by UDP, then ICMP. Other traffic encapsulated directly in IP accounts for very little of the Internet traffic.

The significance of these facts to VoIP is as follows. First, it is important to use small packets for voice traffic. If a packet is lost in the network, the small packet is less likely to contain significant parts of a speech signal. The idea is to divide and conquer. Most low-bit rate voice coders are designed to produce very short voice packets, usually no more than 10–30 ms in duration, and 10–30 bytes in length.

The other reason for a small packet is that it permits the processing node, such as a router, to examine and operate on a small unit of information quickly: it does not have to wait very long for the bits to propagate through the incoming interface. In contrast, a long packet means it takes a while for the bits of the entire transmission to arrive and therefore to be processed.

As you can see, the Internet has been calibrated to use relatively large packets. The fact that almost 50 percent of the packets transported in the Internet are only 40 bytes is not significant. They are not for user traffic, but for connection management operations for TCP.

If a substantial amount of Internet traffic becomes voice traffic, it will require a concomitant increase in Internet capacity, because the smaller packets will consume significantly more of the overall bandwidth: The ratio of overhead to user payload will increase. Some people express concern about this situation, but I do not think it will be a major problem, because the increased use of high-speed SONET links, and the migration to wave division multiplexing (WDM) will provide the needed bandwidth.

A potentially bigger problem is the increased load on the routers in the Internet. After all, the router has to spend as much time processing the fixed-length header of a 10-byte packet as it does in processing the same length header of a 576-byte packet. This situation can be ameliorated by multiplexing two or three voice samples inside one packet, but taking care not to expand the overall packet size such that succumbs to the large packet problem described earlier.

Moreover, with the migration to high-speed gigabit routers, I believe the overall latency in the Internet will continue to improve.

Figure 2–4(b) points to another potential problem of supporting voice traffic in the Internet. The vast majority of user traffic is transported with the TCP header. As explained later in this chapter, TCP provides extensive support for traffic integrity operations: (a) error checks, (b) acknowledgments of traffic, (c) retransmissions of errored traffic, and (d) flow control.

But voice applications need not use TCP; in fact, they should not use it, because the TCP support features introduce too much delay in the overall procedure, and it is not practicable to achieve real-time performance if some of the errored packets are retransmitted. The overall delay, would be over 400–500 ms, clearly beyond the RTT that is acceptable for speech.

The potential problem is related to TCP flow-control mechanisms. One feature implemented in many TCP products is the ability of TCP to back off from sending traffic when the Internet is congested and experiencing poor RTT.

In this regard, TCP is a "courteous" protocol. It waits if necessary and does not intrude its presence (its packets) into a congested network. But UDP, on which VoIP operates, has no such qualms. It is a "discourteous" protocol in that is has no back-off mechanisms. It will continue sending traffic even if the network is congested.

So, if the network is congested, TCP stands by the door at the network, and does not enter. Indeed, TCP opens the door, and UDP goes through it!.

As seen in Figure 2–4(b), UDP accounts for only 3 percent of traffic that is placed directly in the IP datagram. However, if voice (and video) become heavy users of the Internet, then it is possible that the TCP users will experience degraded performance during periods of high activity of the real-time traffic.

Earlier, I said it is a *potential* problem. If the Internet and internets are built with sufficient bandwidth, there will be no problem.

OVERVIEW OF IP

Scores of books are available that describe IP in detail. The approach here is to provide an overview of IP, and emphasize the aspects of IP that are especially important for the support of voice traffic. I recommend any of the Douglas Comer and Richard Stevens books to the newcomer to TCP/IP.

IP is an example of a connectionless service. It permits the exchange of traffic between two host computers without any prior call setup. (However, these two computers can share a common connection-oriented transport protocol.) Since IP is connectionless, it is possible that the datagrams could be lost between the two end-user's stations. For example, the IP gateway enforces a maximum queue length size; if this queue length is violated, the buffers will overflow. In this situation, the additional datagrams are discarded in the network. For this reason, a higher level transport layer protocol (such as TCP) is essential to recover from these problems.

IP hides the underlying subnetwork from the end user. In this context, it creates a virtual network to that end user. This aspect of IP is quite attractive because it allows different types of networks to attach to an IP node. As a result, IP is reasonably simple to install and because of its connectionless design, it is quite robust.

Since IP is an unreliable, best-effort datagram-type protocol, it has no retransmission mechanisms. It provides no error recovery for the underlying subnetworks. It has no flow-control mechanisms. The user data (datagrams) may be lost, duplicated, or even arrive out of order. It is not the job of IP to deal with most of these problems. As we shall see later, most of the problems are passed to the next higher layer, TCP.

These low-level characteristics of IP translate into a fairly effective means of supporting real-time voice traffic. Assuming the routers are fast, and sufficient bandwidth is available, IP does not introduce significant overhead to the support of VoIP. There are better mechanisms, but as stated in Chapter 1, no other mechanism has the universal presence of IP (and the IP addresses).

Figure 2–5 shows how IP processes an incoming IP datagram [STEV98].[3] The incoming packet is stored in a queue to await processing. Once processing begins, the options field is processed to determine if any options are in the header (the support for this operation varies). The datagram header is checked for any modifications that may have occurred during its journey to this IP node (with a checksum field discussed later). Next, it is determined if the IP address is local; if so, an IP protocol ID field in the header is used to pass the bits in the data field to the next module, such as TCP, UDP, ICMP, etc.

An IP node can be configured to forward or not forward datagrams. If the node is a forwarding node, the IP destination address in the IP datagram header is matched against a routing table to calculate the next node (next hop) that is to receive the datagram. If a match in the table to

---

[3][STEV98]. Stevens, W. Richard. *TCP/IP Illustrated*, Addison-Wesley, 1997. Mr. Steven's figure in his book (page 112) does not contain the error-check operation, which I have added in this figure.

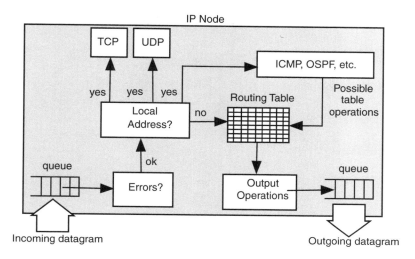

Figure 2–5   Processing an IP datagram

the destination address is found, the datagram is forwarded to the next node. Otherwise, it is sent to a default route, or it is discarded.

Figure 2–6 is an example of a typical routing table found in a router. Individual systems differ in the contents of the routing table, but they all resemble this example. The entries in the table are:

- **Destination:** IP address of the destination node.
- **Route Mask:** Mask that is used with destination address to identify bits that are used in routing.
- **Next Hop:** IP address of the next hop in the route.
- **If Index (port):** Physical port on the router to reach the next hop address.
- **Metric:** "Cost" to reach the destination address.
- **Route Type:** Directly attached to router (direct), or reached through another router (remote).
- **Source of Route:** How the route was discovered.
- **Route Age:** In seconds, since the route was last updated.
- **Route Information:** Miscellaneous information.
- **MTU:** Size of payload

The IP Datagram

A productive approach to analyzing IP is to first examine the fields in the IP datagram (PDU) depicted in Figure 2–7.

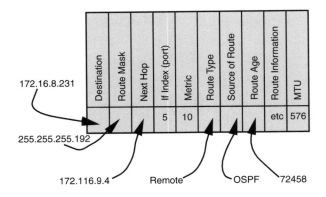

Where:
MTU   Maximum transmission unit size (in bytes, of the L_2 I field)

Figure 2–6   Typical IP routing table

The *version* field identifies the version of IP in use. Most protocols contain this field because some network nodes may not have the latest release available of the protocol. The current version of IP is 4.

The *header length* field contains 4 bits which are set to a value to indicate the length of the datagram header. The length is measured in 32-bit words. Typically, a header without QOS options contains 20 octets. Therefore, the value in the length field is usually 5.

The *type of service (TOS)* field can be used to identify several QOS functions provided for an Internet application. It is quite similar to the

Version	Header Length
Type of Service	
Total Length	
Identifier	
Flags	Fragment Offset
Time to Live	
Protocol	
Header Checksum	
Source Address	
Destination Address	
Options and Padding	
Data	

Figure 2–7   The IP datagram

service field that resides in the OSI-based CLNP (Connectionless Network Protocol) PDU. Transit delay, throughput, precedence, and reliability can be requested with this field.

The TOS field contains five entries consisting of 8 bits. Bits 0, 1, and 2 contain a precedence value which is used to indicate the relative importance of the datagram. Values range from 0 to 7, with 0 set to indicate a *routine precedence*. The precedence field is not used in most systems, although the value of 7 is used by some implementations to indicate a network control datagram. However, the precedence field could be used to implement flow control and congestion mechanisms in a network. This would allow gateways and host nodes to make decisions about the order of "throwing away" datagrams in case of congestion.

The next three bits are used for other services and are described as follows: Bit 3 is the *delay bit (D bit)*. When set to 1, this TOS requests a short delay through an internet. The aspect of delay is not defined in the standard and it is up to the vendor to implement the service. The next bit is the *throughput bit (T bit)*. It is set to 1 to request for high throughput through an internet. Again, its specific implementation is not defined in the standard. The next bit used is the *reliability bit (R bit)*, which allows a user to request high reliability for the datagram. The last bit of interest is the *cost bit (C bit)*, which is set to request the use of a low-cost link (from the standpoint of monetary cost). The last bit is not used at this time.

The *TOS field* is not used in some vendors' implementation of IP. Nonetheless, it will be used increasingly in the future as the Internet's capabilities are increased. Consequently, a user should examine this field for future work and ascertain a vendor's use or intended support of this field.

The *total length* field specifies the total length of the IP datagram. It is measured in octets and includes the length of the header and the data. IP subtracts the header length field from the total length field to compute the size of the data field. The maximum possible length of a datagram is 65,535 octets (2^{16}). Gateways that service IP datagrams are required to accept any datagram that supports the maximum size of a PDU of the attached networks. Additionally, all gateways must accommodate datagrams of 576 octets in total length.

Each 32-bit value is transmitted in this order: (a) bits 0–7, (b) bits 8–15, (c) bits 16–23, and (d) bits 24–31. This is known as big endian byte ordering.

The IP protocol uses three fields in the header to control datagram fragmentation and reassembly. These fields are the *identifier*, *flags*, and *fragmentation offset.* The identifier field is used to uniquely identify all fragments from an original datagram. It is used with the source address at the receiving host to identify the fragment. The flags field contains bits to determine if the datagram may be fragmented, and if fragmented, one of the bits can be set to determine if this fragment is the last fragment of the datagram. The fragmentation offset field contains a value which specifies the relative position of the fragment to the original datagram. The value is initialized as 0 and is subsequently set to the proper number if/when an IP node fragments the data. The value is measured in units of eight octets.

The *time-to-live (TTL)* parameter is used to measure the time a datagram has been in the internet. It is similar to CLNP's lifetime field. Each gateway in the internet is required to check this field and discard the datagram if the TTL value equals 0. An IP node is also required to decrement this field in each datagram it processes. In actual implementations, the TTL field is a number of hops value. Therefore, when a datagram proceeds through a gateway (hop), the value in the field is decremented by a value of one. Some implementations of IP use a time-counter in this field and decrement the value in one-second decrements.

The time-to-live (TTL) field is used not only to prevent endless loops, it can also be used by the host to limit the lifetime that datagrams have in an internet. Be aware that if a host is acting as a "route-through" node, it must treat the TTL field by the router rules. The reader should check with the vendor to determine when a host throws away a datagram based on the TTL value.

Ideally, the TTL value could be configured and its value assigned based on observing an internet's performance. Additionally, network management information protocols such as those residing in SNMP might wish to set the TTL value for diagnostic purposes. Finally, if your vendor uses a fixed value that cannot be reconfigured, make certain that it is fixed initially to allow for your internet's growth.

The *protocol* field is used to identify the next level protocol above the IP that is to receive the datagram at the final host destination. It is similar to the Ethertype field found in the Ethernet frame, but identifies the payload in the data field of the IP datagram. The Internet standards groups have established a numbering system to identify the most widely used upper-layer protocols.

The *header checksum* is used to detect an error that may have occurred in the header. Checks are not performed on the user data stream. Some critics of IP have stated that the provision for error detection in the user data should allow the receiving gateway to at least notify the sending host that problems have occurred. (This service is indeed provided by a companion standard to IP [the ICMP].) Whatever one's view is on the issue, the current approach keeps the checksum algorithm in IP quite simple. It does not have to operate on many octets, but it does require that a higher level protocol at the receiving host must perform some type of error check on the user data if it cares about its integrity.

The checksum is computed as follows (and this same procedure is used in TCP, UDP, ICMP, and IGMP):

- Set checksum field to 0.
- Calculate 16-bit one's complement sum of the header (header is treated as a sequence of 16-bit words).
- Store 16-bit one's complement in the checksum field.
- At receiver, calculate 16-bit one's complement of the header.
- Receiver's checksum is all 1s if the header has not been changed.

IP carries two addresses in the datagram. These are labeled *source* and *destination addresses* and remain the same value throughout the life of the datagram. These fields contain the internet addresses.

The *options* field is used to identify several additional services.[4] It is similar to the option part field of CLNP. The options field is not used in every datagram. The majority of implementations use this field for network management and diagnostics.

TCP AND UDP

Figure 1–10 in Chapter 1 showed that layer four of the OSI Model is the Transport layer. Layer four is where Transmission Control Protocol (TCP) and the User Datagram Protocol (UDP) operate. We shall see that TCP is a connection-oriented protocol, and is responsible for the reliable transfer of user traffic between two computers. Consequently, it uses sequence numbers and acknowledgments to make certain all traffic is delivered safely to the destination endpoint.

UDP is a connectionless protocol and does not provide sequencing or acknowledgments. It is used in place of TCP in situations where the full

---

[4]The option field has fallen into disuse by routers because of the processing overhead required to support the features it identifies. The concepts of this field are well-founded, and a similar capability is found in IPv6, the new IP version.

services of TCP are not needed. For example, telephony traffic, the Trivial File Transfer Protocol (TFTP), and the Remote Procedure Call (RPC) use UDP. Since it has no reliability, flow control, nor error-recovery measures, UDP serves principally as a multiplexer/demultiplexer for receiving and sending traffic into and out of an application.

TCP resides in the transport layer of a conventional seven-layer model. It is situated above IP and below the upper layers. It is designed to reside in the host computer or in a machine that is tasked with end-to-end integrity of the transfer of user data. In practice, TCP is usually placed in the user host machine. Recently, TCP is being loaded into the router in order to provide the router with the ability to examine the TCP header and port numbers. This subject is discussed in the next section.

Notwithstanding, TCP may be placed in the router in some installations. The reasons for this placement vary. As one example, TCP is used in some routers for router-to-router acknowledgment.

TCP is designed to run over the IP. Since IP is a connectionless network protocol, the tasks of reliability, flow control, sequencing, opens, and closes are given to TCP. Although TCP and IP are tied together so closely that they are used in the same context "TCP/IP," TCP can also support other protocols. For example, another connectionless protocol, such as the ISO 8473 (Connectionless Network Protocol or CLNP), could operate with TCP (with adjustments to the interface between the modules). In addition, the application protocols, such as the File Transfer Protocol (FTP) and the Simple Mail Transfer Protocol (SMTP), rely on many of the services of TCP.

Many of the TCP functions (such as flow control, reliability, sequencing, etc.) could be handled within an application program. But it makes little sense to code these functions into each application. Moreover, applications programmers are usually not versed in error-detection and flow-control operations. The preferred approach is to develop generalized software that provides community functions applicable to a wide range of applications, and then invoke these programs from the application software. This allows the application programmer to concentrate on solving the application problem and it isolates the programmer from the nuances and problems of networks.

The Port Concept

One of the jobs of TCP and UDP is to act as the port manager for the user and application residing in layer seven (these operations are performed in concert with the operating system).

Figure 2–8 reinforces those thoughts once more. It shows how the traffic passes from TCP or UDP to the respective application.

A TCP upper-layer user in a host machine is identified by a *port* identifier. The port number is concatenated with the IP internet address to form a *socket*. This address must be unique throughout the internet and a pair of sockets uniquely identifies each endpoint connection. As examples:

Sending socket   = Source IP address + source port number
Receiving socket = Destination IP address + destination port number

Although the mapping of ports to higher-layer processes can be handled as an internal matter in a host, the Internet publishes numbers for frequently used higher-level processes.

Even though TCP establishes numbers for frequently used ports, the numbers and values above 1024 are available for private use. The remainder of the values for the assigned port numbers have the low-order 8-bits set to zero. The remainder of these bits are available to any organization to use as they choose.

Examination of port numbers.   Recently, routers have begun examining the port numbers in order to determine the type of traffic in the user payload. For example, a destination port number might identify a video application and the router could then treat this traffic as a high-priority unit (in contrast to low-priority data traffic).

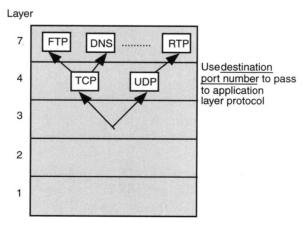

Figure 2–8   The port concept

TCP Traffic Management Operations

TCP acknowledges segments for both interactive traffic and bulk data traffic. However, TCP varies in how these acknowledgements occur. The variability depends on the operating system through which TCP executes, as well as the options chosen for a TCP session. In essence, there is no "standard" TCP operating profile.

Notwithstanding these comments, TCP does use many common procedures that are found in most TCP implementations and versions.

UDP

The User Datagram Protocol (UDP) is classified as a connectionless protocol. It is sometimes used in place of TCP in situations where the full services of TCP are not needed. For example, the Trivial File Transfer Protocol (TFTP) and the Remote Procedure Call (RPC) use UDP.

UDP serves as a simple application interface to the IP. Since it has no reliability, flow control, nor error-recovery measures, it serves principally as a multiplexer/demultiplexer for the receiving and sending of IP traffic.

UDP uses the port concept to direct the datagrams to the proper upper-layer application. The UDP datagram contains a destination port number and a source port number. The destination number is used by UDP and the operating system to deliver the traffic to the proper recipient.

Perhaps the best way to explain UDP is to examine the message and the fields that reside in the message. As Figure 2–9 illustrates, the format is quite simple and contains the following fields:

- *Source Port*: This value identifies the port of the sending application process. The field is optional. If it is not used, a value of 0 is inserted in this field.
- *Destination Port*: This value identifies the receiving process on the destination host machine.
- *Length*: This value indicates the length of the user datagram including the header and the data. This value implies that the minimum length is 8 octets.
- *Checksum*: This value is the 16-bit one's complement of the one's complement sum of the pseudo-IP header, the UDP header, and the data. It also performs a checksum on any padding (if it was necessary to make the message contain a multiple of two octets).

```
                ─────────── 32 Bits ───────────
        ┌──────────────────────┬──────────────────────┐
        │     Source Port      │   Destination Port   │
        ├──────────────────────┼──────────────────────┤
        │        Length        │       Checksum       │
        ├──────────────────────┴──────────────────────┤
        │                    Data                      │
        └──────────────────────────────────────────────┘
```

Figure 2–9   Format for the UDP data unit

There is not a lot more to be said about UDP. It is a minimal level of service used in many transaction-based application systems. However, it is quite useful if the full services of TCP are not needed.

SUMMARY

Data networks in general, and the Internet in particular, are designed to support asynchronous, non–real-time traffic. The variable delay in data networks is usually not a big problem, due to the asynchronous nature of data applications.

The design philosophy of data networks is the opposite of voice networks. Voice networks are designed to support synchronous real-time traffic, with a fixed delay between the sender and the receiver.

Three obstacles must be overcome if the Internet and internets are to be effective bearers of speech: (a) latency must be reduced, (b) jitter must be reduced, (b) traffic loss must be improved.

UDP and IP are the chosen L_4 and L_3 protocols for VoIP. Their choice has nothing to do with their merit (although they are not poor choices). Rather, it reflects the fact that UDP and IP are found in most workstations and personal computers.

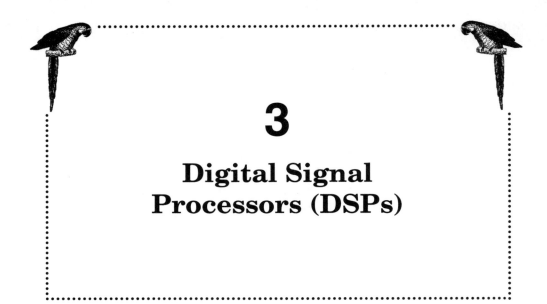

3

Digital Signal
Processors (DSPs)

Digital signal processors (DSPs) are the engines for voice coders and modems, and they are finding their way into many other systems, such as answering machines, and consumer high-fidelity audio systems. In this chapter, we provide an overview of DSPs, and show how they are used to support low-bit rate coders for VoIP.

ROLE OF DSPS IN PACKET-VOICE OPERATIONS

A DSP is a specialized processor that has been in use for many years in other telephony applications such as mobile/wireless networks. They are attractive for internet telephony because they are small, use relatively little power, and are very fast. Packet voice requires computational-intensive operations and special processing, and a standard microprocessor is not up to the task of performing these operations.

In addition, packetized voice requires considerable multiplication and addition functions in a very short period of time. A DSP is designed to support these types of functions. Multiplication operations to estimate the frequency spectrum of a signal are very computationally intensive, and are often performed with a Fast Fourier Transform (FFT) algorithm, a subject discussed shortly.

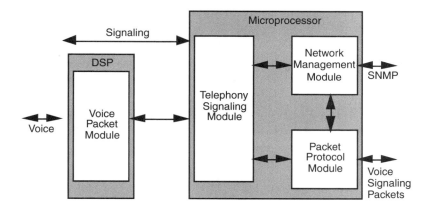

Where:
  SNMP   Simple Network Management Protocol

Figure 3–1   Packet-voice module [KRAP98]

The DSP is the principal machine that performs voice packetization and compression. It works in consonance with other components as depicted in Figure 3–1. The DSP's functions are integrated with other microprocessors. In this example [KRAP98],[1] the DSP supports the voice packet module. It interfaces with a microprocessor containing operations for telephony signaling, network management (the Simple Network Management Protocol [SNMP]), and a packet protocol module, which is used for sending and receiving voice packets.

The DSP component performs compression, voice activity detection, echo cancellation, jitter management, and clock synchronization. The telephony signaling module acts as the communicator between the DSP and the packet protocol module. In turn, the packet protocol module converts the signal information from telephony-based protocols (DS0) to packet-based protocols (IP). The network management protocol monitors the overall activities of the system and allows configuration operations to be performed on various components.

The DSP usually supports more than one telephony channel. The number of channels supported depends on a variety of factors, principally the power of the DSP in millions of instructions per second (MIPS). Another key factor is the amount of memory residing in the DSP. The more memory on the board, the more efficient the operation, but this approach

---

[1][KRAP98] Krapf, Eric. "DSPs: Powering the Packet-Voice Revolution," *Business Communications Review's Voice 2000*. Oct. 1998.

translates into fewer MIPS. Thus, there is a trade-off between MIPS versus memory. As a general practice, manufacturers place considerable memory on the DSP chip for implementations of 1-to-8 ports (interfaces).

Figure 3–2 shows the DSP voice packet module in more detail [KRAP98]. The Pulse Code Modulation (PCM) interface performs conventional G.711 A/D and D/A operations, and this information is used by the voice codec module to perform the compression operations and syntax translations in accordance with G.723.1, G.729A, etc. The PCM interface also contains a tone generator and resampler. The resampler is fed by the comfort noise unit, and packet-loss manager.

On the transmit side, the module employs an ITU-T G.165/G.168 echo cancellor, which is fed into gain control, a voice activity detector, and a tone detector. The output from the voice activity detector is processed by an ITU-T G Series codec, then sent to the packet protocol module for assembly and transmission. On the receive side, the packet protocol module receives the traffic, passes this information to the adaptive playout unit, where a packet loss manager monitors and compensates for the loss of packets. This input is fed to the comfort noise converter, which provides noise to the receiver to simulate a telephone line.

The module may contain the fax interface unit consisting of a V-Series fax specification such as V.17, the fax T.38 protocol, and a network driver.

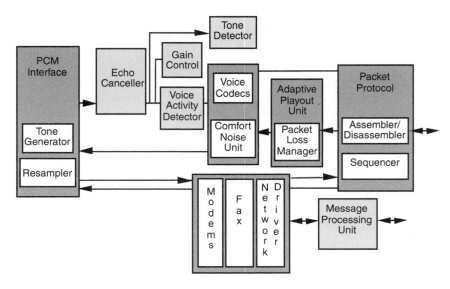

Figure 3–2   Typical DSP-based module [KRAP98]

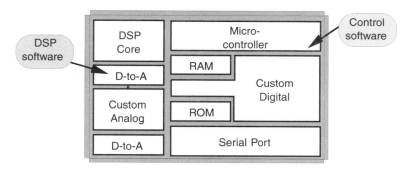

Figure 3–3   DSP–core-based ASICs [LAPS97]

DSP Cores

An approach in the design of a DSP system is to combine the DSP with custom circuits, on a single chip. This approach is attractive, because it allows the manufacturer to use the high-powered DSP as well as custom circuits in one system. Two approaches are used in this endeavor. One approach uses a DSP–core-based application-specific integrated circuits (ASIC), and the other approach uses customizable DSP processors. The overall chip contains a DSP as one part of the chip, and an ASIC as another part. Figures 3–3 and 3–4 provide a functional view of these types of chipsets [LAPS97].[2] Notice that the DSP core logic is part of the overall system, which can support various types of ASICs, such as a speech coder, a high-fidelity ASIC, or a modem ASIC. The configurations shown in Figures 3–3 and 3–4 are general examples, and the vendors differ in how they implement the DSP-based ASICs. Some vendors provide a complete configuration, while others provide a "core", and license the core to the customer. This latter approach allows the customer to customize the circuit to a specific application.

DSP VS. CUSTOMIZED HARDWARE

It is also noteworthy that a DSP implementation may not be as effective as customized hardware. One obvious benefit is that customized hardware can be designed to perform better than a generalized DSP. For example, in systems that need a high sampling rate, customized hard-

---

[2][LAPS97]. Lapsley, Phil. *DSP Processor Fundamentals*, IEEE Press, 1997.

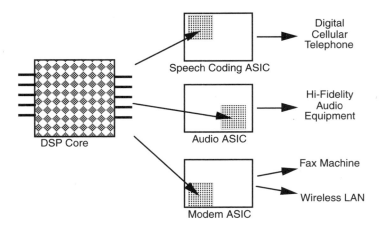

Figure 3–4 Another view of DSP core-based ASICs [LAPS97]

ware may be the best approach. For large volume applications, it may be less expensive to use customized hardware instead of a DSP approach. An application with fewer requirements often does not need the full functionality of a DSP. Therefore, the full operations of the DSP may be too costly for an application with a narrow range of functions. Notwithstanding, the long lead times for the design and manufacturing of customized hardware usually translates into high costs and the inability to meet critical deadlines.

It is not necessary to take an all-or-nothing approach. A variety of hybrid products are available that combine DSPs with application-specific ASICs, customized ICs, as well as field-programmable gate arrays (FPGAs).

FIXED- AND FLOATING-POINT PROCESSORS

As depicted in Figure 3–5, DSPs are organized around a fixed or floating-point architecture. The fixed-point architecture is the simplest approach and was the original way that DSPs were designed. The floating-point architecture uses the conventional mantissa and exponent notations. Just like any other processor, fixed-point operations yield more precision but yield a lesser range of fractions. The fixed-point processors are available in 16-bit, 20-bit, or 24-bit word sizes. In contrast, floating-point processors use a 32-bit word length. For purposes of efficiency and expense, designers attempt to use the smallest word size to support the ap-

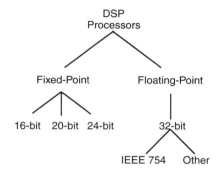

Figure 3–5   DSP arithmetic structure

plication. Currently, the most common word size for a fixed point processor is 16 bits. It is likely the reader has studied the arithmetic of fixed- and floating-point operations, so we will not dwell on these operations here.

One last point is relevant to this discussion. Be aware that as a general practice, the word size of the instruction word size is the same in most processors. However, exceptions do exist, and some implementations support a part 16-bit word size, and a 24-bit instruction word size.

MEMORY ARCHITECTURES

In traditional processors, shown in Figure 3–6, instructions and data are stored in a single memory area, processed in the processor core, through the address bus and the data bus. In a simple implementation of this architecture, the processor takes one instruction cycle to make an access to memory without either a read or write operation. This approach is

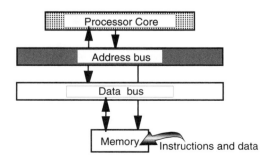

Figure 3–6   Von Neumann architecture

known as the Von Neumann architecture. While this architecture is sufficient for many systems today, it is inadequate for processor-intensive, real-time applications.

One example is the implementation of algorithms to support real-time voice and video [the Finite Impulse Response filter algorithm (FIR) discussed shortly]. In this arrangement, it takes multiple memory accesses for a processor to perform the operations to support typical FIR operations consisting of multiply and accumulate operations. This statement is true even if the processor is designed to perform a multiply and accumulate operation and only one instruction cycle. The fact still remains that four memory accesses are needed to perform the operation.

In contrast to the Von Neumann architecture, DSPs implement a Harvard architecture shown in Figure 3–7. With this approach, two memory spaces may be partitioned with one space to hold instructions and the other to hold data, although there are implementations where the two memory locations store both instructions and data. As the figure shows, there are also two bus sets, thus allowing two simultaneous accesses to the memory. In effect, this architecture doubles the architecture's capacity (known as the memory bandwidth), and it is quite important in keeping the processor core completely occupied with both instructions and data.

It should be emphasized that high-performance generalized processors (the Pentium and the PowerPC) certainly can make multiple memory accesses per instruction, but the generalized processor is just that: a

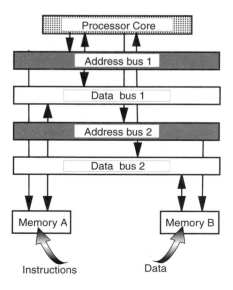

Figure 3–7   Harvard architecture

device built for generic, generalized processing We shall have more to say about this subject shortly.

THE SOFTWARE IS DIFFERENT

The DSP programmer is involved with *each* instruction that passes through the processor. Generalized processor programmers may not know or even specify the instructions and data that reside in caches. In contrast, the majority of DSP processors do not implement cache, but rather rely on chip memory with the multiple bus sets to allow them to rapidly perform several memory accesses with each instruction.[3]

Moreover, data caches are rare for DSPs, because the input data for the DSP is no longer needed once it has be operated on. That is to say, once the DSP operates on a sample (say a voice sample), the sample can be discarded because it is not used in subsequent operations. (It is true that a voice sample is used more than once for sample-to-sample correlations, but after it has been processed, it is not used again.)

FAST FOURIER TRANSFORM (FFT) OPERATIONS

Fast Fourier Transform (FFT) operations are commonly used in DSPs. They were developed in the 1970s to reduce the number of operations in the multiplication of numbers [CRAN97],[4] which is a common operation in digital telephony. Consider two D-digit numbers x and y. The conventional multiplication of x and y consists of multiplying each successive digit of x by every digit of y and then adding the resulting columns. The process takes D^2 operations. FFT reduces the number of operations to $D \log D$. For example, if x and y were 1000-digit numbers, the conventional multiplication would take more than 1,000,000 operations. FFT reduces the number of operations to about 50,000.

The numbers X and Y are treated as signals, and FFT is applied to X and Y in order to break X and Y into their spectral components. The spectra are then multiplied together, frequency by frequency. Then an in-

---

[3]There are exceptions to this statement. Some DSPs do use a very small instruction cache separate from the on-chip memory banks which is used for storing critical instructions for very small looping operations to obviate the processor having to use its on-chip operations to retrieve these critical instructions.

[4][CRAN97]. Crandall, Richard E. "The Challenge of Large Numbers," *Scientific American*, February, 1997.

verse FFT operation and some other final operations are used to yield the product of X and Y.

There are variations of FFT. One method treats the digital signals as bipolar, which permits both positive and negative digits to be used. Another approach is to weight the signals by first multiplying x and y by some other special signal. I refer you to [CRAN97] for more information on FFT, as well some fascinating information on large numbers.

SIGNAL FILTERS AND THE FINITE IMPULSE RESPONSE (FIR) FILTER

One of the main operations of the DSP is signal filtering. The operation is used to improve the quality of the signal, such as the signal-to-noise ratio.

The Finite Impulse Response (FIR) filter is a common digital filter. It implements a 31-tap filter, which is shown in Figure 3–8. This illustration is the most widely used in the literature and further information is available from [EYRE98] and [LAPS97]. Both these references use the same examples, and identical textual explanations. I quote directly from [EYRE98].[5]

> The blocks labeled D [in Figure 3–8] are unit delay operators; their output is a copy of the input sample, delayed by one sample period. A series of storage elements (usually memory locations) are used to implement a series of these delay elements (this series is called a delay line).
>
> At any given time, N-1 of the most recently received input samples reside in the delay line, where N is the total number of input samples used in the computation of each output sample. Input samples are designated X_N; the first input sample is x_1, the next is x_2, and so on.
>
> Each time a new input sample arrives, the FIR filter operation shifts previously stored samples one place to right along the delay line. It then computes a new output sample by multiplying the newly arrived sample and each of the previously stored input samples by the corresponding coefficient. In [Figure 3–8], coefficients are represented as C_k, where k is the coefficient number. The summation of the multiplication products forms the new output sample, Y_n.
>
> We call the combination of a single delay element, the associated multiplication operation, and the associated addition operation a tap. The number of taps and the values chosen for the coefficients define the filter characteristics. For

---

[5][EYRE98] Jennifer Eyre and Jeff Bier, "DSP Processors Hit the Main Stream," *Computer*, August 1998.

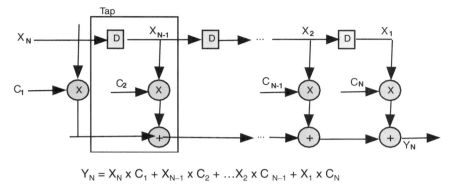

$$Y_N = X_N \times C_1 + X_{N-1} \times C_2 + \dots X_2 \times C_{N-1} + X_1 \times C_N$$

Figure 3–8   The finite impulse response filter (FIR) [EYRE98]

example, if the values of the coefficients are all equal to the reciprocal of the number of taps, $1/N$, the filter performs an averaging operation, one form of a low-pass filter.

To summarize briefly, N represents the total number of input samples used for the specific computation for each output sample. The concept works with a shift register concept. When a new input sample arrives, the previously stored samples are shifted one place to the right through the delay line. A new output sample is then computed by multiplying the new sample with each of the previously stored input samples by the corresponding coefficient.

As you can see, the DSP is organized around the multiple and accumulate (MAC) operation. Because multiple accumulate operations are quite common in applications such as packet telephony, the efficient design of a DSP to perform multiply accumulates is quite important. Because MAC is indeed important, DSPs provide specialized MAC operations.

PREDICTABILITY OF PERFORMANCE

Earlier, we discussed the critical need for DSPs to support real-time applications. Therefore, they must exhibit predictable execution performance because of the tight time constraints involved in real-time execution. In contrast, some generalized processors use code that may consume a different number of instruction cycles depending on what branching operations may take place. Consequently, it is quite difficult with these architectures to predict how long it will take for certain operations to take place. This lack of predictability makes it difficult to optimize code or to predict the timing of the execution of the code in certain situations.

Since the DSP programmer determines the exact set of instructions when they are processed, it is a relatively easy task to predict the time required in executing the code on a DSP. In a nutshell, DSPs do not use the general processor's concepts of branch predictions and speculative execution. The DSP executes highly specialized instruction sets to perform certain functions in a very efficient manner.

An interesting aspect of this situation from a programming standpoint is that the code is certainly less than intuitive, and may require some retraining on the part of a conventional application programmer. To illustrate this point, consider this instruction based on the Motorola DSP 56300 system [EYRE98]. X and Y represent two Harvard architecture memory spaces:

$$\text{MAC } X0, Y0, A \ X: (R0) + , X0 \ Y: (R4) + N4, Y0$$

This instruction directs the DSP to do the following:

- Multiply the contents of registers $X0$ and $Y0$.
- Add the result to a running total stored in accumulator A.
- Load register $X0$ from X, pointed to by register $R0$.
- Load register $Y0$ from Y, pointed to by register $R4$.
- Postincrement $R0$ by one; and
- Postincrement $R4$ by the contents of register $R4$.

It is tight code, and is quite specialized. This single line of code encompasses all the operations to calculate an FIR filter trap.

Compilers are available to allow programmers to write in C or C++ for translations for execution on DSPs. Generally, they do not work very well because the use of multiple memory spaces, irregular instruction sets, and the use of multiple buses and memory locations makes it a particularly big challenge to write efficient compilers for DSPs.

ANOTHER EXAMPLE OF DSP CODE

The previous example is a bit difficult to read and takes some thought for a programmer to use. Let us take a look at another example which may be a bit easier to analyze. The code shown in Figure 3–9 is

```
Entry  fir
fir:   CNTR=30;  ....................................../Instruction 1
*/
       MR=0, MX0=DM(I1,M1), MY0=PM(I4,M4); ............*Instruction 2
*/
       Do sop Until CE;  ............................./*Instruction 3
*/
sop:   MR=MR+MX0*MY0, MX0=DM(I1,M1), MY0=PM(I4,M4);..../*Instruction 4
*/
       MR=MR+MX0*MY0;  .............................../*Instruction 5
*/
       RTS;  ......................................../*Instruction 6
```

Figure 3–9   FIR filter routine [STEV98]

from an analog device's ASP-21xx DSP and I guide you to [STEV98][6] if you need more information on these operations.

The example shown deals with the FIT operation introduced earlier. One of the most important functions in communication DSPs is signal filtering. This concept is simple in that the operation manipulates an input signal to improve its characteristics. Examples that come to mind in filtering improving the signal-to-noise ratio on a telephone line or to remove unwanted noise or static from the input signal. Digital filtering has replaced most analog filtering because it is less expensive, easier to define operation tolerances, and not subject to environmental factors (such as temperature).

Here is an explanation of what the code does:

- Instruction 1: Load loop counter with the filter length minus 1, so the example is for a 31 tap-FIR filter.
- Instruction 2: The accumulator register MR is set to 0, and a prefetch of a sample in memory location (DM) is loaded into register MX0. In addition, a filter coefficient is loaded into MY0 from memory location (PM). I1 and I4 contain the address of the data samples and filter coefficients respectively. M1 and M4 contain modifier values, and are set to 1 here. The code meaning may not be obvious, but each time instruction 2 is executed, I1=I1+M1, and I4=I4+M4.

[6][STEV98] Stevens, Jeff. "DSPs in Communications," *IEEE Spectrum*, September 1998.

- Instruction 3: A do loop is set up to end at label sop. With each loop execution, the loop counter decrements by one, and the loop is exited upon counter expiration.
- Instruction 4: Perform the multiply-accumulate in MR, then fetch the next data sample and filter coefficient.
- Instruction 5: Perform the last multiply-accumulate.
- Instruction 6: Exit the routine

COMING UP

It is known that in the future DSPs will become much faster. It is expected that by the turn of this century, a 200 MIPS equipment will be common with 300- to 400-MIPS machines available in the year 2001. A conventional 64-kbit/s voice signal can be produced in a high-quality manner by the use of a 2-MIPS machine and the ITU-T is examining a standard for a 4-kbit/s voice signal which is expected to require 40–45 MIPS. The processor to support this low-bit rate coder is on the way and likely to be announced in 1999 or 2000.

Furthermore, PCs and workstations will have DSPs installed (or a new generalized chip that performs well enough to produce low-bit rate and high-quality audio signals), thus providing for toll-quality signals from the user appliance.

SUMMARY

Digital signal processors (DSPs) are the engines for voice coders and modems, and an important variable in the VoIP equation. They rely now on Harvard architectures, very compact code, FFT, and other advanced techniques. It is reasonable to say that the new generalized processors (the Pentiums, etc.) will be of sufficient horsepower to compete with DSPs. This may be so, but the generalized processors will likely be tied up with other operations. So, it seems reasonable to say that DSPs and the new chips will both reside in the end-user PC.

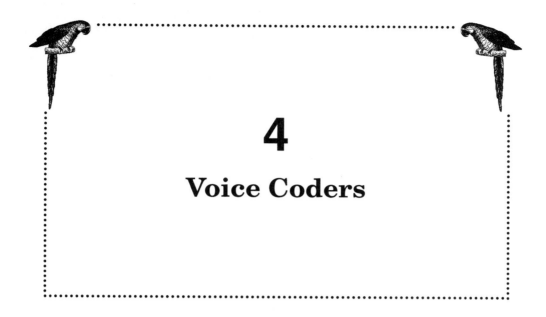

4

Voice Coders

This chapter provides an overview of the prevalent coders/decoders (codecs) used in VoIP. They are also known as codecs, speech, coders, voice coders, or simply coders. There is a wealth of information on this subject, and it is not my intent to rehash these sources. Some recommendations for reading are [MINO98],[1] any of John Bellamy's books, and the *BT Technology Journal*. Several of BT's issues in the past two years have focused on voice coders, and the ITU-T specifications.

The approach in this chapter is to provide a brief tutorial on the major coder functions, provide a brief classification of coders, and then explain three coders used for VoIP: ITU-T G.723, ITU-T G.728, and ITU-T G.729 voice coders.

FUNCTIONS OF THE VOICE CODER

The principal function of a voice coder is to encode pulse code modulation (PCM) user speech samples into a small number of bits (a frame) in such a manner that the speech is robust in the presence of link errors,

---

[1][MINO98] Minoli, Daniel. *Delivering Voice over IP Networks*, John Wiley & Sons, 1998.

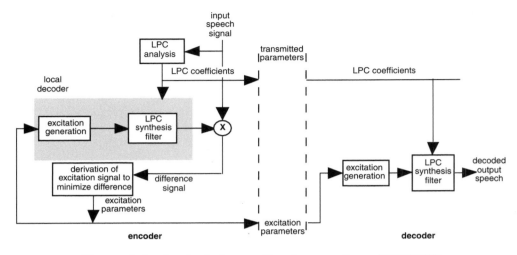

Figure 4–1   Analysis-by-synthesis operations [WEST96]

jittery networks, and bursty transmissions. At the receiver, the frames are decoded back to the PCM speech samples, and then converted to the waveform.

CLASSIFICATION OF SPEECH CODERS

Speech coders are classified into three types: (a) waveform coding, (b) vocoding, and (c) hybrid coding. Waveform coders reproduce the analog waveform as accurately as possible, including background noise. Since they operate on all input signals, they produce high quality samples. However, waveform coders operate at a high bit rate. For example, the ITU-T G.711 (PCM) specification uses a 64-kbit/s rate.

Vocoders (voice + coders) do not reproduce the original waveform. The encoder builds a set of parameters, which are sent to the receiver to be used to drive a speech production model.[2] Linear prediction coding (LPC) is used to derive parameters of a time-varying digital filter. This filter models the output of the speaker's vocal tract [WEST96].[3] The quality of vocoders is not good enough for use in telephony systems.

---

[2]This concept has been around for many years. Homer Dudley of Bell Labs demonstrated it at the World Fair in 1939.

[3][WEST96] Westall, F. A., Johnston, R. D., Lewis, A. V., "Speech Technology for Telecommunications," *BT Journal*, Vol. 14, No. 1, January, 1996.

The prevalent speech coder for VoIP is a hybrid coder, which melds the attractive features of waveform coders and vocoders. They are also attractive because they operate at a very low bit rate (4–16 kit/s). These coders use analysis-by-synthesis (AbS) techniques.

To illustrate, consider a speech pattern produced by the human vocal tract: voiced sounds (phonemes like pa, da, etc.), and unvoiced sounds (phonemes like sh, th, etc.) are produced during talking to produce the signal. An excitation signal is derived from the input speech signal in such a manner that the difference between the input and the synthesized speech is quite small. The use of LPC, the excitation operation, and the difference checks for AbS is shown in Figure 4–1, and we examined the filter concepts in Chapter 3.

Toll-quality coders easily operate at 8 kbit/s as shown in Figure 4–2. As explained in Chapter 1, toll quality speech must achieve a MOS (mean opinion score) of 4 or above. Conventional PCM speech deteriorates significantly at rates less than 32 kbit/s. PCM is not the issue here. Hybrid coding and vocoding exhibit acceptable MOS ratings for fairly low bit rates. At this stage, most VoIP-based coders operate at a range of 5.2–8 kbit/s. Research points to standardized coders that will provide acceptable MOS ratings at 4 kbit/s, and some proprietary systems operate at 4.8 kbit/s with a MOS of 3.8.

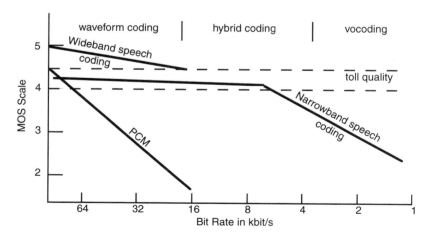

Figure 4–2 MOS ratings versus bit-rate for low bit-rate coders [WEST96]

Vector Quantization (QT) and Code Excited Linear Prediction (CELP)

An enhancement to the operation is to use a pre-stored codebook of optimized parameters (a vector of elements) to encode a representative vector of the input speech signal. This technique is known as vector quantization (VQ).

Coding performance can be improved further by combining VQ with AbS. The AbS VQ technique forms the basis for code excited linear predictive (CELP) coding. The main difference between VQ and AbS VQ is the definition of the quantization distortion measure in the VQ codebook search [WONG96].[4]

LINEAR PREDICTION ANALYSIS-BY-SYNTHESIS (LPAS) CODERS

The most popular class of speech coders for bit rates between 4.8 and 16 kbit/s are model-based coders that use an LPAS method. A linear prediction model of speech production is excited by an appropriate signal in order to model the signal over time. The parameters of both the speech model and the excitation are estimated and updated at regular time intervals (e.g., every 20 ms) and used to control the speech model. Two LPAS coders are discussed next: the forward-adaptive and backward-adaptive LPAS coders.

Forward-Adaptive LPAS coders: 8-kbit/s G.729 and 6.3- and 5.3-kbit/s G.723.1

In a forward-adaptive AbS coder, the prediction filter coefficients and gains are explicitly transmitted. To provide toll-quality performance, these two coders rely on a source model for speech. The excitation signal, in the form of information on the pitch period of the speech, is transmitted as well. The coder provides a good model for a speech signal but is not an appropriate model for some noises or for most instrumental music. Thus, the performance of LPAS coders for noisy backgrounds and music is of poorer quality than that produced by G.726 and G.727 coders.

---

[4][WONG96] Wong, W. T. K., Mack, R. M., Cheetham, B. M. G., Sun, X. Q., "Low Rate Speech Coding for Telecommunications," *BT Journal*, Vol. 14., No. 1, January, 1996.

G.723.1. ITU-T G.723.1 provides toll-quality speech at 6.4 kbit/s.[5] A lower quality speech coder operating at 5.3 kbit/s is also included. G.723.1 was designed with low-bit-rate video telephony in mind. For this application, the delay requirements are less stringent because the video coding delay is usually larger than that of speech. The G.723.1 coder has a 30-ms frame size and a 7.5-ms lookahead. When combined with processing delay to implement the coder, it is estimated that the coder would contribute 67.5 ms to the one-way delay. Additional delays result from the use of network and system buffers.

The G.723.1 coder is designed to perform conventional telephone bandwidth filtering (based on G.712) of the voice signal, sample the signal at the conventional 8000-Hz rate (based on G.711), and convert the 16-bit linear PCM code for input to the encoder. The decoder part performs a complementary operation on the output to reconstruct the voice signal.

The system encodes the voice signal into frames based on LPAS coding. A coder is capable of producing two rates of voice traffic: (a) 6.3 kbit/s for the high-rate, and (b) 5.3 kbit/s for the low-rate. The high-rate coder is based on Multipulse Maximum Likelihood Quantization (MP-MLQ), and the low-rate coder is based on Algebraic-Code-Excited Linear-Prediction (ACELP). A coder and decoder must support both rates, and the coder/decoder can switch between the rates between frame boundaries. Music and other audio signals are compressed and decompressed as well, but the coder is optimized for speech.

The encoder operates on frames (blocks) of 240 samples each to support the 8000-kHz sampling rate. Further operations (a high-pass filter to remove the DC component) result in four subframes of 60 samples each. A variety of other operations occur, such as the computation of an LPC filter, unquantized LCP filter coefficients, etc. resulting in a packetization time of 30 ms. For every subframe, an LPC filter is calculated using the unprocessed input signal. The filter on the last subframe is quantized with a predictive split vector quantizer (PSVQ). As stated earlier, the "lookahead" takes 7.5 ms, so the coding delay is 37.5 ms. This delay is a significant factor in evaluating coders, especially for transporting speech through a data network, since less delay in the coding (and decoding) process means more latitude to deal with the inevitable delay (and variable delay) found in internets.

---

[5]Some of my clients would not agree with this statement. They find G.723.1's speech signals "tinny." I have found some systems that are good and some that are poor.

The decoder operates also on a frame basis. The decoding process occurs as follows (a general summary of G.723.1):

- The quantized LPC indices are decoded.
- The LPC synthesis filter is constructed.
- On each subframe, the adaptive codebook excitation and fixed codebook excitation are decoded and input to the synthesis filter.
- The excitation signal is input into a pitch postfilter, and then into a synthesis filter.
- This is input into a formant postfilter, which uses a gain scaling unit to maintain the energy at the input level of the formant postfilter.

Silence compression has been used for a number of years to exploit the fact that silent periods in a voice conversation occupy about 50 percent of the total time of the conversation. The idea is to reduce the number of bits sent during these silent intervals and save in the overall number of bits transmitted.

For many years in the telephony network, selected analog speech signals have been processed through Time-Assigned Speech Interpolation (TASI). This technology places other speech or data signals into the silent periods of a conversation which provides additional capacity on multichannel links. Today, the concepts of TASI are applied to digital signals and tagged with new names—one example is TDMA (Time Division Multiple Access). To review briefly, TDMA breaks down the conventional signals into small, digitized segments (slots). These slots are time division multiplexed with other slots into one channel.

G.723.1 uses silence compression by executing discontinuous transmission operations, which means that artificial noise (at reduced bit rates) is inserted into the bit stream during silent periods. In addition to conserving bandwidth, this technique keeps the transmitter's modem in continuous operation, and avoids the tasks of switching the carrier on and off.

G.729. G.729 is designed for low-delay applications, with a frame size of only 10 ms, a processing delay of 10 ms, and a lookahead of 5 ms. This yields a 25-ms contribution to end-to-end delay and a bit rate of 8 kbit/s. These delay performances are important in an internet, because we have learned that any factor decreasing delay is important.

G.729 comes in two versions: G.729 and G.729A. The original version is more complex than G.723.1, while the Annex A version is less complex than G.723.1. The two versions are compatible but their performance is somewhat different, the lower complexity version (G.729) having slightly lower quality. Both coders include provision for dealing with frame erasures and packet-loss concealment, making them good choices for use with voice over the Internet. Cox et. al. [COX98][6] state that the G.729 performance for random bit errors is poor. They do not recommend them for use on channels with random bit errors unless there is a channel coder (forward error correction and convolutional coding, discussed in the wireless section of this book) to protect the most sensitive bits.

Backward-Adaptive LPAS Coding: 16 kbit/s G.728 Low-Delay Code Book Excitation Linear Prediction (LD-CELP)

G.728 is a hybrid between the lower bit rate linear predictive analysis-by-synthesis coders (G.729 and G.723.1) and the backward ADPCM coders. G.728 is a LD-CELP coder and operates on five samples at a time.

CELP is a speech-coding technique in which the excitation signal is selected from a set of possible excitation signals through an exhaustive search. While the lower rate speech coders use a forward adaptation scheme for the sample value prediction filter, LD-CELP uses a backward adaptive filter that is updated every 2.5 ms. There are 1,024 possible excitation vectors. These vectors are further decomposed into four possible gains, two possible signs (+ or −), and 128 possible shape vectors.

G.728 is a suggested speech coder for low-bit-rate (56–128 kbit/s) ISDN video telephony. Because of its backward adaptive nature, it is a low-delay coder, but it is more complex than the other coders because the fiftieth-order LPC analysis must be repeated at the decoder. It also provides an adaptive postfilter that enhances its performance.

PARAMETER SPEECH CODERS: 2.4-KBIT/S MIXED-EXCITATION LPC (MELP)

Parametric speech coders assume a generic speech model with a simplified excitation signal and thus are able to operate at the lowest bit rates. All of the speech coders discussed previously can be described as *waveform following*. Their output signals are similar in shape and phase to the input signal.

---

[6][COX98]. Cox, R. V., Hassle, B. G., Lacuna, A., Shahraray, B., and Rabiner, L., "On the Applications of Multimedia Processing to Communications," *Proceedings of the IEEE,* Vol. 86, No. 5, May 1998.

Parametric speech coders are different and do not exhibit waveform following. They are based on an analysis-synthesis model for speech signals that can be represented using relatively few parameters. These parameters are extracted and quantized, usually on a regular basis from every 20–40 ms. At the receiver, the parameters are used to create a synthetic speech signal. Under ideal conditions, the synthetic signal sounds like the original speech. Under harsh enough background noise conditions, any parametric coder will fail because the input signal is not well modeled by the inherent speech model. The 2.4 kbit/s MELP was selected as the U.S. government's new 2.4-bit/s speech coder for secure telephony.

For multimedia applications, the study from [COX98] states that parametric coders are a good choice when there is a need for low bit rates. For example, parametric coders are often used for simple user games. This keeps down the storage requirements for speech. For the same reason, they also are a good choice for some types of multimedia messaging. They tend to be lower in absolute quality for all types of speech conditions and particularly noisy background conditions. This shortcoming can be overcome when the speech files can be carefully edited in advance. At the present time, most of the parametric coders used in such applications are not standards. Rather, they are proprietary coders that have been adapted to work for such applications.

G.723.1 Scaleable Coding for Wireless Applications

Annex C of G.723.1 specifies a channel-coding scheme, which can be used with a triple-rate speech codec. The channel codec is scaleable in bit rate and is designed for mobile multimedia applications as a part of the overall H.324 family of standards.

A range of channel codec bit rates is supported ranging from 0.7 kbit/s up to 14.3 kbit/s. The channel codec supports all three operational modes of the G.723.1 codec, namely high rate, low rate and discontinuous transmission modes.

The channel codec uses punctured convolutional codes. Based on the subjective importance of each class of information bits, the available channel codec bit rate is allowed optimally to the bit classes. This allocation is based on an algorithm which is known by the encoder and decoder. Each time the system control signals either a change in the G.723.1 rate or in the available channel codec bit rate, this algorithm is executed to adapt the channel codec to the new speech service configuration.

If a low-channel codec bit rate is available, the subjectively most sensitive bits are protected first. When increasing the channel codec bit rate, the additional bits are used first to protect more information bits and second to increase the protection of the already protected classes.

Prior to the application of the channel encoding functions, the speech parameters are partly modified in a channel adaptation layer to improve their robustness against transmission errors.

EVALUATING CODERS

In evaluating the performance of codecs, several factors come into play. A summary of these factors is shown in this list:

- *Frame size:* Frame size represents the length of the voice traffic measured in time. It is also called frame delay. Frames are discrete parts of the speech, and each frame is updated based on the speech samples. The codecs covered in this chapter process a frame at a time. This traffic is placed in voice packets and sent to the receiver.
- *Processing delay:* This factor represents the delay incurred at the codec to run the voice and coding algorithm on one frame. It is often simply factored into the frame delay. Processing delay is also called algorithmic delay.
- *Lookahead delay:* Lookahead delay occurs when the coder examines a certain amount of the next frame to provide guidance in coding the current frame. The idea of lookahead is to take advantage of the close correlations existing between successive voice frames.
- *Frame length:* This value represents the number of bytes resulting from the encoding process (the value excludes headers).
- *Voice bit rate:* This parameter is the output rate of the codec when its input is standard pulse-code modulation voice images (at 64 kbit/s).
- *DSP MIPS:* This value specifies the minimum speed for the DSP processor to support the specific encoder. Be aware that DSP MIPS do not correlate to MIPS ratings of other processors. These DSPs are designed specifically for the task-at-hand in contrast to general purpose processors that operate in workstations and personal computers. Consequently, to achieve the operations discussed in this analysis requires a much greater MIPS capability from a general processor than from a specially designed DSP.

Table 4–1   Speech coding standards [RUDK97]

Standard	Coding type	Bit rate kbit/s	MOS	Complexity	Delay (ms)
G.711	PCM	64	4.3	1	0.125
G.726	ADPCM	32	4.0	10	0.125
G.728	LD-CELP	16	4.0	50	0.625
GSM	RPE_LTP	13	3.7	5	20
G.729	CSA-CELP	8	4.0	30	15
G.729A				15	
G.723.1	ACELP	6.3	3.8	25	37.5
	MP-MLQ	5.3			
US Dod FS1015	LPC-10	2.4	synthetic	10	22.5

- *Required RAM:* This value describes the amount of RAM needed to support a specific encoding process.

A key evaluation factor is the time required for the encoder to do its work. This time is referred to as one-way latency or one-way system delay. It is computed as the sum of frame size + processing delay + lookahead delay. Obviously, decode delays are important as well. In practice, the decode delays are about one-half the time of the encode delays.

COMPARISON OF SPEECH CODERS

To conclude the discussion on standardized coders, Table 4–1 [RUDK97][7] compares several coders with regard to bit rate, MOS, complexity (with G.711 as the base), and delay (frame size and lookahead time).

SUMMARY

Speech coders are the engines for the creation and processing of the VoIP packets. They, in turn, are driven by DSPs, discussed in Chapter 3.

The old DS0, TDM G.711 coder of 64 kbit/s will eventually be phased out of the industry and replaced with the low bit-rate coders.

---

[7][RUDK97] Rudkin, S., Grace, A., and Whybray, M. W. "Real-Time Applications on the Internet," *BT Journal,* Vol. 15, No. 2, April 1997.

5

Connecting to Service Providers through the Local Loop

T his chapter explains how the VoIP user is connected to the Internet or an internet through the telco local loop. The role of the telephone network is explained, and we examine ISP configurations, as well as Network Access Point (NAP). An analysis is provided of where the user's modem analog signal is terminated.

Due to the major problem of the limited capacity of the local loop, the chapter also provides an overview of the Integrated Services Digital Network (ISDN), the emerging xDSL (X Digital Subscriber Line) and the HFC (Hybrid Fiber Coax) technologies, as well as a proprietary high-speed modem from Nortel. All these schemes are designed to give the Internet user more bandwidth on the local loop to and from the service provider.

We conclude the chapter by showing how the telco facilities (and the telco circuit switch) can be bypassed.

PATH BETWEEN AN INTERNET USER AND THE INTERNET

Figure 5–1 shows a typical configuration employed between the user customer premises equipment and an internet. The user employs a conventional V Series modem to modulate the analog signals on the local loop to the local telephone office. At the telephone office, the analog sig-

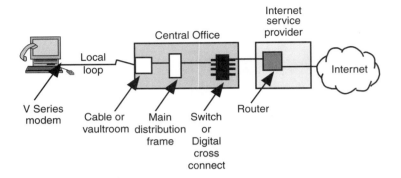

Figure 5–1   Connecting to the Internet Service Provider

nals are digitized in some type of T1 frame (T1, T3, etc.), and sent through the telephone digital backbone to a designated ISP. The telephone company performs the analog-to-digital (A/D) and digital-to-analog (D/A) conversion operations. Therefore, the interface between the telephone system and the Internet Service Provider (ISP) node is digital if the telco backbone is used.

The ISPs connect to each other through Network Access Points (NAPs) see Figure 5–2. The NAP's job is to exchange traffic between ISPs and other networks. NAPs must operate at link speeds of 100 Mbit/s, and thus their local networks have been implemented with FDDI (the Fiber Distributed Data Interface), 100BASE-T (Fast Ethernet at 100 Mbit/s, or 1000Base-T) (Gigabit Ethernet at 1 Gbit/s). Many of them have ATM switches and SONET links to other NAPs and the larger ISPs.

Figure 5–2 lists eleven NAPs currently running in the U.S. Some of them are called Metropolitan Area Exchanges (MAEs). Some are named based on the Federal Internet Exchange (FIX), others based on the Commercial Internet Exchange (CIX). FIXs were set up by the NSF to support federal regional networks. The CIX was set up by the public Internet service providers.

The NAP concept was established by the National Science Foundation (NSF) when it was managing the Internet. Originally, there were four NAPs (NSF-awarded NAPs), but due to the growth of the Internet, additional NAPs have been created, as shown in Figure 5–2.

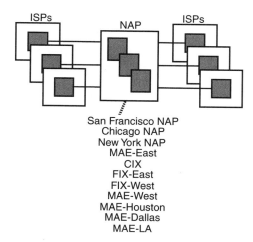

San Francisco NAP
Chicago NAP
New York NAP
MAE-East
CIX
FIX-East
FIX-West
MAE-West
MAE-Houston
MAE-Dallas
MAE-LA

Figure 5–2   The Network Access Point (NAP)

If you wish more information on NAPs, the MAEs, as well as topology maps of the Internet, check www.boardwatch.com.

The ISP or NAP node can range from a simple configuration (for a small ISP) to one that has scores of routers, servers, LANs, and ATM/Frame Relay switches (for larger ISPs and NAPs). A typical ISP site will have high speed LANs, multiple servers and high-speed access to the wide area networks, as shown in Figure 5–3. This site is where the bottlenecks can often occur. If LANs such as FDDI or Fast Ethernet in-

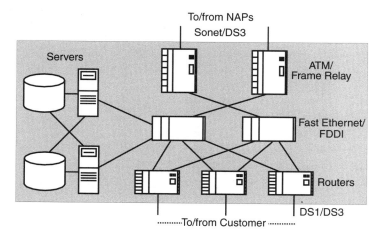

Figure 5–3   Typical NAP or large ISP configuration

side the ISP site are not fast enough, or if the routers become over-loaded, then bottlenecks can occur. If the server farm is not large enough, then the servers may be buffering the data too long. Regardless of the type of equipment, the overall ISP system must be tuned frequently to deliver steady streams of traffic into and out of the site. If this does not happen, then congestion will occur [BATE99].[1]

THE BANDWIDTH PROBLEM AT THE LOCAL LOOP

If I had to cite the biggest problem in deploying high-quality VoIP applications, along with data and video to the masses (the general consumer), it would be the limited bandwidth on the local loop. Because of this problem, we spend time on it in this chapter.

For today's analog voice transport systems, the present structure on the local loop provides adequate capacity, but that capacity is insufficient for other applications, such as data and video. Voice has a modest bandwidth requirement, about 3.5 kHz of the frequency spectrum. The local loop (the distribution plant) is designed to support voice bandwidths.

The problem is that many applications that are now in the marketplace, or are being developed, are significantly handicapped by local loop bottlenecks. As one example, file transfer, and database accesses take too long with current technology. As another, Internet access and browsing is often a chore, due to the limited bandwidth of the local loop. One of the reasons that so much research and development has been expended on low bit-rate coders (Chapter 4) is because of the limited capacity of the local loop.

The present structure is not conducive to building multiapplication (multimedia) networks, because voice, video, and data are difficult to run concurrently on the local loop.

In addition, the present digital systems retain the T1 legacy of using 64 kbit/s DS0 slots that are allocated with fixed, symmetrical bandwidth. This approach is not in line with today's applications that need dynamic, asymmetrical bandwidth.

Help is on the way. It is taking a long time, but it is surely coming. Let us now examine some of the new technologies purported to relieve the local loop bottleneck. The next discussion will not help the local loop problem, but it will help remove bottlenecks at the telco nodes and the telco backbone network.

---

[1][BATE99] Bates, Bud. *Data Communications: A Business View.* Published by TCIC International, Phoenix AZ, 1999.

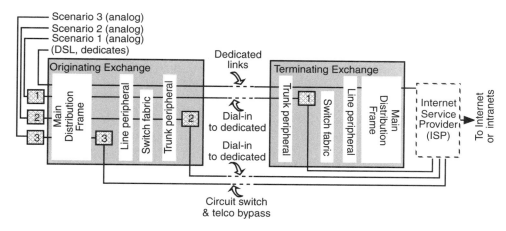

Where:
DSL   Digital Subscriber Line

Figure 5–4   Possible modem terminations

TERMINATING THE MODEM ANALOG SIGNAL

As a general rule, voice and data service providers attempt to terminate the modem analog signal and convert it to a digital signal as soon as practicable. Figure 5–4 shows three scenarios in how the analog modem termination can be handled.[2] The goal is provide this termination as close to the subscriber as possible, which allows more efficient techniques to be used on the remainder of the link to the Internet or corporate node. The shadowed boxes in the figure that are numbered 1, 2, or 3 symbolize the demarcation point at which the modem signals (modem connection) are terminated. Thereafter, digital signaling is employed at the physical layer, with Frame Relay or ATM operating over the physical layer, and IP then operating over Frame Relay or ATM.

In scenario 1, the modem termination occurs at the trunk side of the terminating central office (CO) that is servicing the ISP. A data access switch is installed as a trunk-side peripheral at this CO. This configuration bypasses the line side of the remote CO, but this configuration is not a conventional method to terminate the modem interfaces because it entails sending the analog signal through the telco backbone, which is usually digital-based. Nonetheless, if parts of the telephone network are still analog-oriented, this configuration is used.

---

[2]Additional information on these operations is available from *Telesis*, Issue 102, published by Nortel, telesis@barcam.com

In scenario 2, the modem termination occurs at the trunk side of the originating CO. The benefit of this approach is that it reduces or eliminates the need to upgrade the network's trunks to handle data traffic. The traffic is diverted to data networks before it hits the voice network. The data networks are designed to handle asynchronous data traffic. However, with this approach, the CO voice switch is still involved in the processing of the data call, which results in tying up a port and resources on the local circuit switch.

Scenario 3 is the best approach. It terminates the analog connection before it enters the local voice switch. This example uses a front-end processor to intercept the user signal (this processor is not shown here but is explained later in this chapter). If the called party is an ISP customer, the call is diverted away from the CO facilities and sent directly to the ISP.

ALTERNATIVES TO THE MODEM-BASED LOCAL LOOP ACCESS

The conventional modem access to the Internet is the most popular way of getting a connection to a service provider. It is also one of the most inefficient ways as well. The high-speed modems (discussed in Chapter 6) cannot operate at speeds greater than 56 kbit/s. While this bit rate may seem adequate, it is not of sufficient capacity for large data transfers.

Several alternatives to modem access are emerging in several countries. The ISDN alternative has been around for a few years, but it does not solve the bandwidth problem, because most commercial implementations are set for 64 kbit/s or (for a steep price) 128 kbit/s. The next section explains ISDN, but the emphasis in discussing alternatives in this chapter is on the Digital Subscriber Line (DSL) and Hybrid Fiber Coax (HFC) technologies.

THE INTEGRATED SERVICES DIGITAL NETWORK (ISDN)

In the 1960s and 1970s, as digital technology began to find its way into the telephone providers' networks, and as the costs of digital technology declined, the telephone industry began to look for ways to move this technology into the local loop. The telephone service providers' view was that the superior characteristics of digital technology (over analog) would make it attractive to the customer.

Additionally, the use of analog signaling over the local loop was quite limited with regard to data rates (in bit/s). In fact, when ISDN was first introduced in 1984, the V.22 bis modem was just introduced, operating at only 2400 bit/s! So, a 64 kbit/s rate sounded very attractive to the data user.

Then there was the recognition that the digital T1 technology was proving to be effective within the telephone carriers' backbone network— so why not use some version of T1 at the local loop? This "version" is ISDN.

These factors lead to the deployment of ISDN in the local loop in the mid-1980s, especially in Europe. ISDN was not deployed much in North America until recently.

In the early 1990s, the Regional Bell Operating Companies (RBOCs) launched what is called National ISDN. It is a U.S. plan for a nationwide, standardized implementation of ISDN technology. It places strict requirements on the vendors, and manufacturers who build the ISDN equipment, and on the ISDN service providers.

As part of the plan, each Bell Operating Company set up deployment goals for: (a) number of access lines that support ISDN, (b) number of wire centers to have ISDN presence, (c) total number of switches to have ISDN capabilities, (d) total number of switches to have SS7 capabilities. These goals were tracked each year with each RBOC publishing its progress report.

For more information on the National ISDN services, Bellcore document SR-3476 summarizes all the National ISDN features and capabilities that had to be available by 1996, and the telcos did a good job in meeting the deadlines.

ISDN Bearer Services

The ISDN device connects to the ISDN through a twisted pair four-wire digital link, see Figure 5–5. This link uses time division multiplexing (TDM) to provide three channels, designated as the B, B, and D channels (or 2 B+D). The B channels operate at a speed of 64 kbit/s; the D channel operates at 16 kbit/s. The 2 B+D is designated as the basic rate interface (BRI). ISDN also allows up to eight user devices to share one 2 B+D link. The purpose of the B channels is to carry the user payload in the form of voice, compressed video, and data. The purpose of the D channel is to act as an out-of-band control channel for setting up, managing, and clearing the B channel sessions.

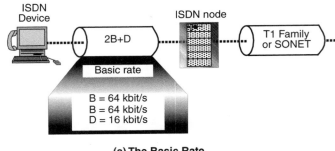

(a) The Basic Rate

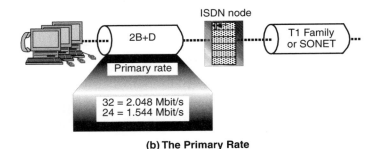

(b) The Primary Rate

Figure 5–5   ISDN services

For higher bandwidth needs, the interface can be a primary rate interface (PRI), which operates at the T1 rate of 1.544 Mbit/s or the E1 rate of 2.048 Mbit/s.

In other scenarios, the user device may not have ISDN installed. If this is the situation, a terminal adapter (TA) is used. The TA allows non-ISDN terminals to operate over ISDN lines. The user side of the TA typically uses a conventional physical layer interface such as EIA-232 or the V Series specifications. It is packaged like an external modem or as a board that plugs into an expansion slot on the user devices.

Does ISDN Solve the Local Loop Bottleneck Problem?   I am not a big proponent of ISDN. I was a supporter until the V.34, and (later) the V.90 modems made it possible to pump 28.8 to 56 kbit/s (maybe) across the local loop to my ISP—at no additional charge. The ISDN B channel gives me 64 kbit/s, at an additional price of twenty to sixty dollars per month, depending on my location in the United States. The marginal increase in the data rate may not be worth the additional fee, but I recommend you investigate your local ISDN service provider before you make a decision.

Nonetheless, ISDN is here. If the 128 kbit/s rates are reduced, the technology will be quite attractive. Moreover, since 1997, ISDN line installations (BRI and PRI) have been growing at an annual rate of over 25 percent.

So, what technology solves the local loop bandwidth problem? And, it is a big problem. Two technologies solve the problem, or at least ameliorate it (it is too soon to know if they are complete solutions). They are discussed next.

ROLE OF DIGITAL SUBSCRIBER LINE (DSL) TECHNOLOGIES

The point was made earlier of the need to terminate the inefficient (and older) modem signals and convert them to digital signals (or to more efficient analog signals). Part of the motivation for this transition is to take advantage of the higher bandwidths that are available with newer technologies. The technologies are known collectively as the Digital Subscriber Line (DSL).

DSL distribution systems refers to a variety of systems that are designed to provide more capacity on the current embedded telephone-based copper loop plant. The Asymmetric Digital Subscriber Line (ADSL), Very-high-bit DSL (VDSL), and High bit-rate DSL (HDSL) are examples of DSL technologies. They are often grouped under the term "xDSL." Table 5–1 summarizes the xDSL technologies, including their bandwidth capacities, and their intended deployment.

The installation of ADSL on the local loop does not disturb the existing cable in the distribution plant, nor does it necessitate taking the customer's phone service out for a long time. As shown Figure 5–6, the customer's location is outfitted with a plain old telephone service (POTS) splitter and an ADSL remote unit. These interfaces allow the existing copper wire to be split in to multiple channels: (a) Forward: central office to customer (upstream to downstream), and (b) Return: customer to central office (downstream to upstream).

The Evolving ADSL Technology

Figure 5–7 shows the reference model for ADSL. The interfaces are noted with dashed lines. This model is just that, a model. Some of the interfaces may not exist in a commercial product. For example, the T-SM

Table 5–1   Digital Subscriber Line (DSL) technologies

xDSL Technology	Capacity	Deployment
Symmetrical Digital subscriber Line (SDSL)	Ranges from 64 kbit/s to 2,048 Mbit/s	Conventional T1/ E1 symmetrical systems
High Bit-rate Digital Subscriber Line (HDSL)	1/2 of T1/E1 in each direction	T1 lines, with ISDN line coding
ISDN Digital Subscriber Line (IDSL)	128 kbit/s in each direction	Proprietary xDSL
Asymmetrical Digital Subscriber Line (ADSL)	*Downstream:* 6.144 Mbit/s, 384 kbit/s, 160 kbit/s, 64 kbit/s *Upstream:* 384 kbit/s, 160 kbit/s, 64 kbit/s	QAM techniques on twisted-pair
Rate adaptive ADSL (RADSL, or RDSL)	As above, and adapts to conditions on link	ADSL
Very High-rate Digital Subscriber Line (VDSL)	Variation of ADSL	Variation of ADSL

interface might not exist, or might be the same as the T interface. Also, the T interface might not exist if the terminal equipment (TE) is part of the ADSL transmission unit, remote side (ATU-R). The U interfaces might not exist if the splitter (S) is part of the ATUs, or if the splitter is eliminated, which is the inclination in the industry.

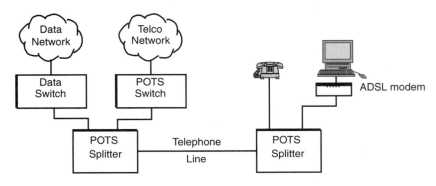

Figure 5–6   The ADSL setup

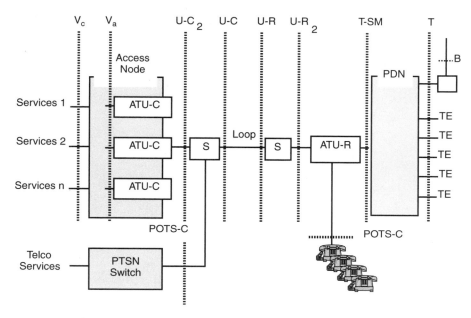

Figure 5–7   The ADSL reference model [GORA98]

Here is a list of names for the interfaces and other ADSL components shown in Figure 5–7 [GORA98]:[3] First, the return channel (to the customer) operates at much lower frequency than the forward channel(s) (an asymmetrical configuration). Consequently, crosstalk is not so great a problem in comparison to conventional symmetrical configurations. The POTS voice signals are isolated from the ADSL signals by the low-pass voiceband splitter filter. It can be packaged with the interface card at the central office or CPE, or it can be packaged separately.

Be aware that some ADSL equipment manufacturers are building systems that eliminate the splitter.

The functions of the ADSL components are:

ATU-C   ADSL transmission unit, CO side
ATU-R   ADSL transmission unit, remote side
B   Auxiliary data input (set top box)
PDN   Premises distribution network
POTS-C   Interface between PSTN and splitter, CO side

[3][GORA98].   Goralski, Walter. *ADSL and DSL Technologies*, McGraw-Hill, New York, 1998.

POTS-R	Interface between PSTN and splitter, remote side
S	Splitter
T	Interface between terminal equipment and PDN
TE	Terminal equipment (user device)
T-SM	T interface for service module
U-C	U interface, CO side
$U\text{-}C_2$	U interface, CO side from splitter to ATU-C
U-R	U interface, remote side
$U\text{-}R_2$	U interface, remote side from splitter to ATU-R
V_A	V interface, access node side from ATU-C to access node
V_C	V interface, CO side from access node to network service

Status of the DSL Deployments

Unfortunately, there are not many DSL offerings at this time. They are beginning to emerge, but it remains to be seen how far the technologies will penetrate into the residential neighborhood. Estimates vary, with some studies predicting a penetration rate of 40 to 50 percent by 2002, and others predicting only 5 to 30 percent.

THE HYBRID/FIBER COAX (HFC) APPROACH

Hybrid/fiber coax (HFC) systems have been deployed in some suburban neighborhoods in several countries, and they are now slowly finding their way into the North American market. The supporters of this approach believe that ADSL technology (over the conventional twisted pair) does not provide enough bandwidth in relation to its costs. The HFC technology exploits the bandwidth capacity of fiber and coax.

As shown in Figure 5–8, the HFC network has an optical fiber facility running from the central office (the headend) to a neighborhood node. The fiber has forward and return paths. At the node, users are connected by coaxial cable.

Figure 5–9 shows a typical hybrid fiber coax system that uses the telco-based GR-303 and TR-08 standards. At the residence is a wall-mounted unit that supports typically two connections. This is labeled in the figure as coax/twisted pair node. This node connects the coaxial cable to the fiber/coax node in the distribution plant, which in turn connects the fiber to the central office. At the central office is a digital terminal

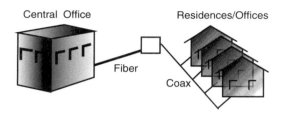

Figure 5–8   The HFC configuration

that is composed of (a) access bandwidth manager, (b) cable modems, and (c) spectrum manager.

On the downstream path (network-to-user), the cable modems are capable of receiving DS0 signals from the access bandwidth manager and converting them into RF signals suitable for transmission on a 2-MHz carrier path to the subscriber over the hybrid fiber/coax network. The modems also receive RF signals from the subscriber (upstream path) via the fiber/coax network and convert them into DS0 signals. The access bandwidth manager maps these DS0 signals to DS1 signals for communicating with the digital switch at the central office.

The cable modem shelf also has a maintenance and control interface which relays OAM information between the access bandwidth manager and the voice ports. As an example, this interface relays provisioning information to the line cards, asends and receives alarms, as well as performance data, to and from the access bandwidth manager. This system typically also maintains inventory information about equipment and facilities between the cable modem shelf and the outside wall of the subscriber locations.

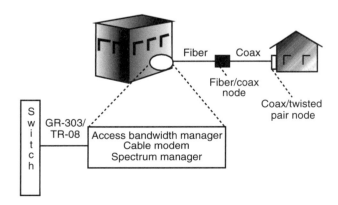

Figure 5–9   The HFC interfaces

The access bandwidth manager contains several circuit packs that perform the following functions:

- Transmitting 2–28 DS1 signals to and from the digital switch
- Mapping the DS0 signals from the cable modem to DS1 signals for transmission to the digital switch and vice versa
- Gathering and distributing performance and alarm data
- Providing an interface for diagnosticians to review this information
- Performing typical call control functions such as call processing and digital switching communications

The spectrum manager is a passive monitoring and information-gathering device.

Figure 5–10 shows one view of how the 750 MHz bandwidth can be allocated. In addition to the analog signals just discussed, HFC can carry digital transmissions such as DS0 at 64 kbit/s or video-telephony at 384 kbit/s (6 DS0s), with quadrature phase-shift keyed (QPSK) digital signals. Digital video transmissions can be carried with a 64-state QAM scheme (64-QAM) at rates of 30 Mbit/s.

Status of the HFC Deployments

The deployment of HFC has also been slow because of the need to reconfigure the CATV one-way (half-duplex) architecture, and other technical problems. However, as of this writing, it has a larger growth rate than its principal competitor, ADSL.

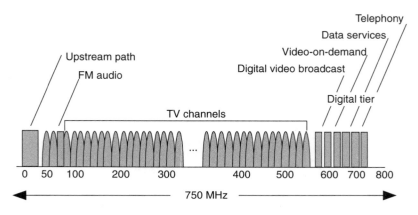

Figure 5–10   HFC spectrum

A HIGH-SPEED PROPRIETARY SOLUTION

Not everyone is waiting for the ADSL and HFC standards to evolve, and the resulting deployment of these standards. Some companies are developing two product lines: (a) one based on the standards, and (b) one based on a proprietary design. Nortel is an example of one of these companies.

Nortel has introduced a high-speed modem to be deployed on the local loop. It is known as the 1-Meg Modem™ and it is designed to offer a high-speed data over voice over existing telephone lines. In addition, it does not require the rewiring of any customer site, and a POTS splitter is not needed. Although it does require some equipment changes in the central office, these changes can be done with only two plug-in circuit packs. Figure 5–11 shows the 1-Meg Modem™ configuration.

The initial release of the 1-Meg Modem™ supports 1-Mbit/s downstream, 120 kbit/s upstream, and the simultaneous use of voice and data over any existing telephone jack at the customer location. Data connections are supported through the use of a standard 10BaseT Ethernet support on the modem. In addition, a pass through RJ-11 jack on the unit permits a fax and analog modem or telephone to coexist with the unit.

The phones remain network powered, and if the modem loses power, the ongoing residential service continues to be supported. Current local loops are supported with a distance of 18 kilofeet on 24-gauge wire and 15 kilofeet on 26-gauge wire.

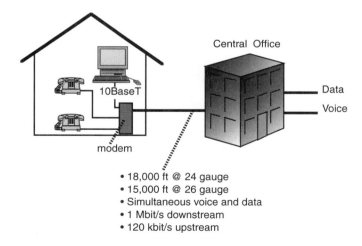

Figure 5–11   Nortel's 1-Meg modem

The service is available on Nortel's DMS-100, DMS-500, and MSL-100 equipment. With the eventual use of Nortel's AccessNode Express™, the modem services can be deployed on non-DMS switches. In addition, it is planned that in 1999, a 1.3-Mbit/s downstream service will be available as well as a 320-kbit/s upstream service. As part of this upgrade, ATM will be used to support the system.

BYPASSING THE CIRCUIT-SWITCHED TECHNOLOGY TO REACH THE INTERNET

For several years, the telephone network will continue to operate with circuit-switched technologies, as explained in Chapter 1. In order to relieve the load on the telephone facilities, a number of vendors have built systems that are installed in the telephone local exchanges. These systems intercept calls destined for Internet or intranet users, and divert them to data facilities, thus avoiding the telco network and switches altogether. Figure 5–12 shows the general idea of circuit-switch bypass (CSB).

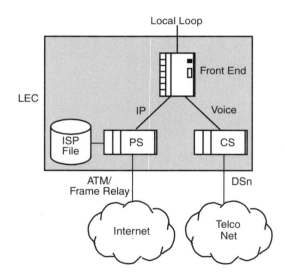

Where:
    CS   Circuit switch
    ISP   Internet Service Provider
    PS   Packet switch

Figure 5–12   The circuit switch bypass

At the local exchange a special machine (I call it a front end, for lack of a better term) monitors incoming calls. If it detects a called number for a data user, it converts the analog signal into a digital signal, encapsulates the traffic into a Frame Relay frame or an ATM cell and forwards the traffic to the appropriate next node, which could be either an ISP or a private network. Otherwise, it passes the call to the conventional circuit switch for transport through the telco network.

This bypass approach is a very attractive means of (a) relieving the load on the telco facilities and (b) passing the packet traffic to facilities designed to support it.

SUMMARY

For the next few years, the conventional modem will be the main way to connect at the physical layer to the Internet. The modem is slow, and will eventually be replaced by DSL or HFC alternatives. In the long run, ISDN will not be a major factor if the DSL and HFC technologies are finally brought into the mass marketplace.

Most of the user's sessions with the Internet occur by connecting through the telephone company local exchange carrier (LEC) and the telco central office. This approach is also less than optimal, and a number of LECs are installing front ends at the central office to filter data calls and route them to an appropriate ISP.

The ISPs are connected with each through peering arrangements, usually through a Network Access Point (NAP). The number of NAPs continues to grow as internets proliferate.

6

Modems, LAPM, PPP, and the V.100 Series

In this chapter, we examine the newer high-speed modems, with an emphasis on V.34 and V.90 (the 56 kbit/s modem). Many Internet users are using the layer-2 link protocol, Link Access Procedure for Modems (LAPM), so we will examine LAPM as well. The Point-to-Point Protocol (PPP) is used in most dial-up connections to the Internet, so we must examine the PPP also. Some PPP-based products do not use LAPM, and instead utilize a similar protocol, named Link Access Procedure, Balanced (LAPB); it is covered, too. Since ISDN services are available in most cities today, we will take a look at how the V.100 Series supports the ISDN user.

The reader may wonder why I am including information on modems in a VoIP book. After all, modems are designed to transport data over analog links, and VoIP is voice. We need to keep in mind that VoIP voice samples are represented as data bits, and these data bits are contained in data packets. Therefore, if a telco analog local loop is used by the VoIP customer, the modem is the instrument used to get the VoIP data packets across this link. If the local loop is ISDN based, the modem may be still involved at the customer site.

Of course, if the VoIP packets are being transported across a native digital network such as an Ethernet, then the modem is not employed. But for point-to-point dialup links, the modem is quite important, and the VoIP gateways stipulate the types of modems the customer must use for the gateway interface.

One other point before we proceed into the chapter. I have chosen to explain outboard modems in this chapter; that is, modems that are not housed inside the user's terminal. These examples are relevant to an installation that has a modem pool, with banks of modems in use. An in board modem may not implement all the operations that are described in this chapter, specifically the use of some of the V.24 interchange circuits.

ANOTHER LOOK AT THE LAYERED ARCHITECTURE FOR VoIP

We have now assimilated enough information to have another look at the VoIP protocol stack that was introduced in Chapters 1 and 2, as depicted in Figure 6–1. In this chapter, we will adjust the model described in the introductory chapters and provide some more details. For this part of the book, I am going to focus on layers 1 and 2 of this model.

In Chapter 5, the roles of ISDN, ADSL, and HFC were explained. This chapter examines the V Series modems, as well as the layer-2 protocols shown here. You might wish to refer back to Figure 6–1 as you read this chapter.

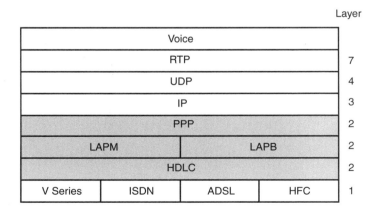

Figure 6–1   The VoIP layered protocol suite

PREVALENT MODEMS

The ITU-T is the prevalent standards organization for the publication of modem specifications. Indeed, I doubt a commercial modem can be purchased which does not adhere to ITU-T specifications. These modems are published under the ITU-T V Series recommendations.[1]

The architecture for the recent V Series modems is based on the V.34 specifications. More recent variations of V.34 are published in V.90 (more commonly known as the 56 kbit/s modem). A later section in this chapter describes the architectures of these modems.

ROLE OF DSPS IN THE MODEM'S OPERATIONS

Chapter 3 was devoted to a discussion of DSPs. Modern modems employ programmable DSPs. Previously, modem DSPs were read-only-memory (ROM) based. This approach required implementing new hardware for any upgrade or for the support of a new modem standard. Programmable DSPs allow changes, upgrades, etc. to be downloaded to the user device. Then from the user device, the upgrade can be loaded onto the DSP.

TYPICAL LAYOUT

Figure 6–2 shows a typical layout for a data communications link. Several of the prominent physical layer (L_1) standards do not specify the complete physical interface between to user devices (called Data Terminal Equipment (DTE) in the ITU-T specifications). Specifically, the span between the modems may not be defined. Prominent examples are the EIA-232 and V.24 standards. Fortunately, this part of the physical interface is standardized through the ITU-T V Series modem specifications. Figure 6–2 shows the relationship of these specifications to the physical layer interface.

---

[1]For more information on V Series recommendations see *V Series Recommendations* by Uyless Black, *The V Series Recommendations: Standards for Data Communications over the Telephone Network,* 2nd Edition, McGraw Hill, 1995.

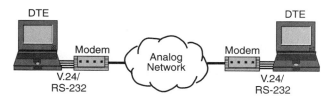

Figure 6–2   Analog configuration

The cables and wires between the DTE ports and the modems are joined to connectors that take the shape of small metal pins. The pins serve as "plugs" into the computers and modems. These connectors are called *interchange circuits*. Figure 6–3 shows two choices for the physical interchange circuits, as well as the International Standards Organization (ISO) mechanical connectors. The connectors' interchange circuits are identified by numbers, by alphabetic identifiers (AB, AC, etc.), or by functional descriptions (transmit data circuit, request-to-send circuit, etc.). You may not see these connectors on your PC or workstation. Some manufacturers use a proprietary connector, and many have migrated to a conventional telephone jack.

V.24

V.24 is used on the vast majority of modems to describe the functions of the interchange circuits ("pins" or circuits) on the interface. Many products use this standard, principally in modems, line drivers, multiplexers, and digital service units. The V.24 interchange circuits are listed in Table 6–1, with a brief description of their functions.

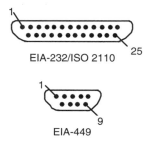

Figure 6–3   Physical connector examples

Table 6–1   **V.24 Interchange Circuits**

Interchange Circuit Number	Interchange Circuit Name
102	Signal ground or common return
102a	DTE common return
102b	DCE common return
102c	Common return
103	Transmitted data
104	Received data
105	Request to send
106	Ready for sending
107	Data set ready
108/1	Connect data set to line
108/2	Data terminal ready
109	Data channel received line signal detector
110	Data signal quality detector
111	Data signal rate selector (DTE)
112	Data signal rate selector (DCE)
113	Transmitter signal element timing (DTE)
114	Transmitter signal element timing (DCE)
115	Receiver signal element timing (DCE)
116	Select standby
117	Standby indicator
118	Transmitted backward channel data
119	Received backward channel data
120	Transmit backward channel line signal
121	Backward channel ready
122	Backward channel received line signal detector
123	Backward channel signal quality detector
124	Select frequency groups
125	Calling indicator
126	Select transmit frequency
127	Select receive frequency
128	Receiver signal element timing (DTE)
129	Request to receive
130	Transmit backward tone
131	Received character timing

(continued)

Table 6–1 *Continued*

Interchange Circuit Number	Interchange Circuit Name
132	Return to nondata mode
133	Ready for receiving
134	Received data present
136	New signal
140	Loopback/maintenance test
141	Local loopback
142	Test indicator
191	Transmitted voice answer
192	Received voice answer

THE EIA-232 INTERFACE

The RS-232/EIA-232 standards have been widely used throughout the world and are functionally aligned with the ITU-T V.24 recommendations. During the last two revisions, RS-232-C was redesignated as EIA-232-D, then EIA-232-E. One revision includes the definition of three testing circuits, a redefinition of ground, and some other minor changes. Another revision made other changes to align EIA-232 with V.24. Table 6–2 summarizes the EIA-232 standard and its relationship to the ITU-T V.24 circuits.

Figure 6–4 summarizes several key points about the point-to-point physical layer and provides an example of how the EIA-232/V.24 interchange circuits are employed for the transfer of the data packet across the interface between the DTE and the modem. Be aware that the packets noted in Figure 6–4 may occupy the full duplex channel at the same time.

The following interchange circuits are on, thus permitting a handshake to take place between the modems: (a) DTE ready, (b) Data set ready, (c) Request to send, (d) Clear to send. The activation of these circuits means the modem and the user terminal are powered-up, have completed several diagnostic checks, and are ready to engage in a full duplex connection. The signal detect interchange circuits are turned on only after the modems have completed their handshakes. As explained later, the handshake entails analyzing the quality of the link between the modems, and the associated decision as to the appropriate bit rate to be used. Other parts of the handshake include the possible use of LAPM as well as data compression.

Table 6–2   EIA-232 and ITU-T V.24 Interchange Circuits

EIA Interchange Circuit	V.24 ITU-T Equivalent	Description
AB	102	Signal ground/common return
BA	103	Transmitted data
BB	104	Received data
CA	105	Request to send
CB	106	Clear to send
CC	107	DCE ready
CD	108.2	DTE Ready
CE	125	Ring indicator
CF	109	Received line signal detector
CG	110	Signal quality detector
CH	111	Data signal rate selector (DTE)
CI	112	Data signal rate selector (DCE)
DA	113	Transmitter signal element timing (DTE)
DB	114	Transmitter signal element timing (DCE)
DD	115	Receiver signal element timing (DCE)
SBA	118	Secondary transmitted data
SBB	119	Secondary received data
SCA	120	Secondary request to send
SCB	121	Secondary clear to send
SCF	122	Secondary received line signal detector
RL	140	Remote loopback
LL	141	Local loopback
TM	142	Test mode

You may have noticed that it takes few seconds for you to get a connection to your ISP after you have clicked the "Sign On" button; the modems are going through a rather elaborate ceremony to set up a good connection for your traffic.

After all these preliminary operations are complete, packets are exchanged between the DTEs. Notice that the modems are providing clocking information to the DTEs, through the V.24 114/115 interchange circuits. The clocking keeps the bits aligned in time and phase between the modem and the user device.

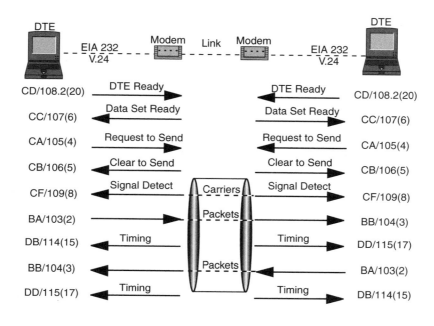

Where: XX/YYY(ZZ)
      xx = EIA-232 Circuit Designators
      YYY = V.24 Circuit Designators
      (ZZ) = ISO 2110/EIA Pin Assignments
      = Full Duplex Channel, carrying
        Packets in Both Directions

Figure 6–4 Conventional analog signaling

TYPICAL LAYOUT FOR THE MODEM

Figure 6–5 shows a typical layout for a V Series modem [STEV98]. The architecture is divided into the controller and the data pump. The controller is responsible for compression/decompression operations as well as handling the AT command set.[2] It is also responsible for the V.42 operations, also known as Link Access Procedure for Modems (LAPM). LAPM is a conventional data link protocol. In some situations, Link Ac-

---

[2]The AT (attention) commands are based on the old Hayes modems. The commands are used to "adjust" the operations of the modem and DTE. The commands are used to control registers and buffers within the personal computer port and the modem. For more information see [BLAC96] Black, Uyless. *Physical Layer Protocols and Interfaces,* Washington, DC; IEEE Computer Society Press, 1996.

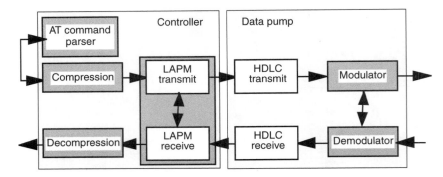

Figure 6–5   Typical modem layout [STEV98]

cess Procedure, Balanced (LAPB) may be used instead of LAPM. They are quite similar to each other and are responsible for the following operations:

- They perform the layer-2 handshake, after the layer-1 handshake is completed.
- They use the HDLC error check to acknowledge the receipt of traffic.
- They insure the proper sequencing of the traffic.
- If frames arrive out of order, or are missing, they notify the sending modem in order to correct the problem, by resending the problem frames.

The data pump contains the HDLC flag/framing, error calculations, and bit stuffing/unstuffing operations for both transmit and receive as well as the V Series modulation and demodulation operations.[3] LAPM uses the HDLC operations; as a whole LAPM and HDLC form the layer-2 link protocol. The DSP operates at this part of the modem.

ROLE OF THE POINT-TO-POINT PROTOCOL (PPP)

PPP is also classified as a layer-2 protocol, but it relies on HDLC for the basic L_2 framing, error-checking, and bit-stuffing operations. It may also rest on top of LAPM or LAPB, if error correction and retransmission

---

[3]For more details on the operations of HDLC, see [BLAC93], Black, Uyless. *Data Link Protocols*. Englewood Cliffs, NJ: Prentice Hall, 1993.

operations are to be used. As depicted in Figure 6–1, an Internet session may entail the execution of three L_2 protocols: (a) HDLC, (b) LAPM or LAPB, and (c) PPP.

The Point-to-Point protocol (PPP) was implemented to solve a problem that evolved in the industry during the last decade. With the rapid growth of internetworking, several vendors and standards organizations developed a number of network-layer (L_3) protocols. The Internet Protocol (IP) is the most widely used of these protocols. However, machines (such as routers) typically run more than one network-layer protocol. While IP is a given on most machines, routers also support network-layer protocols developed by companies such as Xerox, 3Com, Novell, etc. Machines communicating with each other did not readily know which network-layer protocols were available during a session.

In addition, until the advent of PPP, the industry did not have a standard means to define a point-to-point encapsulation protocol. Encapsulation means that a protocol carries or encapsulates a network layer packet in its I field and uses another field in the frame to identify which network layer packet resides in the I field. The PPP standard solves these two problems. Moreover, until PPP was developed, the industry relied on older, less-efficient protocols, such as SLIP (the Serial Link IP).

PPP encapsulates network-layer datagrams over a serial communications link. The protocol allows two machines on a point-to-point communications channel to negotiate the particular types of network-layer protocols (such as IP) that are to be used during a session. If a user is using dial-up access to an ISP, PPP is also used by the ISP to assign the user an IP address for the Internet session.

PPP also allows the two machines to negotiate other types of operations, such as the use of compression and authentication procedures. After this negotiation occurs, PPP is used to carry the network layer packets in the I field of an HDLC-type frame.

This protocol supports either bit-oriented synchronous transmission, byte-oriented transmission, or asynchronous (start/stop) transmission. It can be used on switched or dial-up links. It requires a full duplex capability.

THE PROTOCOL DATA UNIT ON THE LINK BETWEEN THE USER AND THE ISP

The traffic that is sent between the user and the ISP is known by various names. The most general term is protocol data unit (PDU). Most people in the industry call a L_2 PDU a frame. Figure 6–6 shows the for-

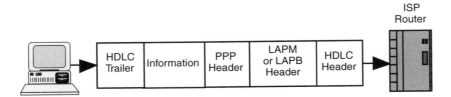

Figure 6–6   The layer-2 frame

mat of this frame. The frame may contain three L_2 headers, and the HDLC trailer. If this implementation is used, the headers and the trailer perform these functions:

- *HDLC header:* Contains a specific set of bits (the flag) that are used at the receiver to detect the beginning of the frame.
- *LAPM or LAPB header:* Contains sequence numbers, flow control bits, ACK and NAK bits, as well as bits that identify the type of frame (user data, control frame, etc.).
- *PPP header:* Contains information to negotiate a variety of services, as well as an encapsulation field that identifies the L_3 protocol residing in the information field of the frame.
- *HDLC trailer:* Contains an error check field, called the frame check sequence (FCS).

V SERIES MODEMS

The V Series recommendations (also called standards by many people) have become some of the most widely used specifications in the world for defining how data are exchanged between computers and communications equipment such as modems and multiplexers. In the past, the V Series recommendations were used principally in Europe because of the influence of the Postal, Telephone, and Telegraph (PTT) administrations in each European country. However, with the growing recognition of the need for international communications standards, the V Series recommendations have found their way into most countries of the world and into practically all vendors' modem products. Their use has paved the way for easier, more efficient, and less costly communications between users' computers, terminals, and other data processing machines.

The V.34 Operations

In the continuing quest to gain more bandwidth from the local sub-scriber loop, the ITU-T has been publishing specifications for high-speed modems for many years. A recent entry is V.34. V.34 retains some of the features of other modems, such as V.17, V.29, V.32, V.32 bis, and V.33, and at the same time adds many of its own unique characteristics. This list explains some of its major attributes.

- Operates on two-wire, point-to-point telephone circuits (or circuits that meet telco specifications)
- Operates on dial-up (switched) or leased circuits
- Operates in half-duplex or duplex modes
- Channel separation is achieved by echo cancellation
- Utilizes QAM on each channel
- Operates in synchronous mode
- Employs trellis coding
- Provides for an optional 200-bit/s asynchronous secondary channel
- Provides adaptive signaling (in bit/s) through line probing by adjusting to channel quality/capacity
- Uses conventional V.24 interchange circuits
- Supports the following signaling rates (bit/s):

2400	12000	21600
4800	14400	24000
7200	16800	26400
9600	19200	28800

Unlike the previous high-speed V Series modems, V.34 uses symbol rates other than 2400.[4] The following symbol rates are supported: 2400, 2743, 2800, 3000, 3200, 3429, with symbol rates of 2400, 3000, and 3200 mandatory. Furthermore, the carrier frequencies can also vary, ranging from 1600 to 2000 Hz.

Both the symbol rate and the carrier frequency are selected during the modem startup and handshaking procedure. During this procedure, the modems can select one or two carrier frequencies for each symbol rate.

---

[4]You may be more familiar with the term baud, instead of symbol rate. They describe the same function, but the term baud is falling in to "disrepute," since many people incorrectly use baud to mean bit rate. Bit rate and baud are not the same.

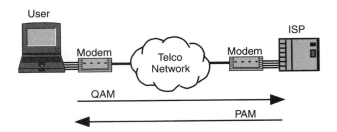

Figure 6–7   Setup for the 56 kbit/s modem

For the reader who wishes to know the details of how modern modems operate, I have prepared Appendix C. I place this information in an Appendix because it is tangential to the subject of VoIP, and I also know that some of the readers will find this information useful. However, to keep with the main theme of this book, we now turn our attention to the principal modem used today, the 56 kbit/s modem, published by the ITU-T as V.90.

THE 56 KBIT/S MODEM (V.90)

The 56 kbit/s modem is the next step up from the V.34 modem. My description of this technology is based on the ITU-T V.90 Recommendation, [WEXL98], and a paper by P. Michael Henderson [HEND96].[5] I recommend Mr. Henderson's work to those readers who wish to delve into the details of 56 kbit/s modems.

The 56 kbit/s modem is really an evolution from the V.32 and V.34 quadrature amplitude modulation (QAM) concepts of placing more bits onto the voice-grade local loop. But there is one big difference. Modified digital pulse code modulation (PCM) techniques are used from the service provider, such as the telco and or ISP (downstream), and QAM is used from the user to the service provider (upstream). The configuration is shown in Figure 6–7.

There are several reasons why the 56 kbit/s modem operates at this rate. First of all, Shannon's theorem is not being violated. The technology

---

[5][WEXL98] Wexler, Joanie. "56k Modems: A Bandwidth Bird in the Hand," *Business Communications Review*, October, 1998.
    [HEND96] Henderson, P. Michael. "56kbps Data Transmission Across the PSTN," A paper published by Rockwell Semiconductor Systems. No date given.

works with the assumption that the signal-to-noise ratio on the line must not exceed 45 dB in order to support 56 kbit/s. This ratio can be achieved on local loop lines.

In the United States, the FCC limits the transmit power on local links. Consequently, some quantization points are not available. The circuit may also experience nonlinear distortion which also cuts down the possible data rate. Another problem deals with the T1 technology. Certain T1 samples have bits robbed from them for signaling purposes. This means the full eight-bit per sample may not be available. Remember that PCM operations rely on quantization and some of these levels are given up due to the inability of the customer's modem to detect all possible quantization levels.

In effect, the downstream transmission does not use all of the conventional PCM steps. All these factors join together to limit the data rate to 56 kbit/s.

For the 56 kbit/s modem to operate successfully, both modems on the link must use the same technology. In addition, the modem pool at the service provider must have a digital connection to the network. Furthermore, no intermittent conversions can be performed on the traffic. These requirements do not create serious problems since most Internet access involves the connection to a local Telco, so the telco bearer services can be invoked.

V.90: Consolidates the Technologies

Before the V.90 agreement, two proprietary specifications (which were incompatible) were deployed in the marketplace: (a) X2, developed by the U.S. Robotics Inc. (acquired by 3Com Corp.), and (b) k56flex, developed by Lucent Technologies and Rockwell Semiconductor Systems. V.90 offers a standardized compromise between the two.[6]

THE V.110 AND V.120 RECOMMENDATIONS
FOR ISDN INTERFACES

Several of the ITU-T V Series recommendations contain specifications on how certain signals are exchanged (and changed) between different types of networks. These standards have become increasingly impor-

---

[6]Until just recently, the V.90 document was not available to the general public. The ITU-T needs to look to the Internet methods of disseminating information about their standards. Appendix D contains more information on V.90.

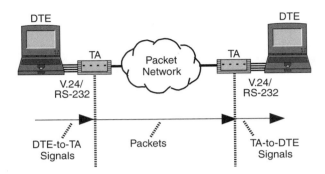

Figure 6–8   Transporting the signals through the packet network

tant in the past few years as networks, carriers, and telephone administrations have implemented the ISDN and other digital-based systems, and the ISDN standards require the use of the specifications described here. On a conventional analog-based link (see Figure 6–2), V.110 and V.I120 define how certain V.24-interchange signals are carried on the modulated analog signal. Both user data and modem control signals are carried across the link.

They are also applicable for systems in which modem signals must be tunneled through a packet data network, such as an internet, and Figure 6–8 shows this situation.[7] A machine called a terminal adapter (TA) is responsible for mapping the incoming V.24 signals to the appropriate bits in a packet, and sending this packet to the receiving TA.[8] At the receiving TA, the process is reversed.

A modem modulates an analog carrier signal to convey information to another modem. This information may be user data, or it may be modem control signals. The user data is relatively straightforward: The TA maps between the analog signals and the digital bits. Control signals are more complicated. The TA must be intelligent enough to know which signals on the V.24/EIA-232 interface are to be mapped and transmitted

---

[7]The V Series recommendations discussed in this text are offered in some vendor products, but not in all of them. If they are not available, other operations are used to perform the same types of functions.

[8]The term *terminal adapter* is used by the ITU-T. In the Internet VoIP specifications, the term *gateway* is used. Both machines are responsible for mapping and syntax conversion operations between analog and digital systems. The TA is ISDN-oriented, and designed to use the ISDN B and D channels. The internet gateway can be ISDN-oriented, but it need not be, and it can be configured to interface with IP, SS7, and conventional telephony signals, such as onhook and offhook.

in the packets to the receiving TA, and of course, the receiving TA must be able to perform the reverse operation.

The ITU-T defines the following specifications to perform these operations. We concentrate on V.110 and V.120 in this part of the book:

- *V.100:* Interconnection between public data networks (PDNs) and the public-switched telephone network
- *V.110:* Support by an ISDN of data terminal equipment with V Series type interfaces
- *V.120:* Support by an ISDN of DTEs with V Series type interfaces with provision for statistical multiplexing
- *V.230:* General data communications interface layer-1 specifications

V.100

The connection of user workstations to data networks through the public telephone network is quite common today. To ensure that the dial-and-answer telephone procedures are consistent across different manufacturers' equipment, the ITU-T has published V.100. This recommendation describes the procedures for physical-layer handshaking between answering and calling modems. The recommendation defines procedures for both half- and full-duplex procedures.

V.100 requires that the dial-and-answer procedures of V.25 or V.25 bis be used to perform the initial handshaking between the modems. Among other requirements, the receiving modem must send back to the transmitting modem an answer tone. Once it has transmitted this tone to the receiving modem, it enters the operations defined in V.100.

Once the modems have exchanged the dial and answer tones, the answering modem transmits what is known as the S1 signal. This signal is of a certain frequency, depending upon the type of modem used.

Upon sending signal S1, the modem remains silent until it detects a signal S2. Based on its response to S2, it either disconnects or conditions itself to the selected mode as indicated in S2. To continue the example, the originating modem sends an S1 signal to indicate it is the modem type and the receiving modem sends back an S2 signal to complete the handshake.

V.110

The V.110 recommendation has received considerable attention in the industry because it defines procedures that have been incorporated into several vendors' ISDN terminal adapters (TAs). Among other fea-

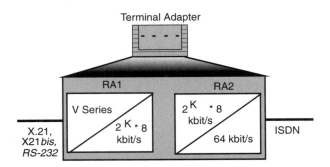

Figure 6–9   The terminal adapter

tures, V.110 establishes the conventions for adapting a V Series data rate to the ISDN 64 Kbit/s rate. Figure 6–9 illustrates the scheme used by V.110.

The V.110 terminal adapter consists of two major functions: rate adapter 1 (RA1) and rate adapter 2 (RA2). The RA1 produces an intermediate rate (IR) which is then input into RA2. RA1 accepts standard V Series interface data rates, ranging from 600 bit/s to 38,400 bit/s.[9] The k value is 0, 1, 2, or 3. The output of RA2 is always 64 kbit/s, in conformance with the ISDN B-channel rate.

The B-Channel Problem.   It is the 64 kbit/s channelized architecture that makes the V.100–V.110 series (and ISDN) rather inefficient and inflexible with regard to the transport of VoIP traffic. We have learned VoIP is based on low bit-rate coders whose signals are not aligned on the B channel (or a DS0) boundary. Nonetheless, ISDN is a big factor on many point-to-point, dial-up links, at least for the next few years, so ISDN is a pertinent subject for this book. Anyway, let us continue the analysis.

RA Frame

Figure 6–10 illustrates the output of RA1, which is an 80-bit frame. The user data are placed into this frame, and some of the bits in the frame are also used for a variety of control functions:

- Seventeen bits are used for synchronization to provide frame alignment patterns.

---

[9]The standards always lag behind the commercial industry. Obviously, 38.4 kbit/s is cited in this standard, but commercial products have higher rates.

1	2	3	Bit Position 4	5	6	7	8	Octet Number
0	0	0	0	0	0	0	0	0
1	D1	D2	D3	D4	D5	D6	S1	1
1	D7	D8	D9	D10	D11	D12	X	2
1	D13	D14	D15	D16	D17	D18	S3	3
1	D19	D20	D21	D22	D23	D24	S4	4
1	E1	E2	E3	E4	E5	E6	E7	5
1	D25	D26	D27	D28	D29	D30	S6	6
1	D31	D32	D33	D34	D35	D36	X	7
1	D37	D38	D39	D40	D41	D42	S8	8
1	D43	D44	D45	D46	D47	D48	S9	9

Figure 6–10   The frame structure

- Several bits are used to convey information about the status of V.24 circuits 105, 106, 107, 108, and 109.
- Several bits are used for network independent clocking information.

A maximum of 48 user bits can be sent in each frame. Therefore, up to 19.2 kbit/s can be placed in the intermediate frame, which has a maximum rate of 32 kbit/s. This value can be derived from a simple calculation: A 32-kbit/s channel allows 400 frames to be transmitted per second (32,000 divided by 80 equals 400). A maximum of 48 bits can be placed in each frame; therefore, 400 times 48 equals 19,200.

If a smaller data signaling rate is used, some of the positions in the frame are not relevant, and they are simply padded out with redundant data bits. For higher bit rates, RA2 creates a frame structure to handle rates of up to 64 kbit/s. For example, the user rate of 38.4 kbit/s.

We now examine how the bits in the frame are used. First, the synchronization bits are used to synchronize the machines' transmissions. The first octet serves as the initial synchronization signal and is set to all 0s. Thereafter, bit 1 of each of the following 9 octets (set to 1) completes the synchronization pattern.

The S and X bits are called status bits, and they are used to provide mapping functions of several of the V.24 interchange circuits that exist at the user device (DTE) and the TA. The state of these interchange circuits is mapped into the S and X bits, sent across the channel to the remote TA-DTE interface, and then used to operate the V.24 interchange circuits on the other side of the interface. With this approach, the system operates with digital bits in the frame, and no modems are required for the traffic inside the ISDN or packet network. The mapping scheme is as follows:

Circuit	Bit Map	Circuit
108	S1,S3,S6,S8 = SA	107
105	S4,S9 = SB	109
106	X	106

This mapping table is extracted from V.110, and can benefit from a few more explanations. The two circuit columns in the table represent the V.24 circuits at the two DTE-TA interfaces. The middle bit map column represents how the V.24 circuits are mapped into the bits in the frame. The state of the circuits (ON or OFF) are mapped to binary 0s and 1s respectively. Several of the bits are used together and are called SA and SB.

The E bits provide several functions. Some of them are used to identify the intermediate rate that is being used in the frame. Some optional E bits are used to carry network-independent clock-phase information. As an example, a modem on a public telephone network may not be synchronized to the ISDN. These bits can be used to develop phase measurements for signaling synchronization.

V.110 Handshaking

Next we discuss the operations for V.110 handshaking. Figure 6–2 is shown in two parts. Figure 6–11(a) shows the interfaces during an idle state, and Figure 6–11(b) shows the interfaces during a data transfer state. This example assumes the B channel has been established between the TAs, and they are awaiting the user DTEs to send traffic. Thus, they are in an idle state.

During the idle state, the DTEs are transmitting and receiving binary 1s on circuits 103 and 104. The TAs in turn send these 1s to each other in the B and D channels. The other pertinent circuits at the DTE-TA interfaces are ON or OFF, as depicted in the figure.

In order to send data, circuit 108/1 must be placed in the ON state, as shown in Figure 6–11 (b). This change on circuit 108/1 will cause the TAs to send the frame synchronization pattern. When this pattern is recognized, then the S and X bits are sent in the ON condition. The receipt of these bits at the TAs will cause the circuits that were OFF previously

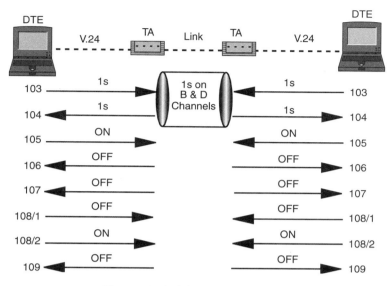

Figure 6–11(a)   The idle state

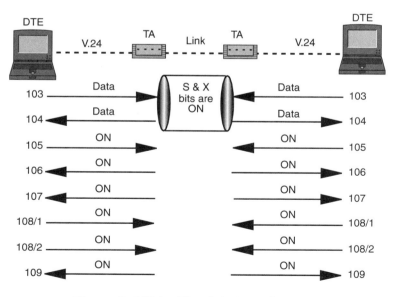

Figure 6–11(b)   The data transfer state

to be placed in the ON condition. There are other rules (and timers) associated with these operations, but the end result is the use of circuits 103 and 104 to pass packets between the user devices.

The interface is torn down by a DTE turning to OFF circuit 108/1. The TA will then send the frame with S = OFF. The result will be turning circuits 106, 107, and 109 to the OFF condition, and the disconnection is complete.

V.120

V.110 is the main subject for this part of the chapter, but a few words on V.120 are in order for those readers using ISDN interfaces. In recognition that the V Series will be in existence for a considerable period and in view of the need for ISDN devices (terminal equipment type 1 or TE1) to interwork with non-ISDN devices (TE2), the ITU-T has published the V.120 recommendation. V.120 supports an ISDN interface with a DTE and its associated physical layer interface. The DTE must operate with the V Series interfaces. V.120 also supports the multiplexing of multiple user data links onto the ISDN S/T interface. V.120 uses a link-level protocol based on the modification of Link Access Procedure for the D Channel, LAPD, published as Q.921. LAPD is similar to LAPM and LAPB, discussed earlier in this chapter.

V.120 describes the use of a TA for the ISDN-to-V Series DTE interworking. However, this TA performs more functions than the TA we examined with V.110. It must perform the following services:

- Electrical and mechanical interfaces conversions
- Adaptation of bit transfer rate (as in V.110)
- End-to-end synchronization of traffic
- Call management between the two end-users

Three modes of operations are supported with the V.120 terminal adapter: (1) asynchronous, (2) synchronous, and (3) transparent. The reader is probably aware that asynchronous mode terminals (async TE2s) use start/stop bits and parity checks. The TA accepts the asynchronous stream from the user device and removes the start/stop bits. As an option, parity may be checked by the TA. In either case, the user data characters are placed in a frame for transmission to a peer entity. The peer entity is another TA or a TE1.

SUMMARY

It is obvious that VoIP means much more than the sole use of IP to support speech traffic. This chapter has explained several widely used layer-1 and layer-2 technologies to support IP, operating at layer 3, as shown in Figure 6–1. A few hardware and software vendors may use proprietary schemes, but they are in the minority. The ability of the user and an ISP to communicate with each other at the physical and data link layers rests on the standardized implementation of the V Series recommendations and PPP.

7

Putting the Pieces Together

We have reached a turning point in our study of VoIP. With the exception of the introductory chapters, most of the material thus far in the book has concentrated on individual pieces of the VoIP puzzle, and most of these pieces reside at the physical and data link layers of the layered model. The bulk of the information in the remaining chapters will focus on the upper layers, with the concentration on layer 3 (the network layer) and layer 7 (the application layer).

But before we delve into these other pieces of VoIP, it should prove useful to take stock of where we have been and try to put together the pieces of the puzzle—those pieces that have been examined thus far.

YET ANOTHER LOOK AT THE LAYERED ARCHITECTURE FOR VoIP

We have assimilated enough additional information to have another look at the VoIP protocol stack that was introduced in Chapters 1, 2, and 6. And as we did in Chapter 6, we will adjust the model described in the introductory chapters, and provide some more details.

STEPS TO THE EXCHANGE OF VoIP TRAFFIC

Figure 7–1 represents a summary of several key points made in previous chapters, plus some additional information. It shows the major steps involved in setting up a connection between a user and a service provider. In this example, the service provider is running a router, and the user machine is a native mode VoIP device [configurations (b) or (c) in Figure 1–2, Chapter 1]. Here is a description of each event depicted in the figure:

- *Event 1:* The user enters a local telephone number for the service provider. The modem dials this number. It is relayed through the local exchange carrier (LEC, not shown here) to the called party: a router serving at the service provider.

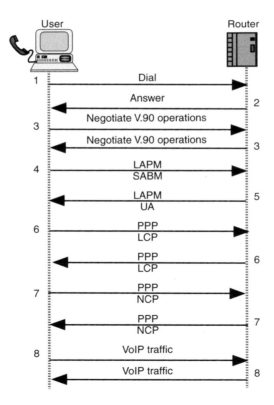

Figure 7–1   An example of the handshakes

- *Event 2:* The gateway has a modem pool available, and one of these modems is selected for this session. It sends back a requisite answer signal to the user.

- *Event 3:* The modems perform the functions explained in Chapter 6.

- *Event 4:* After the modems have finished their handshakes, the physical layer informs the data link layer that it can commence operations. This operation occurs when the carrier detect V.24 interchange circuit is turned on. Assuming the use of LAPM, a Set Asynchronous Balanced Mode (SABM) frame is sent to the service provider. This is the initial handshake at layer 2, and most link protocols use this frame to initialize the link.

- *Event 5:* The service provider returns an unnumbered acknowledgment (UA) frame to the user. The effect of the SABM and UA exchanges is to initialize the link layer. Sequence numbers are set to 0, retransmission timers are initialized, and buffer space is reserved for the sending and reception of user traffic. Some of these operations may be set up with another exchange of frames (not shown here). They are called the exchange ID (XID) frames.

- *Event 6:* After LAPM completes its operations, PPP takes over and executes its Link Control Protocol (LCP). This protocol defines the operations for configuring the link, and for the negotiation of options. As part of LCP, an authentication option can be invoked, as well as a compression operation.

- *Event 7:* Next, PPP executes its Network Control Protocol (NCP) to negotiate certain options and parameters that will be used by a L_3 protocol. The IPCP (The IP Control Protocol), is an example of a specific NCP, and is used to negotiate various IP parameters, such as IP addresses.

- *Event 8:* After all the preliminary operations have been completed, the VoIP traffic is exchanged between the user and the gateway.

In this example, the router does not need to know about the VoIP traffic, because the user node has performed all the voice packetization routines and placed the voice traffic in the IP datagrams. To the router, the IP datagrams are just that: datagrams, and the router makes no special allowance for the VoIP traffic. Well, perhaps this is the case. The router can be configured to handle the real-time voice traffic differently from data traffic. The easiest way to set this feature up is to configure the router to recognize voice traffic by using the Type of Service (TOS) field in the IP header.

ANOTHER LOOK AT THE VoIP PROTOCOL SUITE

Figure 7–2 shows a more detailed view of the VoIP protocol suite that is used to support the operations in Figure 7–1. Once again, the routers are not processing the VoIP traffic. Their job is to use IP to forward this traffic from user A to user B. In this simple example, three routers operate across four links between the users.

The lower layer protocols and interfaces differ, depending on the placement of the router. On links 1 and 4, the lower layer interfaces with the user nodes and the routers are V.90, HDLC, and LAPM. But, between the routers, on links 2 and 3, these protocols are not executed. They are replaced with another L_1 system, typically a DS1, DS3, or SONET trunk, and the two ATM layers: (a) ATM, and (b) the ATM Adaptation Layer (AAL). The replacement of these lower layers allows the use of more efficient and powerful technologies between the routers. Links 2 and 3 form the backbone part of this topology.

Assuming the VoIP traffic is flowing from user A to user B, the voice packets are passed from the voice application down through the layers in the user A node, across link 1 to router 1. Then traffic is then passed up the layers on the receive side of router 1 to IP. IP examines the IP destination address in the IP header and makes a forwarding decision: The next node to receive this traffic to reach user B is router 2, connected to link 2. Consequently, router 1 passes the traffic down the layers to the link-2 interface. In so doing, it encapsulates the IP traffic into AAL, ATM, then the L_1 unit. This process is repeated at each backbone router.

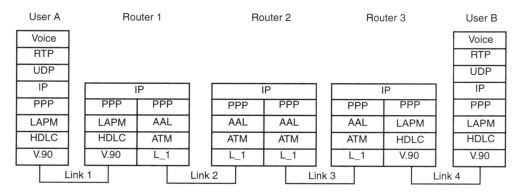

Figure 7–2   The VoIP layered protocol suite in user machines and routers

When the traffic reaches the router that is attached to the destination user (router 3 for user B), router 3 reinserts LAPM, HDLC, and uses the V.90 modem to communicate with the end user at the lower layers.

Remember from our discussions in Chapter 6, that V.110 (or a comparable method) may be used to convey certain V.90 analog signals from user A across the data network to the remote analog interface to user B.

THE VoIP TUNNEL

The internet in this example does not process the voice packets, nor the upper layer headers. They are sent through the internet without being examined. This idea is called a VoIP tunnel and Figure 7–3 depicts the concept. Two points should be noted here. First, the dotted lines in the figure represent the logical communications that occur between the peer layers through the exchange of the protocol headers (protocol control information). Physically, the traffic is moving down the layers when it is being sent, and up the layers when it is being received.

The VoIP tunnel is actually a tunnel for the voice packets, RTP and UDP. Strictly speaking, it is not an IP tunnel because IP is being invoked at each node, as suggested by the dotted horizontal lines between the IP modules at each node.

You may wish to refer back to Figure 1–2, and see if you can determine at which point in the various configuration options the VoIP tunnel begins and ends. Here are the answers:

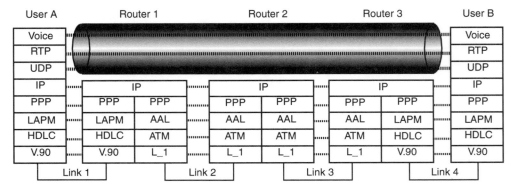

Figure 7–3   The VoIP tunnel

(a) Between the VoIP gateways

(b) Between the user nodes (end-to-end)

(c) Between the user nodes (end-to-end)

(d) Between the VoIP gateways

(e) Between the user node and the VoIP gateway

UNDUE PROCESSING OVERHEAD

We are beginning to tread into waters that are beyond the subject of this book, but a few more comments can be made. The protocol stack in Figure 7–3 can be improved. The problem is that the backbone is running IP in each node. To get a sense of why this configuration is not efficient, assume that the traffic is coming into router 2's incoming interface on link 2. This router must execute AAL to reassemble the small ATM cells into the PPP and then IP data units. Then, IP performs a route lookup to make a forwarding decision. After these operations, the IP datagram is passed back to PPP, then AAL, ATM, and the outgoing L_1 interface. This process is repeated at each node in the backbone, and the time and resources expended to process execute AAL, PPP, and IP can be significant.

Figure 7–4 shows a better approach. The backbone nodes no longer process IP, PPP, or AAL. The ATM cell header is used to make the forwarding decision. The upper layers are all tunneled through an ATM backbone. Moreover, the cumbersome IP addressing and address-matching operations are eliminated, and a fast ATM switch is used instead.

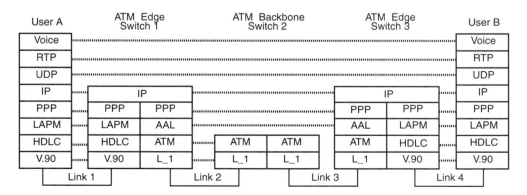

Figure 7–4   Using ATM instead of IP in the backbone.

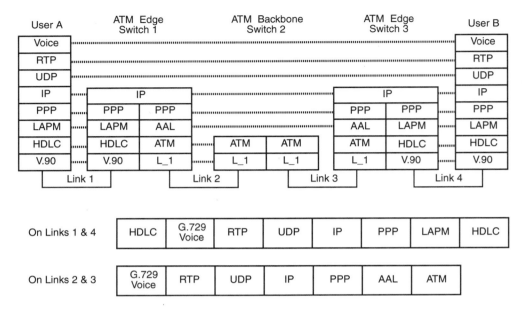

Figure 7–5   The layers and the frames and cells

The ATM edge switches are responsible for mapping the IP address into an ATM address and/or an ATM virtual circuit number. Thereafter, the ATM virtual circuit number is used in the backbone to relay the traffic. This approach is much more efficient and much faster than the IP-based routing configuration, and will reduce delay and jitter in an internet.

To conclude this chapter, Figure 7–5 shows the contents of the data units that are sent across the links. On links 1 and 4, the HDLC frame is conveying the traffic. On links 2 and 3, the ATM cell is conveying the traffic. Notice that the placement of the headers in the frame or cell are aligned in relation to the position of the layers in the sending and receiving nodes.

SUMMARY

This chapter has tied together several individual pieces of the VoIP puzzle from the perspective of the physical and data link layers of the layered model. It can be seen that VoIP has many supporting elements, interfaces, and protocols. It is time to turn our attention to more of those supporting systems, But first, we pause and examine some performance considerations for VoIP applications.

8

Performance Considerations

This chapter examines several issues pertaining to the performance of VoIP networks. The first part of the chapter examines the trade-offs of packet size, buffer size, packet loss and packet latency. The next part of the chapter provides a summary of three studies conducted on VoIP performance in private internets, and in the public Internet.

PACKET SIZE, BUFFER SIZE, LOSS, AND LATENCY

The VoIP designer must pay attention to buffer sizes, packet sizes, and the packet loss rate. The larger the packet loss, the worse the audio quality will be at the receiver. On the other hand, large packet sizes increase the delay and so do large buffers. To see why, let us examine a simple G.711 64 kbit/s voice signal.

First, consider the loss of user traffic. The size of the packet is quite important for speech because of the concept of packet length (the duration of the packet on the channel). Packet length is a function of the number of user bits in the packet, and the coding rate of the signal (for example, 64 kbit/s). Studies reveal that losing traffic that is around 32–64 ms (for G.711 traffic) in duration is disruptive, because it means the loss of speech phonemes. On the other hand, cell loss of a duration of some 4–16 ms is not noticeable nor disturbing to the listener. Therefore, a payload size of anywhere around 32–64 octets would be acceptable to an audio listener. The actual perception of audio loss is a function of other factors such as the compression algorithms used, etc. But for this general example, the following examples show loss for G.711 traffic. It can be seen that the longer packets suffer more loss. The examples are for packets with 32, 48, and 64 bytes of user voice traffic.[1]

$$32 \text{ octets} * 8 \text{ bits per octet} = 256 \text{ bits}$$
$$256 / 64{,}000 = .004$$

$$48 \text{ octets} * 8 \text{ bits per octet} = 384 \text{ bits}$$
$$384/64{,}000 = .006$$

$$64 \text{ octets} * 8 \text{ bits per octet} = 512 \text{ bits}$$
$$512 / 64{,}000 = .008$$

Next, consider buffer size. A larger buffer will increase delay, and decrease the loss rate, because the larger buffer allows more flexibility in playout, and the machine does not have to discard as many packets. But the continued decrease of the buffer size, while decreasing delay, means more packets will be discarded. In effect, as the buffer size approaches 0, the machine operates at wire speed, but will experience more loss of traffic. So, it is a catch-22 situation. Figure 8–1 shows the relationships between packet loss and unidirectional delay [COX98]

In the next section of this chapter, we examine tests conducted on VoIP products in private intranets. I will use one of these tests here to make some other points about the subject of packet size, latency, and voice quality [MIER99].[2] As just mentioned, the voice packet should be small, in order to reduce latency and improve quality. To amplify this thought, large packet sizes are inversely proportional to interactive voice

---

[1]These examples are from studies performed on ATM cells. After extensive deliberations in the ATM standards working groups, it was agreed that a cell size between 32 and 64 octets would perform satisfactorily in that it (a) worked with ongoing equipment (did not require echo cancellers), (b) provided acceptable transmission efficiency, and (c) was not overly complex to implement. Japan and the United States favored a cell size with 64 octets of user payload; Europe favored a size of 32 octets.

[2][MIER99] Mier, Edwin, E. "Voice-Over-IP: Better and Better," *Business Communications Review*, January, 1999.

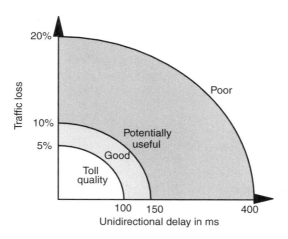

Figure 8–1   Traffic loss versus traffic delay [COX98]

quality. One could take this idea to the extreme and postulate a packet of say 1 byte (or even 1 bit!). Obviously, there is a point of diminishing returns where the overhead of headers to the miniscule user packet is so high that it militates against building an efficient network.

Another consideration is to attempt to build the packet size in consonance with the output of the codec. For example, the G.729 and G.729a codecs produce a 10-ms sample (10 bytes, with 1 byte per ms). In so far as possible, it is a good idea to package the packets in 10-ms bundles.

But this approach may not be possible. For example, if these voice packets are placed inside a fixed-length frame, they may not fit exactly in the fixed payload of the frame. If this is the situation, and the payload size of the frame cannot be altered, the system should be able to break the sample into even-byte boundaries and place it into successive frames in order to best use the payload bandwidth. This approach is common today, and I provide some examples in Chapter 12.

PERFORMANCE OF VoIP IN PRIVATE SYSTEMS

Our focus for this part of the chapter is to examine two studies conducted by Mier Communications Inc. on VoIP products. The general results of the first study are available from Mier Communications

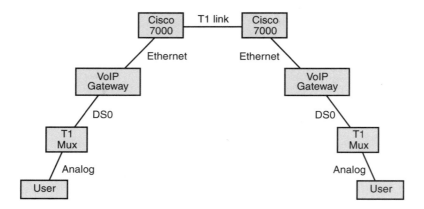

Figure 8–2   Topology for study [MIER98]

[MIER98].[2] The second study is also available from [MIER99] and [MIER99a]. Mier Communications can be reached at ed@mier.com. After we examine the first test, we then look at the new test, and compare the differences.

Figure 8–2 shows the topology layout and configuration for the first study conducted by Mier Communications. The voice traffic was exchanged between two Cisco 7000 routers over an unchannelized T1 link. The voice traffic was created through a simulated analog line and fed into a T1 mux where it was digitized into 64 kbit/s DS0 slots. This signal was fed into the voice-over-IP (VoIP) gateway (the products under test) where they were then input into the Cisco router across an Ethernet 10 Mbit/s channel. The signals were then transported across the unchannelized T1 link to the receiving router where the signal then was sent through an Ethernet interface to the receiving VoIP gateway, then via a DS0 slot to a T1 mux. The mux converted the signal back to analog and transported the signal to the user at either a telephone handset or a speaker.

The study was performed with various voices (female speakers, male speakers, etc.). All speakers recited common voice images such as *do*, *re*, *me*, and so on.

---

[2][MIER98] Mier, Edwin, E. "Voice-Over-IP: Sounding Better," *Business Communications Review*, February, 1998.

[MIER99a] Mier, Edwin, E. "VoIP Gateways-Tradeoffs Affecting Voice Quality," *Business Communications Review Voice 2000*, January, 1999.

Keep in mind that this study did not test voice quality over the Internet. The test was run over the T1 link between the routers. Consequently, you should not infer that these tests state anything about the performance of the Internet in supporting telephony. But the study does provide an interesting and useful assessment of VoIP products. As we shall see, the test reveals that high-quality products are available to run voice over what is essentially data-based protocols, and offer an attractive alternative to public-switched toll services.

Several tests were performed on four products. According to Mier Communications, all four products performed well and provided high-quality telephony images to the end-user. The four products tested were Lucent Technologies, Micom (now part of Nortel), Nuera Communications, and Selsius Systems.

Figure 8–3 reflects the assessment of the quality of these systems when operating under ideal network conditions, The definition of ideal network conditions is a fully available T1 channel which is then unchannelized (not restricted to DS0, TDM slots). In addition, the media operated under relatively error-free conditions without adding delay or latency across the system. That is to say, any latency or delay in the test

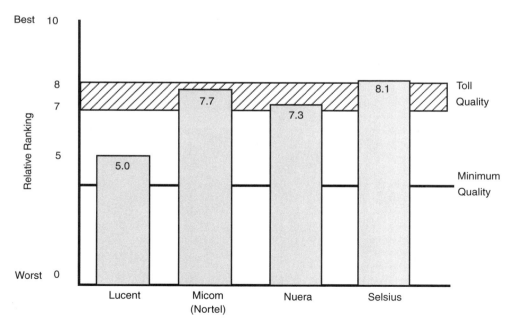

Figure 8–3   Voice quality under ideal conditions [MIER98]

was introduced as a result of the components in the topology and the operations of the VoIPs.

Obviously, the evaluation of the tests is subjective, but the evaluation of voice quality on the telephone network is subjective as well. Notwithstanding, as this figure shows, all products were evaluated as exceeding a minimum quality for the signal. The scale of 0 to 10 was devised with the expectation that a score between 7 and 8 represented the current "toll quality" exhibited in the telephone network. The evaluation of 10 would reflect the best possible telephone voice connection wherein the analog loop is terminated into a digital system one time only, sent a very short distance, and then converted back to an analog signal.

Next, the test was conducted in an environment that exhibited poor quality conditions. To simulate these poor conditions, Mier Communications applied burst errors to the T1 line. The approach was to cycle a 5-ms burst of random errors at a rate of 1×10^2, followed by 50 ms of transmissions with a bit error rate of 1×10^6. The 1×10^6 value is a reasonable assumption for BER performance on a typical local loop. The result of this operation is the introduction of errors in about 10 percent of the IP telephony datagrams. As Figure 8–4 shows, Micom and Nuera

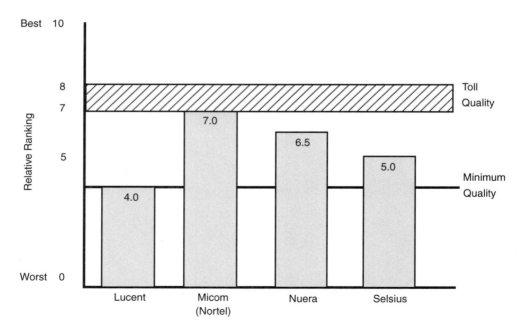

Figure 8–4   Voice quality under poor conditions [MIER98]

continue to exhibit high-quality performance and Lucent and Selsius still exhibited somewhat acceptable quality.

Figure 8–5 shows the bandwidth utilization of the four tested products working under relatively error-free conditions and on a full-unchannelized T1 link. The Nuera system scored the highest with a bandwidth requirement of 14 kbit/s followed by Micom with 18 kbit/s. The Nuera performance approaches that of the sophisticated mobile/wireless vocoders that operate in a range of 13 kbit/s.

Not shown in this figure is the underlying fact that voice quality improved with those systems that used smaller protocol data units (with one exception). Micom's packet size is 91 bytes; Nuera's packet size is 93 bytes; Lucent's packet size is 77 bytes; and Selsius system uses 300 bytes.

In fairness, it should be stated that the performance of Nuera and Micom is partially attributable to the fact that they are using proprietary vocoding techniques whereas Lucent employs the ITU-T G.723.1 and Selsius uses ITU-T G.711. All organizations that belong to the VoIP and the International Media Teleconferencing Consortium (IMTC) have all selected G.723.1 for their basic vocoder.

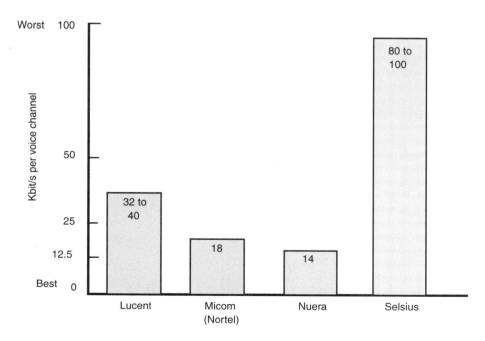

Figure 8–5 Bandwidth used under ideal conditions [MIER98]

It is reasonable to assume that the Lucent and Selsius performance would improve with proprietary schemes.

The trade-off of proprietary versus standardized schemes pertain to the fact that private systems might opt for proprietary schemes because of their superior performance. But if different vendor systems are to interoperate with each other, the standards must be used.

Figure 8–6 shows the latency introduced by the tested systems. All operated within the 250-ms threshold (which is not considered very good performance), and none operated in accordance with the telco standard for one-way latency of 100 ms. The 250-ms delay is considered by some to be the threshold at which it becomes noticeable and disturbing to the users of the system.

In addition, the general study did not focus on where the delay was encountered. Recent tests with voice-over-telephony, in some products (not those cited in the study), indicate that significant delay is occurring in the line card located at the customer premises. Therefore, a clear analysis must focus on the specific components that create the delay because the VoIP may not be the actual culprit for these delay performances.

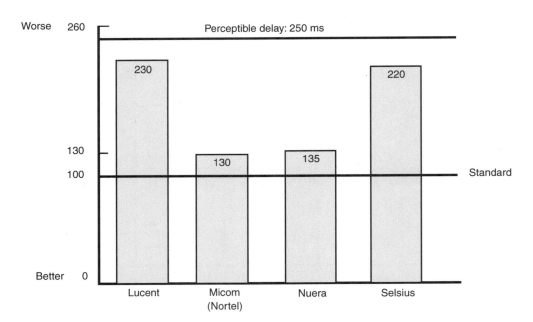

Figure 8–6   Latency: One-way delay [MIER98]

As a result of the interest shown in Mier's first test, the company conducted another test [MIER99]. You can reach Mier at (609) 275–7311 if you need more information about these studies.

Figure 8–7 shows the layout for the study, and notations of the vendors' testing equipment (the tested systems are not shown here). Several points should be emphasized here. First, the test layout is more elaborate and sophisticated than the earlier test. Second, G.723.1 and G.711 were not used by the vendors in this test. Instead, G.729 and G.729a were used. Third, H.323 was part of a test, and it is considered an important component of VoIP by all the tested vendors. Fourth, the results of the test were considerably higher than the earlier test, reflecting better coders and the overall maturation of the technology.

The analog voice files were prerecorded and sent through an Adtran TSU/100 T1 mux, where they were converted to DS0 signals, then to a

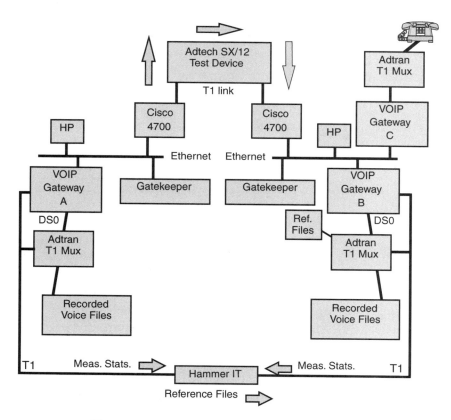

Figure 8–7   Revised test topology [MIER99]

VoIP gateway (Gateway A). Here they were subjected to the vendor's codec and VoIP operations. The resultant VoIP packets were sent through a Cisco 4700 router across an unchannelized T1 (and through an Adtech SX/12 test device) to the receiving site. At this site, the process was reversed (Gateway B), with the voice message rerecorded onto the voice files. A back-to-back T1 line was used to provide reference signals at the receiver. These toll quality samples were compared (by a panel of people) against the tested samples. Gateway C was used to test real-time quality and latency between two people.

The original voice files were sent to the receiver to act as reference (ref.) files for the comparison tests. A scope from Fluke Corp. was used to measure the latency that each vendor's product added (not shown in the figure). A Hammer IT VoIP Test System also measured latency and generated loads on the gateways, as well as measured voice quality and a variety of other statistical support.

The testing for voice quality was performed by Mier's staff by listening to the rerecorded voice samples, as well as using interactive tests between two people. As Figure 8–8(a) shows, all vendors' products performed very well, under ideal conditions (the higher bars for each vendor). All scored well above minimum toll quality. Mier's conclusions are that the reception of packet voice with the tested VoIP gateways cannot be distinguished from POTS services. The lower bars in Figure 8–8(a) show the quality during poor conditions, in which periodic error bursts were placed on the link.

The figure also shows the codecs used for the tests. The vendors used G.729, G.729a, or proprietary coders. All vendors have products with other codecs, such as G.711, and most of them have or are planning to support G.723.1.

Figure 8–8(b) shows the one-way latency for the tested products. Mier's ongoing tests have made them attuned to quality vs. latency, and they conclude that once latency drops below 90 to 80 ms, a person cannot tell the difference between the vendors, or for that matter, between the vendors and the public switched network. After all the tests, the testers could actually tell the differences between latencies under 100 ms, slightly more than 100 ms, and considerably more than 100 ms.

This study was amplified further in [MIER99a]. As you might expect if you read the first part of this chapter, the vendors whose traffic experienced the lowest latency also experienced the best quality. What you might also be thinking is how large a packet do the vendors' products produce? After all, we learned that larger packets lead to more loss on noisy links, and they increase latency.

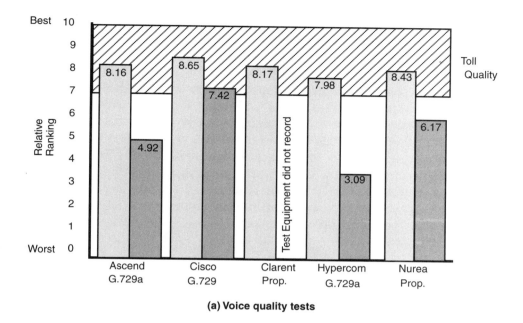

(a) Voice quality tests

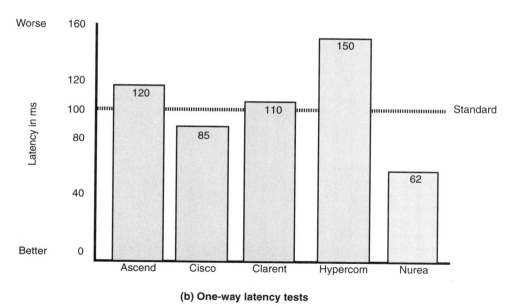

(b) One-way latency tests

Figure 8–8   Voice quality and latency [MIER99]

Then it should come as no surprise that the vendors (with some minor exceptions) whose product gave the best voice quality also exhibited the lowest latency. The number and size of the voice samples in each packet are shown in Figure 8–9.

From these tests, it seems prudent to construct a small packet if one is interested in voice quality. Indeed it is, but there is a price to pay. As stated in the introductory part of the chapter, the packet that contains a small number of samples suffers from more overhead than a packet that contains more samples. This is so, because number of bytes in the associated headers (protocol control information) remain the same for a small or larger user payload—the IP header is always 20 bytes, etc.

Mier's study corroborates these claims, as shown in Figure 8–10. The bandwidth consumption was tested on the LAN and a simulated WAN. Statistics were gathered on the LAN by an HP Internet Advisor, and on the WAN by an Adtech SX-12. In addition, on the WAN, the Adtech gradually reduced the amount of bandwidth available (to the point where the quality was unacceptable). As expected, the systems that

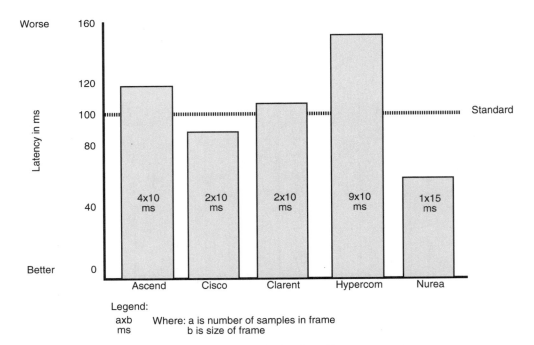

Figure 8–9   Latency and frame size [MIER99]

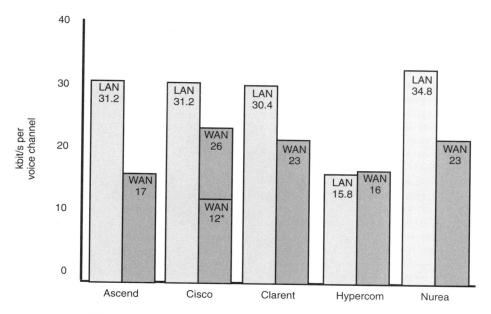

Figure 8–10   Bandwidth consumption [MIER99]

had larger packet sizes and more latency also had a more efficient use of bandwidth.

As stated in the first part of this chapter, there is a tradeoff of latency, packet size, and perceived voice quality. If bandwidth is plentiful, one would opt for the system that provides higher quality, and so on.

In addition, these vendors' gateways are configurable. Frame packing (number of samples per frame) can be set on most of them, as can the jitter buffer. Many other factors come into play in evaluating VoIP gateways, such as costs and ease of use (configuration). So, it is best to delve into more detail about a vendor's product, but the Mier studies are excellent places to start.

PERFORMANCE OF VoIP IN PUBLIC SYSTEMS

This part of the chapter examines a test conducted by 3Com on the performance of VoIP in the public Internet. The source for this study is [COX98].

The study entailed sending and receiving traffic between three nodes: University of California, Davis; University of Illinois, Chicago;

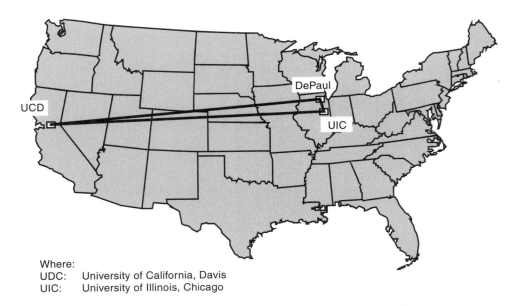

Where:
UDC: University of California, Davis
UIC: University of Illinois, Chicago

Figure 8–11   Topology for the study [KOST98][3]

and DePaul University, see Figure 8–11. The tests were run for a six-
month period. During these tests, a client would transmit once per hour
to a server for three minutes. The transmissions involved a trace which
allowed the analysts to judge RTT as well as packet loss. The engineers
designed their own "ping" program and did not rely on internet pings in
order to control how routers handle conventional ping packets. Observations were made in the evenings as well as various times during the business day, and on weekends.

In addition, different codecs were employed in the tests with the emphasis on G.723.1 and G.729A. Tests were done using PC-to-PC communications and VoIP gateways.

We can summarize several key aspects of the study with the examination of the three figures depicted in Figure 8–12. Figure 8–12 (a) compares the average RTT (in ms) in relation to the hop count. The hop
count represents the number of nodes traversed between the client and
the server. This figure reveals some interesting facts. The first fact is
that RTT exceeds 200 ms. This conclusion is borne out by other studies.

---

[3][KOST98] Kostas, T. J., Borella, M. S., Sidhu, I., Shuster, G. M., Grabiec,
J., and Mahler, J. of a 3Com, paper "Real-Time Voice Over Packet Switched Networks, *IEEE Network*, January, February 1998.

The second fact is that the delay is highly variable. On occasion a delay going through the same number of nodes is, say, 100 ms and on another occasion it may be 200 ms.

Keep in mind that these data represent RTT measured with a ping only and does not include analog-to-digital conversion, codec operations, or other factors that would increase RTT.

Figure 8–12(b) is the same figure as that of 8–12(a). The oval is placed on the figure to emphasize that despite the variability in the RTT in relation to hop count, increased hop counts do indeed contribute to delay.

Figure 8–12(c) has some numbers placed around several of the points in the graph. These numbers represent the geographical distances in miles between the sender and receiver of the trace. It is clear that geographical distance cannot be correlated to RTT. Indeed, a short distance of only 477 miles with a hop count of 21 resulted in a 24-ms RTT. Therefore to emphasize, hop distance is a key factor in delay, and geographical distance is less a factor.

Figure 8–13 provides a summary of the 3COM study. Based on the two alternatives of (a) use of the telephone and VoIP gateways, and (b) use of PCs and routers, the study reveals that the telephone/gateway approach provides significantly better performance than the PC/router approach.

Under ideal conditions, option (a) meets the RTT established by the ITU-T specifications. Option (b) does not meet these requirements, but comes close. During less-than-ideal conditions, neither approach meets the requirements, but a large segment of the population would likely find the performance acceptable for option (a). Option (b) pushes the envelope of acceptable quality.

So, is Internet telephony feasible? Yes, but under the present Internet environment, it may not be acceptable to some people, and may be acceptable to others.

Nonetheless, given the attractive features of Internet telephony (one link to the home, integrating voice and data, and low costs), it will surely succeed.

One other aspect of this subject bears examination: the deployment of high-speed (a) ADSL modems, (b) cable modems, or (c) fixed wireless access technologies on the local loop. Once the customer has these technologies available, the equation changes.

First, overhead (headers and trailers) is not as significant a factor, since the increased bandwidth can support this overhead. Second, new PCs will be upgraded to support faster voice coders to take advantage of

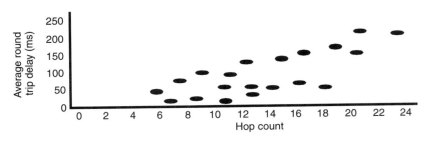

(a) Average delay and hop count

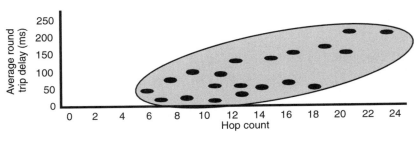

(b) Correlation of delay to distance

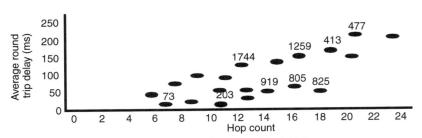

(c) Relationship of delay and geographical distance

(note: numbers represent distance in miles)

Figure 8–12   Round trip delay versus hop count [KOST98]

the higher-speed local loop. Third, the increased pipes into and out of the Internet will force an upgrading of the Internet's capacity. Fourth, the increase of voice (and video) traffic will also force the Internet to look more and more like the telephone network, but with significantly enhanced multiapplication capabilities.

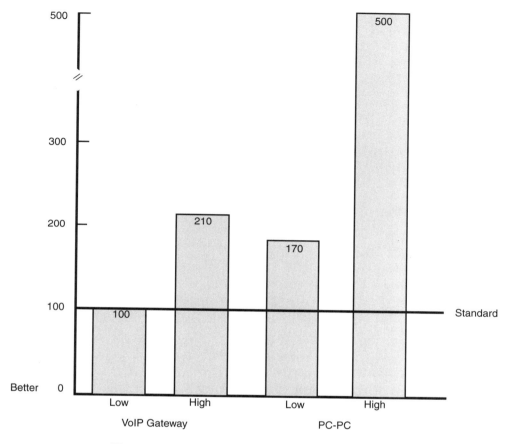

Figure 8–13   Unidirectional delays [KOST98]

SUMMARY

The Mier and Cox studies demonstrate that VoIP is quite feasible in private networks with leased lines, but marginal in the public Internet. It is a good idea to remember that packet voice is in its infancy, and the test results from Mier's labs are impressive. It is reasonable to expect that the Internet will also deliver toll-quality speech—in a few years.

9

VoIP Gateways
and Gatekeepers

As of this writing, the industry is migrating to two protocol suites to support VoIP. They are the H.323 recommendations published by the ITU-T, and the Media Gateway Control Protocol (MGCP), published (in the draft stages) by the Internet Engineering Task Force.

H.323 and MGCP are not "stand-alone" specifications. They rely on many other supporting protocols to complete their operations. The approach taken in this chapter is to concentrate on the core H.323 and MGCP operations, and explain the supporting protocols in the context of H.323 and MGCP.[1]

As a prelude to the examination of H.323 and MGCP, we examine a model that defines the interfaces and functional entities of VoIP Gateways and VoIP Gateway controllers.

THE GATEWAY/GATEKEEPER MODEL

Several terms are used to describe the placement of the VoIP functions in the VoIP physical entities, and we have explained some of them in this book. This aspect of packet telephony can be confusing because

---

[1]A companion book to this series is being written about these protocols, titled: *The Internet Voice and Video Protocols*.

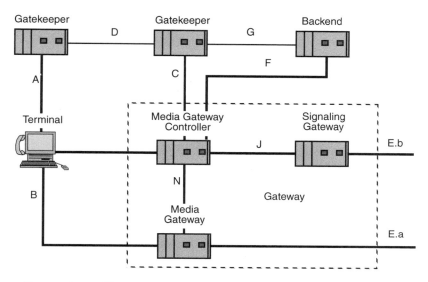

Figure 9–1   The VoIP Gateway/Gatekeeper reference model [VAND98]

the various specifications use different terms to describe the same or similar functions. For example, H.323 uses the term Gatekeeper to describe a nearly similar entity residing in the MGCP as a Call Agent.

To help clarify these terms and concepts, [VAND98][2] has published a model of the Media Gateway Controller and the Media Gateway, which also includes the Gatekeeper, the H.323 terminal, and the signaling Gateway. This model is shown in Figure 9–1. The model is not yet finished, the references (A, B, C, etc.) have not been fully defined.

In this model, the Gateway is made up of the Media Gateway Controller (MGC), the Media Gateway (MG), and the Signaling Gateway (SG). The Gateway is the node in the network that interfaces an IP-based network and the telephony network. It must provide two-way, real-time communications interfaces between the IP-based network and the telephony network. The three components that make up the Gateway are explained here:

---

[2][VAND98] Vandenameele, Jozef. "Requirements for the Reference Point ('N') between Media Gateway Controller and Media Gateway," *Draft-vandenameele-tiphon-arch-gway-decomp-00.txt*, November 1988.

- The *Media Gateway* provides the mapping and translation functions between the IP/telephony networks. For example, it might translate G.711 64 kbit/s speech into G.723.1 6.3 kbit/s speech or vice-versa. These operations are referred to as stream conditioning and may also include echo cancellation, if necessary. For traffic emanating from the IP network, packet media termination is performed since packets do not operate on the telephony side. Therefore, these packets must be mapped into telephony bearer channels (DS0, ISDN B channel). The opposite operations occur when traffic emanates from the telephony network.

  The Media Gateway is also responsible for support services such as playing announcements, and tone generation as necessary. It keeps track of traffic and has statistics available on network usage.

- The *Signaling Gateway* is responsible for the signaling operations of the system. It provides the interworking of the H.323 and SS7 ISUP signaling operations. For example, it might translate an H.323 SETUP message coming from an H.323 Gatekeeper into an SS7 ISUP Initial Address Message (IAM) that is to go to a telephony exchange. These operations may actually be located in the Media Gateway Controller. If they are in the Signaling Gateway, they are controlled by the Media Gateway Controller.

- The *Media Gateway Controller* is the overall controller of the system. That is, it controls the Media Gateway and the Signaling Gateway. It must interwork with the H.232 Gatekeeper, so it is able to process H.225 and H.245 messages (explained later in this chapter). It is also responsible for authentication and network security. It also monitors the resources of the overall system, and maintains control of all connections.

The *Gatekeeper* is also a controller and has some of the same responsibilities as the Media Gateway Controller, except it does not control the Signaling Gateway or the Media Gateway. Its job is to control the H.323 activities on the IP-based network.

The *Backend* may be used by the Gateways and Gatekeepers to provide support functions such as billing, database management, routing and address resolution.

The reference interfaces labeled E are: (a) E.a is the interface for telephony user links (lines and trunks), (b) E.b is the interface for the SS7 signaling links.

THE H.323 SPECIFICATION

Many VoIP vendors are using the ITU-T H.323 recommendation (or a subset) in their products. In a few short years, it has become the standard for deploying VoIP in a local area network.

H.323 for VoIP encompasses considerably more than one H.323 specification. Other H-Series recommendations come into play, such as H.225.0 and H.245. The focus of attention for the first part of this chapter is H.323, but the other pertinent H-Series recommendations are also explained.

The H Series use Abstract Syntax Notation.1 (ASN.1) to describe messages. From previous experience, I know that few readers understand ASN.1. So, I have kept the ASN.1 examples to a minimum. I provide a brief tutorial on ASN.1, and I explain each element (field) in the ASN.1 code.

ARCHITECTURE OF H.323

The H.323 Recommendation assumes the transmission path between the telephony users passes through at least one local area network (LAN), such as an Ethernet or a token ring. It is further assumed that the LAN may not provide a guaranteed quality-of-service (QOS) needed to support the telephony traffic. As shown in Figure 9–2, the H.323 encompasses end-to-end connection between H.323 terminals and other terminals and through different kinds of networks. To gain an understanding of the scope and architecture of H.323, the entities in Figure 9–2 are explained in more detail next.

The H.323 Terminal

The H.323 terminal is an end-user device that provides real-time, two-way voice, video, or data communications with another H.323 terminal. The terminal can also communicate with an H.323 Gateway or a Multipoint Control Unit (MCU). While I cite the ability to support voice, video, and data, the terminal needs to not be configured for all those services, and H.323 does not require the terminal to be multiservice-capable.

The H.323 Gateway

The H.323 Gateway is a node on a LAN that communicates with the H.323 terminal or other ITU-T terminals attached to other networks. If one of the terminals is not an H.323 terminal, the Gateway performs

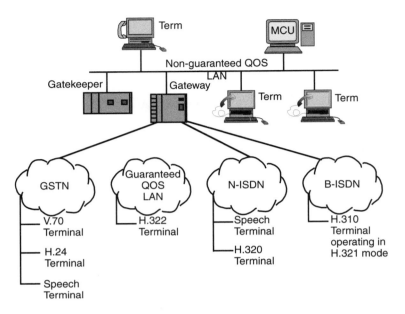

Figure 9–2   H.323 architecture

translation of the transmission formats between the terminals; for example, a translation between G.711 and G.729 voice signals. One H.323 Gateway can interwork with another H.323 Gateway.

In addition, the Gateway can operate with other ITU: (a) switched circuit networks (SCNs); (b) the General Switched Telephone Network (GSTN), (c) the narrowband-ISDN (N-ISDN), and (d) the broadband-ISDN (B-ISDN, an ATM-based network). Also, the Gateway can operate as an H.323 Multipoint Control Unit (MCU), discussed next.

Working in conjunction with the Gatekeeper, the Gateway can set up and clear calls on the LAN and SCN. In effect, it reflects the LAN characteristics to the H.323 terminal on the LAN video and the SCN terminal characteristics on the SCN side. Under certain conditions, the Gateway can be used to bypass a LAN router or a low-bandwidth communications link.

The Multipoint Control Unit (MCU)

The Multipoint Control Unit (MCU) supports multiconferencing between three or more terminals and Gateways. A two-terminal point-to-point conference can be expanded to a multipoint conference. The MCU consists of a mandatory multipoint controller (MC) and optional multipoint processor (MP).

The MC supports the negotiation of capabilities with all terminals in order to insure a common level of communications. It can also control the resources in the multicast operation. The MC is not capable of the mixing or switching of voice, video, or data traffic. However, the MP can perform these services (under the control of the MC). The MP is the central processor of the voice, video, and data streams for a multipoint conference.

MCU Multipoint Conference Control. The MCU may (or may not) control three types of multipoint conferences (see Figure 9–3):

- *Centralized multipoint conference:* All participating terminals communicate with the MCU point-to-point. The MC manages the conference, and the MP receives, processes, and sends the voice, video, or data streams to and from the participating terminals.
- *Decentralized Multipoint Conference:* The MCU is not involved in this operation. Rather, the terminals communicate directly with each other through their own MCs. If necessary, the terminals assume the responsibility for summing the received audio streams and selecting the received video signals for display.

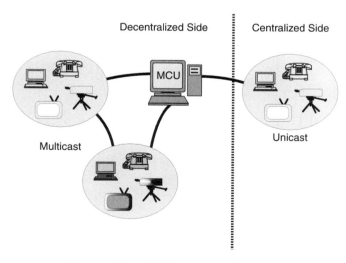

Figure 9–3   Multipoint conferences

- *Mixed Multipoint Conference:* As the name suggests, this conference is a mix of the centralized and decentralized modes. The MCU keeps the operations transparent to the terminals.

The H.323 Gatekeeper

The H.323 Gatekeeper provides address translation and call control services to H.323 endpoints. It also is responsible for bandwidth control, a set of operations that allow endpoints to change their available bandwidth allocations on the LAN.

A single Gatekeeper manages a collection of terminals, Gateways, and MCUs. This collection is called a zone. A zone is a logical association of these components and may span multiple LANs.

CODEC REQUIREMENTS

H.323 establishes the requirements for speech codecs; the video codec is optional. A summary of the requirements follows.

Speech Codecs

All H.323 terminals must have a voice codec. The minimum requirement is the support of recommendation G.711 (the A-law and μ-law). Other speech encoding/decoding standards cited by H.323 are G.722, G.723, G.728, G.729, and MPEG-1 audio.

H.245 is used during an initial handshake between the machines to determine the audio encoding algorithm. The terminal should be capable of sending and receiving different audio streams. After H.245 has completed the agreements on the terminals' capabilities, H.225 is used to format the audio stream.

Video Codecs

If video is supported, the H.323 terminal must code and decode the video streams in accordance with H.261 Quarter Common Intermediate Format (QCIF). Options are available, but they must use the H.261 or H.263 specifications.

Audio Mixing

In a multipoint conference, terminals may be sending different simultaneous audio streams to a terminal. The H.323 terminal must be able to present a composite audio signal to the user, so it must support an audio mixing function.

THE H.323 PROTOCOL STACK

H.323 consists of several standards, and cites the use of others, as shown in Figure 9–4. For audio applications, G.711 is required, and other G Series recommendations are options. However, the preference in recent commercial products is not G.711, because of its 64 kbit/s-bandwidth requirement.

The video standards are H.261 and H.263. Data support is through T.120, and the various control, signaling, and maintenance operations are provided by H.245, Q.931, and the Gatekeeper specification.

The audio and video packets must be encapsulated into the Real-Time Protocol (RTP) and carried on a UDP socket pair between the sender and the receiver. The Real-Time Control Protocol (RTCP) is used to assess the quality of the sessions and connections as well as to provide feedback information among the communicating parties. The data and support packets can operate over TCP or UDP.

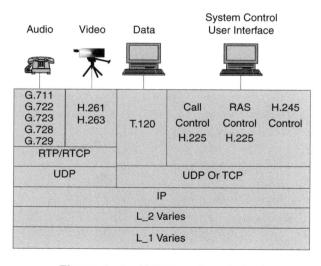

Figure 9–4   H.323 protocol stack

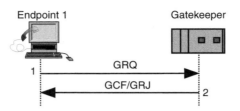

Figure 9–5   Auto discovery

REGISTRATION, ADMISSIONS, AND STATUS (RAS) OPERATIONS

The approach in this section is to describe the H.323 functions pertaining to Gatekeeper discovery, endpoint registration, call management, and other key H.323 operations. I also explain the role of H.225 and H.245. These examples are not all-inclusive, but represent a sampling of the RAS function.

H.323 uses a logical channel on the LAN to manage overall signaling activities. This channel is the Registration, Admissions, and Status (RAS) channel. The RAS signaling function uses H.225.0 messages for a variety of support operations, discussed next.

Gatekeeper Discovery Procedures

The Gatekeeper discovery is a straightforward procedure used by an endpoint to determine with which Gatekeeper it should register. The process is automatic and does not require manual configuration, and allows the association between the endpoint and its Gatekeeper to change over time.

Figure 9–5 shows the messages exchanged for the Gatekeeper discovery operation, which starts in event 1 with endpoint 1 sending a Gatekeeper Request (GRQ) message on the LAN. This message is examined by one or more Gatekeepers who may (or may not, depending on the implementation) respond with a Gatekeeper Confirmation (GCF) message. This message contains the transport address of the Gatekeeper's RAS channel.

The transport address is implemented with a Transport Service Access Point (TSAP), and allows the multiplexing of multiple connections on a TSAP.[3] The transport address is a LAN MAC address and a TSAP.

An alias address can be used as an alternate method for identifying an endpoint. An example of an alias address is E.164 (the ISDN tele-

---

[3]The TSAP is an OSI transport layer SAP. It is equivalent to an Internet socket number. An Internet socket consists of a port number and an IP address.

phony address). If alias addresses are used, they must be unique within a zone; also Gatekeepers, MCs, and MUs cannot use alias addresses.

The endpoint starts a timer upon issuing the GRQ message. If it does not receive a response, the time expires and another GRQ can be issued. If auto discovery fails, the network administrator must do troubleshooting to determine the problem.

Alternatively, the Gatekeeper may return a Gatekeeper Reject (GRJ) message if it chooses not to be the endpoint's Gatekeeper.

H.323 defines the GRQ, GCF, and GRJ messages in a general way. It is left to the H.225.0 to define the contents of these messages using Abstract Syntax Notation.1 (ASN.1). The ASN.1 coding for these three messages are listed below and Box 9–1 describes a few simple rules to help you understand the code.

```
GatekeeperRequest              ::=SEQUENCE-- (GRQ)
{
        requestSeqNum          RequestSeqNum,
        protocolIdentifier     ProtocolIdentifier,
        nonStandardData        NonStandardParameter OPTIONAL,
        rasAddress             TransportAddress,
        endpointType           EndpointType,
        GatekeeperIdentifier   GatekeeperIdentifier OPTIONAL,
        callServices           QseriesOptions OPTIONAL,
        endpointAlias          SEQUENCE OF AliasAddress OPTIONAL,
        . . .
}


GatekeeperReject               ::=SEQUENCE-- (GRJ)
{
        requestSeqNum          RequestSeqNum,
        protocolIdentifier     ProtocolIdentifier,
        nonStandardData        NonStandardParameter OPTIONAL,
        GatekeeperIdentifier   GatekeeperIdentifier OPTIONAL,
        rejectReason           GatekeeperRejectReason,
        . . .
}


GatekeeperRejectReason         ::=CHOICE
{
        resourceUnavailable    NULL,
        terminalExcluded       NULL, —permission failure, not a resource failure
        invalidRevision        NULL,
        undefinedReason        NULL,
        . . .
}
```

Box 9–1   Rules for reading ASN.1 code

::=	Means defined as.
SEQUENCE	Means a sequence of ASN.1 elements. H.325 uses the SEQUENCE statement to explain the fields in the packet, where each line in the code represents a field in the packet.
Words beginning with an upper case	This word describes a field in the packet and somewhere in the code, it must be defined by another ASN.1 descriptor called the "type". A type could be integer, Boolean, etc. In fact, SEQUENCE is a type.
Word beginning with a lower case	This word is supposed to be a "user friendly" description of the associated upper case word. An ASN.1 compiler does not act upon these words.
OPTIONAL	The entry is not required in a message.
CHOICE	One and only one of the fields is present in the message.
NULL	A type stating that information may not be available and therefore not provided.
—-	Comments in the code.
{	Proclaims the start and end of a part of the code.
}	
, after the field	Signifies the continuance of the code.
Words all in CAPS	These are ASN.1 reserved words.
Other concepts	A word is a string of words without spaces in which the initial letter determines its status by being either a capital letter or lower case letter. The individual words in the string are capitalized to aid the reader in understanding the string but do not have any other significance.

```
GatekeeperConfirm              ::=SEQUENCE-- (GCF)
{
        requestSeqNum          RequestSeqNum,
        protocolIdentifier     ProtocolIdentifier,
        nonStandardData        NonStandardParameter OPTIONAL,
        GatekeeperIdentifier   GatekeeperIdentifier OPTIONAL,
        rasAddress             TransportAddress,
        . . .
}
```

The contents of these messages are used primarily for identification purposes and contain the following information:

- *requestSeqNum:* A number unique to the sender, returned by the receiver in any messages associated with this message.
- *protocolIdentifier:* Used to determine version/vintage of implementation.
- *nonStandardData:* An optional parameter whose contents are not defined.
- *rasAddress:* The transport address that this endpoint uses for registration and status messages.
- *endpointType:* Specifies the type(s) of the terminal that is registering.
- *GatekeeperIdentifier:* Identifies the Gatekeeper that the terminal would like to receive permission to register from a missing or null string *GatekeeperIdentifier* indicates that the terminal is interested in any available Gatekeeper.
- *callServices:* Provides information on support of optional Q-Series protocols to the Gatekeeper and called terminal.
- *endpointAlias:* Contains external address (if used), such as E.164.
- *rejectReason:* Codes for why the GRQ was rejected by this Gatekeeper.

Endpoint Registration Procedures

Once the discovery process has taken place, registration procedures are undertaken. These administrative operations define how an endpoint joins a zone and provides the Gatekeeper with its transport (and alias) address(es). Figure 9–6 shows the message exchange, with an endpoint 1 sending the Registration Request (RRQ) message to the Gatekeeper, who was discovered with the auto-discovery operation. Of course, the connect transport address is used in the RRQ message. In event 2, the Gatekeeper responds with the Registration Confirmation (RCF) message or the Registration Reject (RRJ) message.

Either the endpoint or the Gateway can cancel the registration, and end the association between the two entities. The operations in events 3 and 4 show the registration cancellation emanating from the endpoint with the Unregister Request (URQ) message. The Gatekeeper can respond with the Unregister Confirm (UCF) message or the Unregister Reject (URJ) message. The Gatekeeper starts the registration cancellation

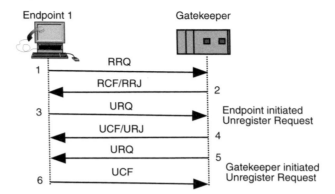

Figure 9–6   Registration

process with the URQ message and the endpoint must respond with the UCF message.

The ASN.1 coding for the terminal and Gateway registration messages is:

```
RegistrationrRequest              ::=SEQUENCE-- (RRQ)
{
    requestSeqNum                 RequestSeqNum,
    protocolIdentifier            ProtocolIdentifier,
    nonStandardData               NonStandardParameter OPTIONAL,
    discoveryComplete             BOOLEAN,
    callSignalAddress             SEQUENCE OF TransportAddress,
    rasAddress                    SEQUENCE OF TransportAddress,
    terminalType                  EndpointType,
    terminalAlias                 SEQUENCE OF AliasAddress OPTIONAL,
    terminalIdentifier            GatekeeperIdentifier OPTIONAL,
    endpointVendor                VendorIdentifier,
    . . .
}


RegistrationConfirm               ::=SEQUENCE-- (RCF)
{
    requestSeqNum                 RequestSeqNum,
    protocolIdentifier            ProtocolIdentifier,
    nonStandardData               NonStandardParameter OPTIONAL,
    callSignalAddress             SEQUENCE OF TransportAddress,
    terminalAlias                 SEQUENCE OF AliasAddress OPTIONAL,
    GatekeeperIdentifier          GatekeeperIdentifier OPTIONAL,
    endpointVendor                VendorIdentifier,
    . . .
}
```

```
RegistrationReject              ::=SEQUENCE-- (RRJ)
{
    requestSeqNum               RequestSeqNum,
    protocolIdentifier          ProtocolIdentifier,
    nonStandardData             NonStandardParameter OPTIONAL,
    rejectReason                RegistrationRejectReason,
    GatekeeperIdentifier        GatekeeperIdentifier OPTIONAL,
    . . .
}


RegistrationRejectReason        ::=CHOICE
{
    discovery required          NULL,—registration permission has aged
    invalidRevision             NULL,
    invalidCallSignalAddress     NULL
    invalidRASAddress           NULL,—supplied address is invalid
    duplicateAlias              SEQUENCE OF AliasAddress,  —alias registered to
                                                    another endpoint
    invalidTerminalType         NULL,
    undefinedReason             NULL,
    transportNotSupported       NULL,  —permission failure, not a resource failure
    . . .
}


UnregistrationRequest           ::=SEQUENCE-- (URQ)
{
    requestSeqNum               RequestSeqNum,
    callSignalAddress           SEQUENCE OF TransportAddress,
    endpointAlias               SEQUENCE OF AliasAddress OPTIONAL,
    nonStandardData             NonStandardParameter OPTIONAL,
    endpointIdentifier          EndPointIdentifier OPTIONAL,
    . . .
}


UnregistrationConfirm           ::=SEQUENCE-- (UCF)
{
    requestSeqNum               RequestSeqNum,
    nonStandardData             NonStandardParameter OPTIONAL,
    . . .
}


UnregistrationReject            ::=SEQUENCE-- (URJ)
{
    requestSeqNum               RequestSeqNum,
    rejectReason                UnregRejectReason,
    nonStandardData             NonStandardParameter OPTIONAL,
    . . .
}
```

```
UnregRejectReason              ::=CHOICE
{
   notCurrentlyRegistered      NULL,
   callInProgress              NULL,
   undefinedReason             NULL,
   . . .
}
```

The contents of these messages are as follows:

- *requestSeqNum:* A number unique to the sender. It is returned by the receiver in any response associated with this specific message.
- *protocolIdentifier:* Identifies the H.225.0 vintage of the sending terminal.
- *discoveryComplete:* Set to TRUE if the requesting endpoint has preceded this message with the Gatekeeper discovery procedure; set to FALSE if registering only.
- *callSignalAddress:* The call control transport address for this endpoint. If multiple transports are supported, they must be registered all at once.
- *rasAddress:* The registration and status transport address for this endpoint.
- *terminalType:* Specifies the type(s) of the terminal that is registering.
- *terminalAlias:* A list of external addresses.
- *gatekeeperIdentifier:* Identifies the Gatekeeper that the terminal wishes to register with.
- *endpointVendor:* Information about the endpoint vendor.
- *callSignalAddress:* An array of transport addresses for H.225.0 call control messages: one for each transport that the Gatekeeper will respond to. This address includes the TSAP identifier.
- *endpointIdentifier:* A Gatekeeper assigned terminal identity string: which is echoed in subsequent RAS messages.
- *callServices:* Provides information on support of optional Q-Series protocols to Gatekeeper and called terminal.
- *endpointAlias:* Contains external address (if used), such as E.164.
- *rejectReason:* Codes for why the GRQ was rejected by this Gatekeeper.

Admission Procedures

H.323 defines the use of a modified Q.931 signaling protocol. An example of how Q.931 is used with RAS is shown in Figure 9–7 to support the Admission procedures. Notice that the RAS messages are used between the terminals (endpoint 1 and endpoint 2) and the Gatekeeper—which, of course, is the purpose of RAS. The Q.931 messages are exchanged between the H.323 terminals.

In events 1/2 and 5/6, the terminals and the Gatekeeper exchange these messages:

- *ARQ:*   The Admission Request message
- *ACF:*   The Admission Confirmation message
- *ARJ:*   The Admission Reject message (perhaps)

Let us examine the content of these messages first and then look at the Q.931 messages. Keep in mind: To this point, the RAS operations have been concerned with discovery and registration procedures. Thus far, there have been no requests for bandwidth or other services.

The ASN.1 coding for the Admission messages are:

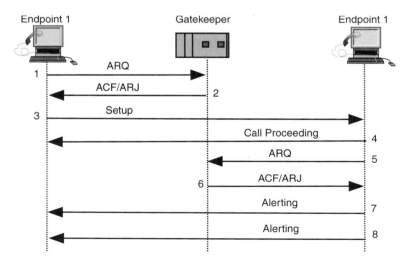

Figure 9–7   The Admission procedures

```
AdmissionRequest                 ::=SEQUENCE-- (ARQ)
{
    requestSeqNum                RequestSeqNum,
    callType                     CallType,
    callModel                    CallModel OPTIONAL,
    endpointIdentifier           EndPointIdentifier,
    destinationInfo              SEQUENCE OF AliasAddress OPTIONAL,
    destCallSignalAddress        TransportAddress OPTIONAL,
    destExtraCallInfo            SEQUENCE OF AliasAddress OPTIONAL,
    srcInfo                      SEQUENCE OF AliasAddress,
    srcCallSignalAddress         TransportAddress OPTIONAL,
    bandWidth                    BandWidth,
    callReferenceValue           CallReferenceValue,
    nonStandardData              NonStandardParameter OPTIONAL,
    callServices                 QseriesOptions OPTIONAL,
    conferenceID                 ConferenceIdentifier,
    activeMC                     BOOLEAN,
    answerCall                   BOOLEAN,  —answering a call
    . . .
}

CallType                         ::=CHOICE
{
    pointToPoint                 NULL,  —Point-to-point
    oneToN                       NULL,  —no interaction (FFS)
    nToOne                       NULL, —no interaction (FFS)
    nToN                         NULL,  —interactive (multipoint)
}

CallModel                        ::=CHOICE
{
    direct                       NULL,
    GatekeeperRouted             NULL,
}

AdmissionConfirm                 ::=SEQUENCE-- (AFC)
{
    requestSeqNum                RequestSeqNum,
    bandWidth                    BandWidth,
    callModel                    CallModel,
    destCallSignalAddress        TransportAddress,
    irrFrequency                 INTEGER (1..65535) OPTIONAL
    nonStandardData              NonStandardParameter OPTIONAL,
    . . .
}

AdmissionReject                  ::=SEQUENCE-- (ARJ)
{
    requestSeqNum                RequestSeqNum,
```

```
    reject Reason               AdmissionRejectReason,
    nonStandardData             NonStandardParameter OPTIONAL,
    . . .
}


AdmissionRejectReason        ::=CHOICE
{
    calledPartyNotRegistered  NULL, —cannot translate address
    invalidPermission         NULL, —permission has expired
    requestDenied             NULL, —no bandwidth available
    undefinedReason           NULL,
    callerNotRegistered       NULL,
    routeCallToGatekeeper     NULL,
    invalidEndpointIdentifer  NULL,
    resourceUnavailable       NULL,
    . . .
}
```

The contents of these messages are as follows:

- *requestSeqNum:* A number unique to the sender. It shall be returned by the receiver in any response associated with this specific message.
- *callType:* The Gatekeeper uses this parameter to determine bandwidth usage. The default value if *pointToPoint* for all calls.
- *callModel:* If direct, the endpoint is requesting the direct terminal to terminal call model. If *GatekeeperRouted*, the endpoint is requesting the Gatekeeper mediated model.
- *endpointIdentifier:* An endpoint identifier that was assigned to the terminal by RCF, probably the E.164 address or H323_ID. It is used as a security measure to help ensure that this is a registered terminal within its zone.
- *destinationInfo:* Sequence of external addresses for the destination terminal, such as E.164 addresses or H323_IDs.
- *destCallSignalAddress:* Transport address used at the destination for call signaling.
- *destExtraCallInfo:* Contains external addresses for multiple calls.
- *srcInfo:* Sequence of external addresses for the source terminal, such as E.164 address or H323_IDs.
- *srcCallSignalAddress:* Transport address used at the source for call signaling.
- *bandWidth:* The number of 100 bit/s requested for the bidirectional call. For example, a 128 kbit/s call would be signaled as a re-

quest for 256 kbit/s. The value refers only to the audio and video bit rate excluding headers and overhead.

- *callReferenceValue:* The CRV from Q.931 for this call; used by a Gatekeeper to associate the ARQ with a particular call.
- *nonStandardData:* An optional value whose contents are not defined.
- *irrFrequency:* The frequency, in seconds, that the endpoint shall send information request response (IRR) messages to the Gatekeeper while on a call, including while on hold.
- *requestSeqNum:* the same value that was passed in the ARQ.
- *rejectReason:* Reason the bandwidth request was denied.
- *callServices:* Information on support of optional Q-Series protocols to Gatekeeper and called terminal.
- *conferenceID:* Unique conference identifier.
- *activeMC:* If TRUE, the calling party has an active MC; otherwise FALSE.
- *answerCall:* Used to indicate to a Gatekeeper that a call is incoming.

The Q.931 messages are similar to the conventional ISDN L_3 messages. The setup message is explained here. First the ASN.1 code is listed, followed by a description of the fields in the message.

The ASN.1 coding for the Q.931 Setup message is:

```
Setup_UUIE                  ::=SEQUENCE
{
    protocolIdentifier      ProtocolIdentifier,
    h245Address             TransportAddress OPTIONAL,
    sourceAddress           SEQUENCE OF AliasAddress OPTIONAL,
    sourceInfo              EndpointType,
    destinationAddress      SEQUENCE OF AliasAddress OPTIONAL,
    destCallSignalAddress   TransportAddress OPTIONAL,
    destExtraCallInfo       SEQUENCE OF AliasAddress OPTIONAL,
    destExtraCRV            SEQUENCE OF CallReferenceValue OPTIONAL,
    activeMC                BOOLEAN,
    conferenceID            ConferenceIdentifier,
    conferenceGoal          CHOICE
    activeMC                CHOICE
    {
        create              NULL,
        join                NULL,
        invite              NULL,
        . . .
    }
}
```

```
callServices          QseriesOptions OPTIONAL,
callType              CallType,
    . . .
}
```

The contents of the Setup message are as follows:

- *protocolIdentifier:* Set by the calling endpoint to the version of H.225.0 supported.
- *h245Address:* A specific transport address on which the calling endpoint or Gatekeeper handling the call would like to establish H.245 signaling.
- *sourceAddress:* Contains the H323_IDs for the source; the E.164 number of the source is in the Q.931 part of SETUP.
- *sourceInfo:* Contains an EndpointType to allow the called party to determine whether the call involved a Gateway.
- *destinationAddress:* The address the endpoint wishes to be connected to.
- *destCallSignalAddress:* Informs the Gatekeeper of the destination terminal's call signaling transport address.
- *destExtraCallInfo:* Needed to make possible additional channel calls, i.e., for 2×64 kbit/s call on the WAN side.
- *destExtraCRV:* CRVs for the additional SCN calls specified by *destExtraCallInfo.* Their use is for further study.
- *activeMC:* Indicates that the calling endpoint is under the influence of an active MC.
- *conferenceID:* Unique conference identifier.
- *conferenceGoal:* Indicates a desire to join an existing conference, start a new conference, or to invite a party to join an existing conference.
- *callServices:* Provides information on support of optional Q-Series protocols to Gatekeeper and called terminal.
- *callType:* The Gatekeeper uses this parameter to determine bandwidth usage. The default value if *pointToPoint* for all calls.

OTHER RAS PROCEDURES

As mentioned earlier, all the RAS procedures are not discussed in this overview. So, here is a brief description of the others.

Terminal Gatekeeper Requests for Changes in Bandwidth

These messages are exchanged for this procedure:

- *BRQ:* Bandwidth Change Request, contains the bandwidth parameter, discussed earlier.
- *BCF:* Bandwidth Change Confirmation, confirms the change request with the bandwidth parameter.
- *BRJ:* Bandwidth Change Reject, rejects the request and provides the reason for the reject.

Location Requests

This procedure is not an actual location request, but a service that the Gatekeeper provides a requester. The service translates an address (say E.104) to transport address (a port or socket).

The location request procedure uses two messages

- *LRQ:* Location Request, contains the endpoint identifier and destination info parameters.
- *LCF:* Location Confirm, contains the call signal address and the ras address.

Disengage Procedures

This procedure is invoked by an endpoint to notify the Gatekeeper that an endpoint is being dropped. If the Gatekeeper invokes the procedure, it forces a call to be dropped. These messages are exchanged for this procedure:

- *DRQ:* Disengage Request, contains the identifiers associated with this endpoint, the ID of the call (endpoint ID, conference ID), and the reason for the disengage.
- *DCF:* Disengage Confirmation.
- *DRJ:* Disengage Reject.

Status Request Procedures

These procedures are used to obtain status information between terminals and Gatekeeper, including information about a call. These messages are exchanged for this procedure:

- *IRQ:* Information Request, contains the call reference value in order to identify the call.
- *IRR:* Information Request Response, contains information about the terminal or Gatekeeper as well as information about the call. The call information provides fields for identifying (a) RTP data, (b) type of call (video, voice), (c) bandwidth usage, etc.

SOME COMMENTS ON H.323 AND H.225.0

You may have noticed that the only RAS/Q.931 information pertaining to bandwidth or QOS is in the bandWidth parameter of the RAS ARQ and ACF messages. This parameter is coded in 100 bit/s increments for a symmetrical two-way call.

The Gatekeeper and the endpoints know about bandwidth, but the endpoints' knowledge of each other's bandwidth requirements is made available by the Gatekeeper with the ACF message.

It would seem reasonable for the bandwidth field in the ACF message in event 2 to be used in the Setup message in event 3 to inform the called party of the bandwidth requirements of the calling party. But, the Setup message has no such field. So, endpoint 2 receives a setup message without any knowledge of the calling party's bandwidth needs. It sends its bandwidth information to the Gatekeeper in event 5 and receives a reply in event 6. I assume the bandwidth field in the ACF message in event 6 is a reflection of the bandwidth field in the ACF message in event 2. However, H.323 does not discuss this situation. Thus, the Gateway acts as the agent between the endpoints, and we can only assume that the bandwidth fields in events 1 and 2 are made available to the messages in events 5 and 6.

T.120

The T.120 specifications define the data (document) conferencing part of a multimedia conference. IMTC,[4] describes T.120 as a protocol that distributes files and graphical information in real-time during a multipoint multimedia meeting. The objective is to assure interoper-

---

[4]International Teleconferencing Consortium, Inc. (IMTC), http://www.imtc.org/main.html

abilty between terminals without either participant assuming prior knowledge of the other system. T.120 permits data sharing among participants in a multimedia teleconference, including white-board image sharing, graphic display information, image exchange, and protocols for audiographic or audiovisual applications.

The T.120 series governs the audiographic portion of the H.320, H.323, and H.324 series and operates either within these or by itself. The T.120 suite consists of a series of recommendations, which are summarized in Table 9–1.

H.245

I made a few comments about H.245 earlier. Its purpose is to specify the syntax of terminal information messages and the procedures to use those messages. It is a "generic" protocol in that it is used by H.222.0, H.223, and H.225.0.

H.245 provides some features that are similar to RTCP, such as the calculation of RTT between two terminals. However, the H Series recommendations provide no guidance on how to (or how not to) interwork H.245 and RTCP. The recommendations contain "informative" appendices describing RTCP but (unfortunately) not in relation to the H Series operations.

I have not shown any H.245 message flows in this chapter (just RAS and Q.931 messages have been shown). Notwithstanding, H.323 describes several scenarios for using the H.245 protocol. If you wish more information on the relationship of H.323 and H.245, I refer you to Section 8 of the H.323 Specification.

H.324

H.324 defines the operations of terminals for low bit-rate multimedia communication using V.34/V.34+ modems operating over the telephone network. H.324 terminals can carry real-time voice, data, and video, or any combination, including video-telephony.

The H.324 suite consists of five recommendations: H.324, H.223, H.245, H.263, and G.723.1. H.261 Video Compression and T.120 operations are also included. Table 9–2 summarizes these Recommendations.

H.324 terminals may be integrated into personal computers or implemented in stand-alone devices such as videotelephones. The ability to

Table 9–1   ITU T.120 Recommendations

Recommendation	Description
T.120	Data protocols for multimedia conferencing: This provides an overview of the T.120 series.
T.121	Generic Application Template: This provides a guide for development of T.120 application protocols.
T.122	Multipoint Communication Service (MCS) Description: This describes the multi-port services available to developers.
T.123	Protocol stacks for audiographic and audiovisual teleconference applications: This specifies transport protocols for a range of networks.
T.124	Generic Conference Control (GCC): This defines the application protocol supporting reservations and basic conference control services for multipoint teleconferences.
T.125	Multipoint Communication Service (MCS) Protocol specification: This specifies the data transmission protocol for multipoint services.
T.126	Multipoint still image and annotation protocol: This defines collaborative data sharing, including " white board" image sharing, graphic display information, and image exchange in a multipoint conference.
T.127	Multipoint Binary File Transfer Protocol: This defines a method for applications to transmit files in a multipoint conference.
T.130	Real time architecture for multimedia conferencing: Provides an overview description of how T.120 data conferencing works in conjunction with H.320 videoconferencing.
T.131	Network-specific mappings: Defines how real time audio and video streams should be transported across different networks (i.e. ISDN, LAN, ATM) when used in conjunction with T.120 data conferencing.
T.132	Real time link management: Defines how real time audio and video streams may be created and routed between various multimedia conferencing endpoints.
T.133	Audiovisual control services: Defines how to control the source and link devices associated with real time information streams.
T.RES	Reservation Services: this is an overview document which specifies how terminals, MCUs, and reservation systems need to interact, and defines the interfaces between each of these elements.

Table 9–2   H.324 and supporting recommendations

Recommendation	Description
H.324	Terminal for low bit rate multimedia communications. It includes T.120 and V.34.
H.263	Speech coding at rates less than 64 kbit/s.
H.223	Multiplexing protocol for two bit rate multimedia terminals.
H.245	Control of data communications between multimedia terminals.
G.723.1	Speech coding for multimedia telecommunications transmitting at 5.3/6.3 kbit/s.

use a specified common mode of operation is required, so that all terminals supporting that media type can interwork.

H.324 uses the logical channel signaling procedures of H.245. Procedures are provided for expression of receiver and transmitter capabilities, so transmissions are limited to what receivers can decode, and so that receivers request a particular desired mode from transmitters. According to the ITU-T, since the procedures of recommendation H.245 are also planned for use by recommendation H.310 for ATM networks, and recommendation H.323 for nonguaranteed bandwidth LANs, interworking with these systems should be straightforward.

SUMMARY OF H.323

H.323 was released in late 1996 and, as we just learned, is organized around four major facilities: (a) terminals, (b) Gateways (which can perform protocol conversions), (c) Gatekeepers (bandwidth managers), and (d) multipoint control units (MCUs), responsible for multicasting. H.323 is a rich and complex specification. As of this writing, user and vendor groups are meeting to define a subset of H.232 to be used in internets and to expand the specifications of the H.323 Gatekeeper and H.323 Gateway to provide detailed information on internetworking with telephony systems—the subject of the next part of this chapter.

MEDIA GATEWAY CONTROL PROTOCOL (MGCP)

The Media Gateway Control Protocol (MGCP) is in the Internet draft stages. The current version (version 0.1) integrates the Simple Gateway Control Protocol (SGMP) and the Internet Protocol Device Control (IPDC) specification. It is quite similar to SGMP, but provides several features beyond that offered by SGMP. For those readers who wish more detail on the specifications, I refer you to [ARAN98], [ARAN98a], and [TAYL98].[5]

MGMP describes an application programming interface (SGCI), and a complementary protocol (MGCP). Its purpose is to control telephony Gateways from external call control elements, known as *Call Agents* or *Media Gateway Controllers* (MGC). The telephony Gateway provides conversion operations between the audio signals used on telephone circuits and data packets used by the Internet or other packet oriented networks.

MGCP is concerned with several types of Gateways, some are shown in Figure 9–8. The trunking Gateway operates between a conventional telephone network and a voice over IP network. The residential Gateway operates between a traditional telephony end user (analog RJ11 interfaces) and the voice over IP network. The ATM Gateway operates the same way as a trunking, except the interface is between an ATM networks and a voice over IP network. The access Gateway provides an analog or digital interface of a PBX into an IP over internet network.

MGCP assumes the bulk of the intelligence for telephony call control operations and resides in an external element, called the Call Agent. This statement does not mean that the Gateways are completely unintelligent. Rather, it means that most of the control operations are performed by the Call Agent. In essence, signaling is the responsibility of a Call Agent. The Call Agents act as masters to the slave Gateways, and the Gateways receive commands that define their operations from the Call Agents. In Figure 9–9, one Call Agent is in control of three Gateways, but the actual configurations depend upon specific installations. The figure also shows that two Call Agents are communicating with each other. MGCP defines the operations between the Call Agents and the Gateways, but does not define the operations between the Call Agents.

As the reader might expect, MGCP is based on a connection model, since telephony operations are basically connection oriented. Connec-

[5][ARAN98] Arango, Mauricio, Huitema, Christian. Simple Gateway Control Protocol (SGCP), Internet Engineering Task Force draft-huitema-sgcp-va-o2.txt.

[ARAN98a] Arango, Mauricio, Dugan, Andrew, Elliott, Isacc, Huitema, Christian, Pickett, Scott. Media Gateway Control Protocol (MGCP). Internet Engineering Task Force draft-huitema-MGCP-v0r1–01.txt

[TAYL98] Taylor, P. Tom, Calhoun, Pat R., Rubens, Allan C. IPDC Base Protocol. Internet Engineering Task Force. Draft-taylor-Ipdc-99.txt.

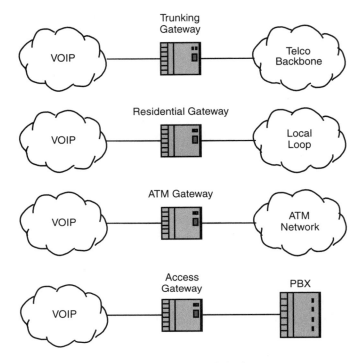

Figure 9–8   Types of MGCP gateways

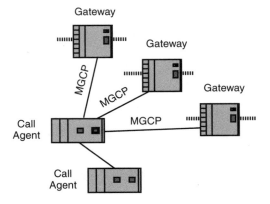

Figure 9–9   The call agents and the gateways

tions are affected between endpoints. These endpoints represent the sources and sinks of data. Endpoints may be physical or virtual. An example of a physical endpoint is a link or trunk connection to a physical node through a line card. An example of a virtual endpoint is a software module operating on the physical endpoint.

Endpoints have two aspects: They represent operations and identifiers. A Gateway is identified by a domain name as well as a local name within that Gateway. In a trucking Gateway, the endpoints identify trucking circuits that connect the Gateway to the telephone switch, such as a T1, ISDN, E1 line. However, these trunks use different identifiers on the telephone side. For example, SS7 uses point codes to identify the same circuits.

MGCP also supports point-to-point or multipoint operations. We will have more to say about multipoint systems later.

OTHER PROTOCOLS

Things can become quite confusing when examining MGCP and other Internet-based VoIP protocols, described in more detail in Chapter 10. Therefore, before we move to a detailed analysis of SGCP, let's pause for a moment to comment on several other multimedia protocols. They are: (a) The Session Description Protocol (SDP), (b) The Session Announcement Protocol (SAP), (c) The Session Initiation Protocol (SIP), and (d) The Real-Time Streaming Protocol (RTSP).

The *Session Announcement Protocol* supports the distribution of multicast session parameters to a group of recipients. The *Session Initiation Protocol* is used to invite a user to take part in a session. The *Real-Time Streaming Protocol* supports the exchange of real-time information between the server and a user. These three protocols are actually signaling protocols. They rely on the Session Description Protocol to describe the actual session.

The Call Agent uses the MGCP and the *Session Description Protocol* to provision and set up the Gateways. The SDP supports and conveys information on: (a) the session name and purpose, (b) time or times the session is active, (c) the media that comprises the session, (d) destination information (addresses, ports), (e) bandwidth requirements, and (f) contact information about the session.

The *Session Initiation Protocol (SIP)* is a major support tool for MGCP (and other signaling systems). It operates with user agents and user agent servers. The main job of the server is to provide for name-to-address resolution and user location. For example, when a user makes a call, the user agent sends an SIP message to a server. The user is unaware of this support operation, but will have given its agent an identifier, such as a phone number. The message is sent to a server by the agent, and at this server, the name may be resolved to an IP address, or the server may redirect (proxy) the message to another server.

SIP allows more than one server to contact the user, and these forked messages are sent to multiple servers. The responses are returned to the agent in such a manner that the agent can make decisions about the best path for the call.

SIP is a very attractive support tool for IP telephony because:

- It can operate as stateless, or stateful. Thus, a stateless implementation provides good scaleability, since the servers do not have to maintain information on the call state once the transaction has been processed. Moreover, the stateless approach is very robust, since the server need not remember anything about a call.
- It uses much of the formats and syntax of HTTP (Hypertext Transfer Protocol), thus providing a convenient way of operating with ongoing browsers.
- The SIP message (the message body) is opaque; it can be of any syntax. Therefore, it can be described in more than one way. As examples, it may be described with the Multipurpose Internet Mail Extension (MIME), or the Extensible Markup Language (XML).
- It identifies a user with a URI (Uniform Resource Identifier), thus providing the user the ability to initiate a call by clicking on a web link.

The Real-Time Streaming Protocol (RTSP) gives the user the ability to control a media server. Perhaps the best way to view RTSP is that it provides the user VCR-type controls, such as fast forward, stop, rewind, record, etc. In addition, a user can direct a media server as to the type of audio (or video) format the media is to use.

RTSP is an excellent tool for controlling the playback rate from a voice-mail server, and it can be used to control the content of a recording.

MGCP incorporates all these protocols and allows a diverse community of users to gain access to MGCP based networks using SDP, SAP, SIP, or RTSP.

These protocols are quite important, but we must leave further discussions of them to another book. Let's redirect our attention back to the main features of MGCP.

CALL AGENTS AND CALLS

Call Agents use configuration databases to keep track of trunk groups and circuits within the trunk. We just learned that the Gateway is identified by a domain name. In addition, each physical interface is also identified by a name. The physical circuit is further identified by a circuit member, which is concatenated to the name to identify unambiguously a specific circuit.

Each call that is managed by the Call Agent must be identified with a name, which is created by the Call Agent. Call identifiers are important not just for the call, but for accounting purposes as well. The use of a domain name is quite important to this architecture. By the use of this name, instead of the address, components can be easily moved across platforms and maintain a unique identity through the domain name. It is then the job of the Domain Name System (DNS) administrator to correlate the names to the proper addresses.

RELATIONSHIP TO H.323

The relationship of MGCP to H.323 is shown in Figure 9–10. Be aware that MGCP does not have to be a part of H.323, but if it is, the MGCP Call Agent acts as an H.323 Gatekeeper. This approach is in keeping with the functions of the H.323 Gatekeeper, who provides address translation and call control services to H.323 endpoints.

The MGCP Call Agent/H.323 Gateway in this example has signaling operations with four networks. These four networks show logical placements of the GMCP, and some of these placements will depend on many factors, such as marketplace acceptance (especially from the LECs) of IP-based protocols in the local loop.

To help you study this figure, the solid lines indicate signaling links and the dashed lines indicate links for user traffic. In some of the network interfaces, the signaling traffic and user traffic can be transmitted on the same physical link. I separate them in this figure for purposes of discussion.

We examine the signaling interfaces first (the solid lines in the figure). For a digital local loop to a remote digital terminal (RDT) into a neighborhood, the MGCP Gatekeeper/H.323 Gatekeeper uses ISDN D channels (and Q.931 operating inside the D channel) for digital local links. If the loop is configured with Belcore's GR-303 (a very common interface in North America), IDLC messages (Integrated Digital Loop Carrier System) are exchanged, or (not shown here) conventional ABCD sig-

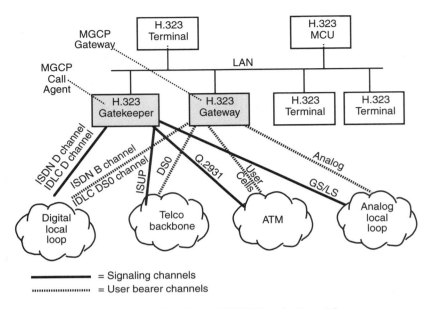

Figure 9–10   H.323 and MGCP relationships

nals in accordance with GR-303. The MGCP Gateway/H.323 Gateway exchanges SS7 ISUP messages with the telco network, Q.2931 messages with the ATM network, and a variety of ground start/loop start (GS/LS) signals on analog local links.

Next, let's consider user traffic (the dashed lines in the figure). The MGCP Gateway/H.323 Gateway handles the user traffic, and provides signal translations as necessary: DS0 signals with the telco network, ATM user cells with the ATM network, and either conventional analog signals on analog local links, or B channels on digital local links.

These four interfaces are not exhaustive. I have not included mobile wireless, fixed wireless, or coaxial systems. I trust this explanation gives you a view of the general relationships of GMCP and H.323. But one other point should be noted before we move on.

The intent of MGCP is for it to act as an internal protocol in a distributed system that to the outside of this system, appears as a single VoIP Gateway. The system contains Call Agents and Gateways. The system interfaces on one side with a telephony system and on the other with an H.323 conformant system. Therefore, the Call Agent must be "conversant" in ISUP and other telephony protocols on one side and H.323 proto-

Figure 9–11   A single view of the MGCP gateway

cols (H.225/RAS and H.225/Q.931) on the other side. This idea is shown in Figure 9–11.

ENDPOINTS, CONNECTIONS, CALLS, EVENTS, PACKAGES, AND NAMES

MGCP supports the conventional telephony operations, such as dial tone, offhook, etc. It also supports telephony-based links, such as DS1. All these components are identified with names. We describe them here, but will not go into the rules for the syntax of each name, which are quite detailed and beyond the general explanation.

Figure 9–12 shows the concepts of endpoints, connections, and calls. Endpoints in MGCP are sources and sinks of data. Endpoints can be physical links, like a T1 trunk. They may be virtual links that operate over the physical links.

Endpoints are identified by names. The name is in two parts. The first part is the domain name of the Gateway that is at the endpoint, and the second part is a local name in the Gateway. The syntax of the local name depends upon the type of endpoint, but a hierarchical name is required, forming a naming path from the Gateway name to the individual endpoint.

Endpoints in MGCP must correlate with comparable entities in SS7. In an SS7 network, endpoints are trunks connecting switches, or a switch to a MGCP Gateway. In ISUP, trunks are grouped into trunk groups and are identified by an SS7 point code. Circuits within a trunk group are identified by a circuit identification code (CIC). It is the job of MGCP to map SS7 identifiers to MGCP names.

Connections are managed at the endpoints (that is, on the trunk). Connections can be grouped into calls. Connections are created by the Gateway, and each connection has a unique connection identifier associ-

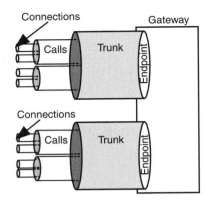

Figure 9–12   MGCP gateway components

ated with it. The connection identifier is within the context of its end-point. MGCP uses an unstructured octet string for the identifier.

Calls also have identifiers, and are created by the Call Agent. They are also unstructured octet strings. Call identifiers must be unique within the system. A Call Agent may build several connections pertaining to the same call, and the connections must be associated with the same call.

In order to manage connections, other identifiers and their associated entities are needed, specifically *events* and *packages*. Figure 9–13 depicts the concepts of events and packages. An event is an occurrence in an endpoint. Examples of events are an off-hook event, and a dial-tone event. Events correspond to associated signals, which are grouped into packages, such as dual tone multiple frequency (with a name of "D"), off hook (with a name of "hu"). A package is the grouping of events and sig-

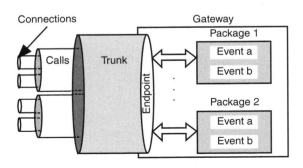

Figure 9–13   Events and packages

nals that are supported by a specific type of endpoint. Event names and package names are used to identify each event and package. Both names are strings of letters.

How These Names Are Applied

A Call Agent uses these names to inform the Gateway what the Gateway is to do. For example, the Call Agent may request Gateway to detect a group of events. It uses MGCP messages containing the event names to so-direct the Gateway.

Wildcarding is supported in MGCP. A wildcard name is used for a number of purposes. In this example, a wildcard name can inform the Gateway to detect *any* event belonging to a package. The wildcard conventions permit names to include "all values of this term," or "any one value of this term" known to the Gateway.

THE CONNECTION MODES

Before we examine the messages that are exchanged between the Call Agent and the Gateway, we need one more piece of information. Each connection is defined by the following modes: (a) send only, (b) receive only, (c) send/receive, (d) conference, (e) data, (f) inactive, (g) loopback, (h) continuity test, (i) network loop test, or (j) network continuity test. The mode of the connection determines how voice signals are handled. The MGCP sets forth the following rules for these modes, and I use [ARAN98a], with amplifying comments:

Voice signals received in data packets through connections in receive, conference, or send/receive mode are mixed and sent to the endpoint. Voice signals originating from the endpoint are transmitted over all the connections whose mode is send, conference or send/receive. In addition to being sent to the endpoint, voice signals received in data packets through connections in conference mode are replicated to all the other connections whose mode is conference.

The loopback and continuity test modes are used during ISUP maintenance and continuity test operations on telephony circuits. They are invoked during a call set up to ensure that the source and sink endpoints are fully connected and exchanging signals correctly. The rules for these tests vary between the SS7 ISUP specifications published by the standards groups.

There are two implementations of the continuity test (COT), one as specified by ITU-T, and one (used in the U.S.), as specified by Bellcore and ANSI. In the ITU-T case, the test is a loopback test. The source switch sends a tone (the go tone) on the bearer circuit and expects the sink switch to loopback the circuit. If the source switch sees the same tone returned (the return tone), the COT has passed. If not, the COT has failed.

In the Bellcore/ANSI case, the go and return tones are different. The source switch sends a certain go tone. The sink switch detects the go tone, it then asserts a different return tone to the source. When the source switch detects the return tone, the COT is passed. If the source switch never detects the return tone, the COT has failed.

In either the ITU-T or Bellcore/ANSI cases, the COT must be performed correctly, or the call set up operations are suspended.

If the mode is set to loopback, the Gateway is expected to return the incoming signal from the endpoint back into that same endpoint. This procedure will be used, typically, for testing the continuity of trunk circuits according to the ITU specifications.

If the mode is set to continuity test, the Gateway is informed that the other end of the circuit has initiated a continuity test procedure according to the Bellcore specification. The Gateway will place the circuit in the transponder mode required for dual-tone continuity tests.

If the mode is set to network loopback, the voice signals received from the connection will be echoed back on the same connection.

If the mode is set to network continuity test, the Gateway will process the packets received from the connection according to the transponder mode required for dual-tone continuity test, and send the processed signal back on the connection.

MGCP COMMANDS: FOR THE API AND THE MESSAGES

The gist of MGCP is the issuance of commands to the Gateway and the Gateway acting on these commands and sending back responses. The purpose of the commands is to control the operations of the Gateway in regard to the creation and termination of connections, and to keep the Call Agent informed of events occurring at the Gateway's endpoints.

Eight commands are defined in the MGCP. These commands are described in two ways: (a) as an application programming interface (API) between a user application and the MGCP software in the Call Agent and Gateway, (b) as messages exchanged between the Call Agent and the

Gateway. This concept is in keeping with layered protocol concepts (see Figure 9–14) where the user application at the sending node invokes a command at the API to the MGCP, which uses the command to construct a message and send to the receiving node. At this node, the message is parsed and the information is passed to the receiving applications by MGCP via the API. The commands are as follows:

- The Call Agent issues a *NotificationRequest* command to instruct the Gateway to watch for specific events such as a specified endpoint.
- The Gateway responds with the *Notify* command to inform the Call Agent when the specific events occur.
- The Call Agent issues the *CreateConnection* command to create a connection that terminates on a specified endpoint in the Gateway.
- The Call Agent issues the *ModifyConnection* command to change the parameters associated with a previously established connection.
- The Call Agent issues the *DeleteConnection* command to delete an existing connection. This command is also used by a Gateway to inform the Call Agent that a connection can no longer be sustained.
- The Call Agent issues the *AuditEndpoint* and *AuditConnection* commands to check on the status of an endpoint and any associated connections and calls.

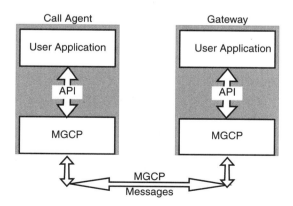

Figure 9–14   The Applications Programming Interface (API) and the MGCP

- The Gateway issues the *RestartInProgress* command to notify the Call Agent that the Gateway (or a group of endpoints) is being taken out of service or is being placed back in service.

Absence of Bootstrapping/Configuration Operations

Notice that the MGCP does not define any messages for the Call Agent and the Gateway to set up a relationship with each other, such as the exchange of authentication and configuration parameters. Prior to the invocation of the MGCP, another protocol is responsible for executing these operations. It is called the IP Device Control (IPDC) Protocol. IPDC is explained in Chapter 10.

Similarities and Differences between the API and Message Information

The parameters passed at the API are similar to the parameters carried in the messages between the Call Agent and the Gateway. However, they are not the same. For example, the API NotificationRequest defines eight parameters for this call, but only one of them is required to be carried in the message to the other node. To explain the API and message set coherently, and to show their relationships, my approach in the next section is to:

- Describe each parameter that is carried in the API call and the message set
- Show each API command and associated parameters
- Show each message and associated parameters

THE MGCP PARAMETERS

These parameters are present in the API and/or an MGCP message. Perhaps the best approach to the analysis is for you to review this section and refer back to it in the next two sections. I think you will recognize many of these parameters as a result of our previous analysis of MGCP. They are sorted in alphabetical order.

- *CallID:* A globally unique parameter that identifies the call to which the connection belongs.

- *ConnectionID:* Value returned by the Gateway during a connection creation. It uniquely identifies the connection within the endpoint.
- *ConnectionIdentifiers:* A list of ConnectionIdentifiers that exist for an endpoint
- *Connection-parameters:* A general term to describe a list of parameters about a connection.
- *DetectEvents:* During the quarantine period, a list of events that are currently detected. The quarantine period is discussed later.
- *DigitMap:* A method to collect digits according to a dial plan.
- *EndPointId:* The name of the endpoint in a Gateway.
- *EndPointIdList*: A list of endpointids, that may be present in an auditing operation to direct the Gateway to report on more than one endpoint.
- *LocalConnectionDescriptor:* A descriptor of the connection assigned by the Gateway, and returned to the Call Agent during the connection creation. It contains addresses and RTP ports, as defined in SDP.
- *LocalConnectionOptions:* Used by the Call Agent to direct the Gateway as to how the connection is to be handled. A wide variety of fields can be contained in this parameter. Some of them are defined in the SDP standard. The fields are discussed along with the CreateConnection command.
- *Mode:* Defines the mode of operation for this side of the connection, as explained earlier.
- *NotifiedEntity:* Specifies where Notify or DeleteConnection commands are to be sent; defaults to the originator of the CreateConnection command.
- *ObservedEvents:* A list of events that the Gateway has detected.
- *QuarantineHandling:* In notification messages, Gateways can receive a list of events that they should watch for and monitor. The Call Agent uses this operation to keep track of the calls, and the state of the endpoint. The events are examined as they occur, and the controlled Gateway accumulates information about the event, and at some point may send a notification to the Call Agent.
- *ReasonCode:* The value indicates the reason for the disconnection.
- *RemoteConnectionDescriptor:* A descriptor of the connection assigned to the Gateway.
- *RequestedEvents:* List of events that the Gateway is requested to direct and report to the Call Agent. Detailed rules stipulate how

the events are handled in the Gateway and how/when/if they are reported to the Call Agent. Examples of parameters here are: (a) accumulate dialed digits according to the Digit Map, (b) ignore the event, (c) notify Call Agent immediately of the event (of delay notification), (d) keep signal active, and so on.

- *RequestedInfo*: Information that is requested with a ConnectionID within an endpoint. This field can contain: CallId, NotifiedEntity, LocalConnectionOptions, Mode, RemoteConnectionDescriptor, LocalConnectionDescriptor, and ConnectionParameters.
- *RequestIdentifier:* A unique value to identify a request.
- *RestartDelay:* The number of seconds before a restart operation is attempted. The number is randomly generated to reduce chances of multiple machines restarting at same time.
- *RestartMethod:* Coded as graceful, forced, or restart.
- *SignalRequests:* Set of signals that the Gateway must apply to the endpoint, such as ringing, off hook, continuity tones, etc.
- *SupportedModes:* List of modes supported.

API COMMANDS AND ASSOCIATED PARAMETERS

This section lists the API commands and their associated parameters. I also add some comments pertinent to these commands and parameters. The explanations are organized as follows: (a) Command and associated parameters and (b) comments.

NotificationRequest

Command and Associated Parameters. The structure for the NotificationRequest command is as follows:

```
NotificationRequest ( Endpointid,
                      NotifiedEntity
                      RequestedEvents
                      RequestIdentifier
                      DigitMap
                      SignalRequests
                      QuarantineHandling
                      DetectEvents )
```

Comments. The Gateway must send a message to the Call Agent upon an occurrence of the event(s) specified in this command. Many events may be identified. As examples, off hook, the type of ITU-T V Series modem signals, line seizure, etc. may be identified as events the Call Agent wishes to know about.

Notify

Command and Associated Parameters. The structure for the Notify command is as follows:

```
Notify ( EndPointId,
         NotifiedEntity
         RequestIdentifier
         ObservedEvents )
```

Comments. The ObservedEvents is a list of events that the Gateway has observed. It may contain only the events that were in the RequestedEvents parameter of the NotificationRequest. It can also contain events that have been accumulated, and events that met a final match in a digit map.

CreateConnection

Command and Associated Parameters. The structure for the CreateConnection command sent by the Call Agent is as follows:

```
CreateConnection ( CallId,
                   EndPointId,
                   [NotifiedEntity]
                   LocalConnectionOptions,
                   Mode,
                   RemoteConnectionDescriptor,
                   RequestedEvents,
                   RequestIdentifier,
                   DigitMap
                   SignalRequests
                   QuarantineHandling,
                   DetectEvents )
```

Comments. The LocalConnectionOptions describes the Gateway's point of view pertaining to the following (a) method of encoding the traffic, (b) packetization period (duration of packet), (c) bandwidth for connection (in kbit/s), (d) type of service (TOS field of the IPv4 datagram header), (e) use of echo cancellation.

The Gateway responds to the CreateConnection command by returning a ConnectionID that identifies the connection within the endpoint. It also returns a LocalConnectionDescriptor.

ModifyConnection

Command and Associated Parameters. The structure for the Modify-Connection command sent by the Call Agent is as follows:

```
ModifyConnection ( CallId,
                   EndPointId,
                   ConnectionId,
                   NotifiedEntity,
                   LocalConnectionOptions,
                   Mode,
                   RemoteConnectionDescriptor,
                   RequestedEvents,
                   RequestIdentifier,
                   DigitMap
                   SignalRequests,
                   QuarantineHandling,
                   DetectEvents )
```

Comments. This command can be used to provide information about the other end of the connection, through the RemoteConnectDescriptor. It can also be used to activate or deactivate a connection. This operation occurs by changing the mode parameter value. Other operations can be modified; for example, echo cancellation, packetization period, etc. can be changed.

DeleteConnection by the Call Agent

A connection can be deleted by the Call Agent or the Gateway. This discussion is on the connection deletion operation emanating from the Call Agent.

Command and Associated Parameters. The structure for the Delete-Connection command sent by the Call Agent is as follows:

```
DeleteConnection ( CallId,
                   EndPointId,
                   ConnectionId,
                   NotifiedEntity,
                   RequestedEvents,
                   RequestIdentifier,
                   DigitMap
                   SignalRequests,
                   QuarantineHandling,
                   DetectEvents )
```

Comments. If two Gateways are involved in the connection, this command is sent to both Gateways. Upon receiving this command, the Gateway responds with a list of parameters (statistics) that describe what happened on the connection. The following information is sent to the Call Agent by the Gateway; I refer you to [ARAN98a] for the rules on how the statistics are tabulated, In addition, RFC 1889 provides information on this topic, and [ARAN98a] also provides additional guidance on how to use these statistics if the connection is through an ATM network:

- Number of packets sent: The total number of RTP packets sent by the Gateway since starting this connection.
- Number of octets sent: The total number of RTP octets (user traffic, headers not included) sent by the Gateway since starting this connection.
- Number of packets received: The total number of RTP packets received by the Gateway since starting this connection.
- Number of octets received: The total number of RTP octets received by the Gateway since starting this connection.
- Number of packets lost: The total number of RTP packets lost by the Gateway since starting this connection.
- Interarrival jitter: An estimate on the variance of the RTP packet interarrival time, expressed in milliseconds.
- Average transmission delay: An estimate of the average network delay, expressed in milliseconds.

DeleteConnection by the Gateway

A connection can be deleted by the Gateway, but only if a problem occurs, such as the loss of a trunk interface, etc. Normal connection deletions are handled by the Call Agent.

Command and Associated Parameters. The structure for the Delete-Connection command sent by the Call Agent is as follows:

```
DeleteConnection ( CallId,
                   EndPointId,
                   ConnectionId,
                   Reason-code,
                   Connection-parameters)
```

AuditEndpoint

Command and Associated Parameters. The structure for the Audit-Endpoint command sent by the Call Agent is as follows:

```
AuditEndpoint ( EndPointIdList,
                NotifiedEntity,
                Requested\Events,
                DigitMap,
                SignalRequests,
                RequestIdentifier,
                NotifiedEntity,
                ConnectionIdentifiers,
                DetectEvents,
                LocalConnectionOptions,
                SupportedModes )
```

Comments. This command allows the Call Agent to audit one or more endpoints. The Gateway is responsible to return to the Call Agent information on the events requested, the current digit map being used, any signals that are being applied to the endpoint, and so on.

AuditConnection

Command and Associated Parameters. The structure for the Audit-Connection command sent by the Call Agent is as follows:

AuditConnection (CallId,
 NotifiedEntity,
 LocalConnectionOptions,
 Mode,
 RemoteConnectionDescriptor,
 LocalConnectionDescriptor,
 ConnectionParameters)

Comments. This command is similar to the AuditEndPoint, except it is used to audit a specific connection.

RestartInProgress

Command and Associated Parameters. The structure for the Restart-InProgress command sent by the Call Agent is as follows:

RestartInProgress (EndPointId,
 RestartMethod,
 RestartDelay)

Comments. The EndPointId identifies one or more endpoints that are being taken out of service. The RestartMethod may be graceful where no ongoing connections are disrupted, or it may be forced, due to problems, in which case the connections are lost.

MGCP MESSAGES AND ASSOCIATED PARAMETERS

We learned earlier that the Call Agent and the Gateway exchange eight types of MGCP messages, and we discussed them in a general way. The messages are called commands when sent to the Gateway, and responses when sent from the Gateway.

Figure 9–15 shows the format for the MGCP message. The messages are coded as lines of text consisting of a command header, followed by a session description. The command header is composed of a command line and a set of parameter lines. Text lines are separated by line feed character. The items in the message are simply strings of ASCII printable characters, separated by an ASCII space (0×20) or tabulation characters (0×09).

The command line contains four fields: (a) the identifier of the message (called a verb), (b) a transaction number, (c) the endpoint towards which the command is requested, and (d) the protocol version number.

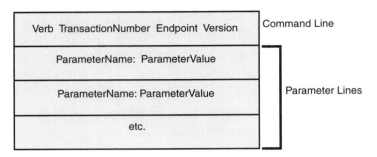

Figure 9–15   Structure for MGCP messages (commands)

The parameter lines are made up of a parameter name, a colon, a space, and the parameter value. Several parameter names have a reserved code (ASCII character) reserved for them. For example, the code "N" is reserved for the NotifiedEntity, and it means the parameter value is coded according to RFC 821. As another example, the code "D" is used for a digit map and is coded in accordance with the digit map rules cited earlier.

The IETF drafts that were referenced earlier have many examples of how to code the GMCP commands, and the many rules for them are beyond this text. However, let's look at one message to get a feel for the simplicity of the message structure:

```
Line 1        RQNT 4561 endpoint-44@tgw-21.infoinst.com MGCP 0.1
Line 2        N: abc@cal.infoinst.com:5777
Line 3        X: 45848484
Line 4        R: hd
```

Line 1 is the command line. RQNT is the verb for a NotificationRequest command; the transaction number is 4561; the directed endpoint is endpoint-44@tgw-21.infoinst.com; and the MGCP version is 0.1.

Line 2 is the NotifiedEntity of : abc@cal.infoinst.com:5777. Line 3 is a hexadecimal string for the RequestIdentifier. Line 4 is code for an event name, and the "hd" code is for offhook transition.

This command is sent by the Call Agent to the Gateway to direct the Gateway to monitor for an offhook transition on endpoint-44 at the trunking Gateway with a domain name suffix of cal.infoinst. The 5777 is the port number.

Table 9–3   The MGCP verbs

Verb	Code
CreateConnection	CRCX
ModifyConnection	MDCX
DeleteConnection	DLCX
NotificationRequest	RQNT
Notify	NTFY
AuditEndpoint	AUEP
AuditConnection	AUCX
RestartInProgress	RSIP

MESSAGES AND MESSAGE PARAMETERS

Each message verb is coded a four character ASCII field, as shown in Table 9–3.

The command and response messages contain the parameters explained earlier. The command messages and parameters are shown in Table 9–4, and the response messages and parameters are shown in Table 9–5. The notations in the tables have these meanings: M = mandatory; O = optional; F = forbidden.

EXAMPLES OF MGCP OPERATIONS

Figure 9–16 presents an example of MGCP in action. I have used SGCP [ARAN98] for this example. Additional examples are provided in [HUIT98a].[6] Figure 9–16 is divided into two parts. The first part in Figure 9–16(a) shows events 1–24; the second part in Figure 9–16(b) shows events 25–37. Two Gateways are involved, a residential Gateway and a trunking Gateway. In addition, the common database is shown, as well as an accounting Gateway. Here is a description of each event:

- *Event 1:* The NotificationRequest command must be sent to the residential Gateway before the Gateway can handle a connection.

---

[6][HUIT98a] Huitema, Christina , Andreasen, Flemming, Arango, Mauricio, "Media Gateway Control Protocol (MGCP) Call Flows." Draft-huitema-mgcp-flows-00.txt, November 11, 1998.l.

Table 9–4   Commands and parameters

Parameter Name	1	2	3	4	5	6	7	8
CallId	M	M	O	F	F	F	F	F
ConnectionId	F	M	O	F	F	F	M	F
RequestIdentifier	O	O	O	M	M	F	F	F
LocalConnectionOptions	O	O	F	F	F	F	F	F
ConnectionMode	M	M	F	F	F	F	F	F
RequestedEvents	O	O	O	O	F	F	F	F
SignalRequests	O	O	O	O	F	F	F	F
NotifiedEntity	O	O	O	O	O	F	F	F
ReasonCode	F	F	O	F	F	F	F	F
ObservedEvents	F	F	F	F	M	F	F	F
DigitMap	O	O	O	O	F	F	F	F
ConnectionParameters	F	F	O	F	F	F	F	F
SpecificEndPointId	F	F	F	F	F	F	F	F
RequestedInfo	F	F	F	F	F	M	M	F
QuarantineHandling	O	O	O	O	O	F	F	F
DetectEvents	O	O	O	O	O	F	F	F
RestartMethod	F	F	F	F	F	F	F	M
RestartDelay	F	F	F	F	F	F	F	O
RemoteConnection Descriptor	O	O	F	F	F	F	F	F

Where:
1 CreateConnection
2 ModifyConnection
3 DeleteConnection
4 NotificationRequest
5 Notify
6 AuditEndpoint
7 AuditConnection
8 RestartInProgress

Be aware that this command is not a crafting (configuration) command. The Call Agents and Gateways must be preconfigured. Let us assume that this command is directing the Gateway to monitor for an offhook condition on a specific endpoint connection.

- *Event 2:* The Gateway acknowledges the command. It uses the same transaction number that was in the command in event 1.
- *Event 3:* Thereafter, the Gateway monitors for this transition, and eventually the user goes offhook to make a call.

Table 9–5   Responses and parameters

Parameter Name	1	2	3	4	5	6	7	8
CallId	F	F	F	F	F	F	O	F
ConnectionId	O	F	F	F	F	F	O	F
RequestIdentifier	F	F	F	F	F	O	F	F
LocalConnectionOptions	F	F	F	F	F	O	O	F
ConnectionMode	F	F	F	F	F	F	O	F
RequestedEvents	F	F	F	F	F	O	F	F
SignalRequests	F	F	F	F	F	O	F	F
NotifiedEntity	F	F	F	F	F	F	F	F
ReasonCode	F	F	F	F	F	F	F	O
ObservedEvents	F	F	F	F	F	O	F	F
DigitMap	F	F	F	F	F	O	F	F
ConnectionParameters	F	F	O	F	F	F	O	F
SpecificEndPointId	O	F	F	F	F	F	F	F
RequestedInfo	F	F	F	F	F	O	F	F
QuarantineHandling	F	F	F	F	F	O	F	F
DetectEvents	F	F	F	F	F	O	F	F
RestartMethod	F	F	F	F	F	F	F	F
RestartDelay	F	F	F	F	F	F	F	F
LocalConnection Descriptor	M	O	F	F	F	F	O	F
RemoteConnection Descriptor	F	F	F	F	F	F	O	F

Where:
1   CreateConnection
2   ModifyConnection
3   DeleteConnection
4   NotificationRequest
5   Notify
6   AuditEndpoint
7   AuditConnection
8   RestartInProgress

- *Event 4:* The Gateway sends a NotificationRequest to the Call Agent, with the message coded to show the offhook event for the monitored endpoint.
- *Event 5:* The Call Agent must acknowledge the Gateway's transmission.

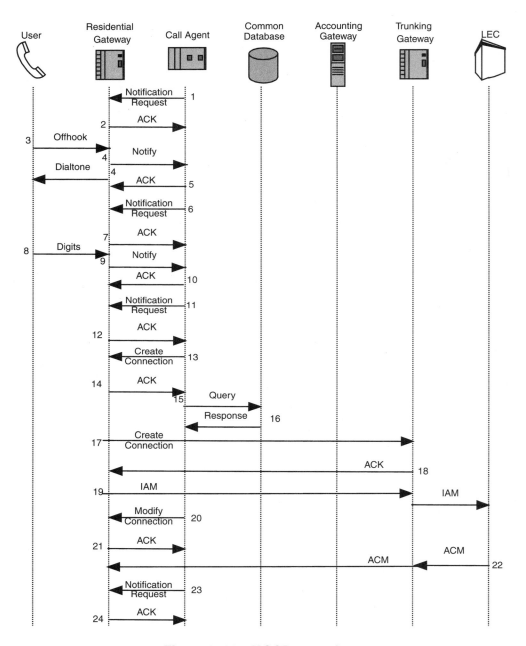

Figure 9–16   MGCP operations

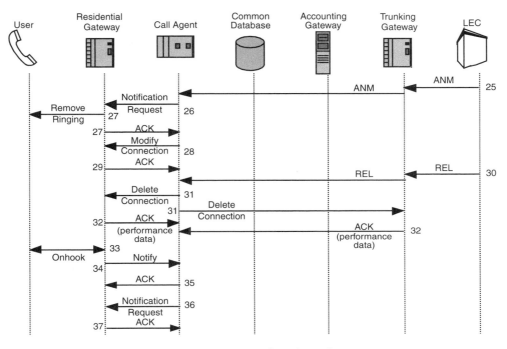

Figure 9–16 *Continued*

- *Event 6:* The Call Agent's decisions on what to tell the Gateway next will depend on the type of line being monitored. Assuming it is a conventional dialup (nondirect) line, it sends a NotificationRequest command directing the Gateway to play a dialtone, and to collect digits.
- *Event 7:* The Gateway responds with an ACK, and gives dialtone to the user. The exact sequence of these two events vary, depending on the specific implementation.
- *Event 8:* Based on the digit map sent to it in event 7, the Gateway accumulates digits.
- *Event 9:* And based on this digit map, the Gateway notifies the Call Agent with a message containing an ObservedEvent parameter. This parameter contains the collected digits.
- *Event 10:* The Call Agent ACKs the message.
- *Event 11:* Next, the Call Agent sends a NotificationRequest command to direct the Gateway to stop collecting digits, and to monitor for an onhook transition.

- *Event 12:* The Gateway ACKs the command.

- *Event 13:* The CreateConnection command is sent by the Call Agent to seize the incoming circuit. This message contains the CallId, LocalConnectionOptions, and the ConnectionMode parameters. Recall that the LocalConnectionOptions are: (a) packetization period in milliseconds, (b) compression algorithm (G.711, G.729, etc.), (c) bandwidth for the connection, and (d) user of nonuse of echo cancellation. The ConnectionMode is set to receive only.

- *Event 14:* The Gateway ACKs the command. In this message the new connection (ConnectionId) is identified, as is the session description (an SDP announcement) that is used to receive the audio traffic. This description may contain the IP address at which the Gateway is ready to receive the audio data, the protocol used to transport the packets (RTP), the RTP port (3456), the audio profile (AVP, in accordance with RFC 1890). The AVP defines the payload type, such as G.711. This message can also be used to inform the Call Agent that the Gateway is ready to use other audio profiles. For example, G.726 for 32 kbit/s ADPCM may also be stipulated.

- *Event 15:* The Call Agent now must determine where to route the call and to which egress Gateway the connection should be established. It sends a query to the common database to obtain this information.

- *Event 16:* The needed information is returned to the Call Agent.

- *Event 17:* The Call Agent has sufficient information to send a CreateConnection command to the egress Gateway, in this example, a trunking Gateway. The parameters in this message mirror the parameters exchanged in events 13 and 14 between the residential Gateway and the Call Agent, and the session description in this message is the same as the description given to the Call Agent by the residential Gateway. There are two differences: (a) the EndPointId identifies the endpoint at the outgoing at the trunking Gateway, and (b) the mode parameter is set to send/receive. The CallId is the same in this message since the two endpoint connections belong to the same call.

- *Event 18:* The trunking Gateway responds with an ACK. In this message is this Gateway's session description such as its IP address, its port, and its RTP profile.

- *Event 19:* Based on the information obtained in event 18, the Call Agent now builds an SS7 ISUP Initial Address Message (IAM) and sends it to the trunking Gateway. This Gateway relays this message to a designated local exchange carrier (LEC). It is the job of the Call Agent to correlate the MGCP endpoints to the SS7's CIC. Some of the information gathered in events 1–18 are used to help build the IAM. For example, calling and called party numbers, echo cancellation, international call, ISUP used end-to-end, and other fields are placed in this message.

- *Event 20:* The information obtained in event 18 is used to create the ModifyConnection command that is sent to the residential Gateway. The parameters in this command reflect the parameters in the ACK in event 18.

- *Event 21:* The Gateway ACKs the command.

- *Event 22:* The LEC returns an SS7 ISUP Address Complete Message (ACM) to the Call Agent. This message contains fields (backward call indicators) to aid the Call Agent in directing the residential Gateway, as explained in the next event.

- *Event 23:* The receipt of the ACM at the Call Agent precipitates the sending of a NotificationRequest command to the residential Gateway. This message directs the Gateway to place ringing tones on the line.

- *Event 24:* The Gateway ACKs the commands and places ringing tones on the line to the user telephone.

- *Event 25:* When the called party answers the call at the remote end, the offhook condition will result in an ISUP answer message (ANM) being returned to the Call Agent.

- *Event 26:* The Call Agent sends a NotificationRequest command to the residential Gateway to instruct it to remove the ring tone from the line.

- *Event 27:* The Gateway removes the ring tone and ACKs the command.

- *Event 28:* To this point, the connection at the local end has been in a receive only mode. To change connection to full duplex mode, the Call Agent sends a ModifyConnection command to the Gateway.

- *Event 29:* The Gateway responds, and sends back an ACK. The connection is now established.

- *Event 30:* In this example, the called party hangs up, and the offhook condition precipitates the ISUP Release message (REL) which is conveyed to the Call Agent.

- *Event 31:* The Call Agent sends a DeleteConnection command to both Gateways. Each message contains the respective EndPointId, and ConnectionID at each Gateway as well as the global CallId.

- *Event 32:* The Gateways respond with the performance data fields in the response.
- *Event 33:* The local line is placed in an onhook state by the local party hanging up.
- *Event 34:* The onhook event is relayed to the Call Agent with a NotificationRequest message.
- *Event 35:* The Call Agent ACKs the message.
- *Event 36:* The Call Agent then "resets" the endpoint by informing the Gateway to monitor for an offhook condition.
- *Event 37:* The Gateway ACKs the command.

SUMMARY

Gatekeepers and Call Agents are the brains of the VoIP network. Gateways are the muscle. The Gateways act on the directions for the Gatekeepers and the Call Agents.

H.232 and the MGCP are based on the user of Gateways, Gatekeepers, and Call Agents. All are partners in setting up, maintaining and tearing down the telephony connections of the VoIP.

10

Internetworking SS7 with IP and H.323

T his chapter explains how SS7, IP, and H.323 can act as partners to support telephony traffic in packet networks.[1] I mention IP here, but once again (as it is in H.323 and the MGCP), IP is a passive party in these operations, and is employed only as the protocol to forward the voice traffic after the connection has been established between the calling and called parties. SS7 and H.323 are responsible for the signaling and connection management operations.

Several task forces are now involved in defining these operations and they are highlighted in this chapter. Be aware that the work is not yet finished, and the Internet specifications are still in the draft stages.

If the reader is unfamiliar with SS7, see a companion book to this series, titled: ISDN and SS7: Architectures for Digital Signaling Networks. Alternately, Appendix B provides you with enough information to understand the SS7 material in this book. You will need to know SS7's ISDN User Part (ISUP) protocol to understand this chapter. Additionally, it is assumed you have read the material in Chapter 9 on H.323.

In Chapter 9, a general model was used to explain the functions of Gateways and Gatekeepers. Be aware that my discussions of SS7, IP,

---

[1]A generic term to identify the interconnection of IP and SS7 networks is IPS7.

and H.323 interworking operations in this chapter use the terms used in these specific specifications, and may not match exactly with the generic model.

WHY COMBINE IP AND SS7?

One of the common criticisms of VoIP that is voiced by some people in the circuit switch telephony industry is the absence of the many service features that are common to telephony systems, such as call forwarding, call screening, caller id, and so forth. These features are quite important to many telephone users and are a vital part of the services that produce revenue for telephony service providers.

The IP protocol suite was not designed to offer these critical services, and any VoIP system that is going to succeed in the corporate environment must do so. Certainly, there will be niche applications that run a sparse set of service features, and certain customers will be content with these services. But for VoIP to become a significant force in telephony, it must provide telephony-type services. To be able to provide these services, it must be able to avail itself to the SS7 technology, the lynchpin for telephony service features, and the foundation for Advanced Intelligent Network (AIN) services.

Otherwise, the services that are part of SS7 must be "reinvented" by the Internet tasks forces—a ridiculous alternative. At any rate, the large SS7 vendors, such as Lucent, Nortel, etc. are developing IPS7, and most products are slated for testing in 1999.

POSSIBLE CONFIGURATIONS

Much work remains to be done on the development of standards for SS7-IP gateways. However, it is evident that the configurations explained in this section will be part of the final standards mix. For example, in Figure 10–1, an SS7 network is adjacent to subnetworks that run IP (labeled internets in the figure). The end-users are SS7, so the traffic being transferred between them is ISUP, SCCP, TCAP, etc. The SS7 nodes may be fully functioning Signaling Transfer Points (STPs), or endpoints, and the full features of MTP-3 are available, such as point code routing, and recovery from failed nodes and links.

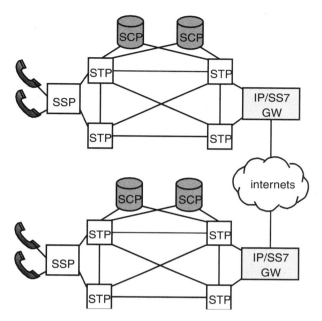

Figure 10–1   A full SS7 topology configuration

Another approach is shown in Figure 10–2, in which MTP-3 is not used. The requirement here is for a simple point-to-point topology. Therefore, MTP-3's routing, route recovery, and point-code operations are not needed. Addressing is provided with IP addresses or an adaptation layer can provide the MTP-3 routing label. The adaptation layer can also be responsible for backup operations in case of a failure of a link between the nodes. MTP-2 at the link layer can be used, but it is not required.

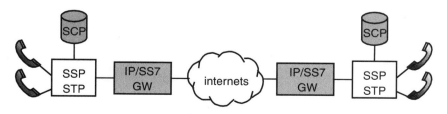

Figure 10–2   A scaled-down point-to-point configuration

THE BASIC FRAMEWORK AND THE INTERNET SPECIFICATIONS

Several Internet Drafts describe the operations of SS7 over IP. [GREE98][2] describes the overall architectural framework for SS7-Internetworking, and [DALI98][3] describes an architecture for an SS7-Internet Gateway. [HOLD98][4] defines a signaling protocol for an SS7-IP gateway, called the Reliable Signaling Gateway Protocol (RSGP). These Internet drafts are related to the Media Gateway Control Protocol (MGCP), discussed in Chapter 9, and since MGCP is emerging as a preferred VoIP protocol suite, the analysis of these specifications are made in the context of MGCP.

Bay Networks has another proposal that is called the Access Signaling Protocol (ASP) [MATO99].[5] The RSGP includes ASP.

H.323 is another preferred VoIP protocol suite, and [MA99][6] discusses the relationships of H.323 and SS7. This chapter also examines the [MA99] Draft in relation to H.323. Finally, another IPS7 draft is published with [MCGR98][7] as the author. I also provide a summary of [MCGR98] in this chapter.

TAKING ADVANTAGE OF SS7 CAPABILITIES

The idea of IPS7 is to transport SS7 messages over IP and at the same time, take advantage of the SS7 protocols MTP and SCCP. The transport of SS7 messages can operate over TCP or UDP. The SS7 messages include ISUP or SCCP or only TCAP. The SS7 or Internet engineer might question why a dual stack of SS7/IP is desirable. I cite [MCGR98] directly to support the rationale for the SS7/ IP dual stack.

---

[2][GREE98] Greene, Nancy. SS7-Internet Internetworking-Architectural Framework. Draft-green-ss7-arch-frame-01.txt., 1998.

[3][DALI98]. Dalias, R. Bay Networks SS7-Internet Gateway Architecture. Draft-ong-ss7-internet-gateway-01.txt., 1998.

[4][HOLD98]. Holdrege, Matt. Reliable Signaling Gateway Protocol (RSGP). Draft-ong-rsgp-ss7-info-00.txt., 1998.

[5][MATO99]. Matousek, J. and Ong, L. Bay Networks SS7-Internet Access Signaling Protocol. draft-long-ss7-signal-00.txt., 1998

[6][MA99]. Ma, Gene. H.323 Signaling and SS7 ISUP Gateway: Procedure Interworking. Draft-ma-h323-isup-gateway-00.txt., 1999.

[7][MCGR98] McGrew, Michael. Transport SS7 Signaling, Over IP. Internet Draft draft-mcgrew-tss7s-00.txt.,1998.

This paper addresses the need to transport over an IP network SS7 signaling between any two network elements which have an SS7 protocol stack at Message Transfer Part (MTP) Level 3 and/or above. In architectures that have been discussed for transport SS7 signaling over IP, a common thread is that the end user protocols need to understand SS7. The motivation is that SS7 users need the interface with IP to give them more flexibility to communicate with a more widely distributed SS7 user community of the future. Some SS7 users might not have the SS7 protocol stack, but instead rely on transport over IP. Other SS7 network nodes will already be on the standard SS7 network and have a full SS7 protocol stack, but have a need to communicate with the nodes that have only IP-based access. When the latter is deployed on SS7 Signaling Transfer Points (STPs), they can act as gateways to open up access to the SS7 nodes on the large installed base of SS7 networks that should need to have no knowledge of the IP network interconnection. All nodes such as Service Switching Point (SSP) nodes and Service Control Point (SCP) database nodes would be included in this new community.

The SS7/IP designers are not suggesting the ISUP be deployed in an internet. The view is to maintain the existing relationship of SS7 components and provide: (a) a mechanism for the transport of SS7 traffic over an IP network, and/or (b) a Gateway to internetwork H.323 and ISUP. IP would operate under the internet layer 4 TCP or UDP. However, TCP conventional ports may not be used for opening and closing connections, due to the delay and overhead involved (but this issue is not yet determined).

THE SS7-IP ARCHITECTURAL FRAMEWORK

A variety of SS7-IP components are being proposed in the Internet standards and are under development by the VoIP vendors. Figure 10–3 reflects the [GREE98] Draft—the Architectural Framework. As you can see, the entities in the "SS7-IP Gateway/Controller" are more numerous than in the MGCP that we examined in Chapter 9 in which H.323 defines only the gateway and the gatekeeper, and MGCP defines only (a) the Gateway and (b) the Media Gateway Controller/Call Agent. In fact, the Architectural Framework (hereafter called the Framework) defines other entities that are not shown in Figure 10–3. We will deal with these other entities later, but for now, we will concentrate on the entities in Figure 10–3 that have not yet been explained in this chapter or in Appendix B. They are:

- *Signaling gateway (SG):* The SG receives and sends public switched telephone system (PSTS) signals, and it may also receive

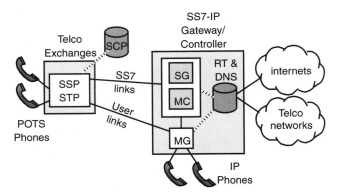

Figure 10–3   The SS7-IP architectural framework

and send SS7 messages. This entity is equivalent to the H.323 gateway and the MGCP gateway.

- *Media gateway controller (MC):* The MG acts as the registration and resource management entity. It is similar to the H.323 gatekeeper and the MGCP Call Agent, but it also may contain capabilities that establish usage of resources based on policies.

- *Media gateway (MG):* The media gateway acts as the physical interface for PSTN lines and trunks. It also is the interface for VoIP links. It also is similar to the H.323 gateway and the MGCP gateway.

- *Routing tables (RT):* The IP routing tables that are accessed with destination IP addresses in order to route the IP traffic through an internet.

- *Domain Name System (DNS):* Database for domain names, and associated IP addresses and SS7 point codes.

These units' functions are straightforward and their operations are apparent. However, the Framework is more complex than the configuration shown in Figure 10–3. First, the Framework includes a *Signaling Agent (SA).* The SA is responsible for signaling mediation within the IP network. As such, it is responsible for MG-MG, MG-SG, and SG-SG interworking. An MGCP Call Agent is an instance of an SA.

The Framework also defines the Network Access Server (NAS), which is responsible for allocating and deallocating resources. So, it has some of the capabilities of the H.323 gatekeeper and the MGCP Call Agent. It encompasses both an SG and MC.

It is left to an implementor to determine how some of these entities are arranged and how they internetwork with each other.

Reason for the Many Entities in the Framework

While these many entities may appear to make an SS7-IP configuration overly complex, they are placed in the Framework because several Internet Drafts propose different methods of implementing SS7-IP internetworking. The Framework explains each of the alternatives in the context of these entities, and therefore provides an excellent archetype for the SS7-IP designers. I leave you to [GREE99] if you wish to pursue the subject further.

THE RELIABLE SIGNALING GATEWAY PROTOCOL (RSGP)

The Framework model sets the stage for the Reliable Signaling Gateway Protocol (RSGP), as defined in [HOLD98]. RSGP encompasses the SS7-Internet Access Signaling Protocol (ASP) [MAT99], so we need not explain ASP separately here.

RSGP uses the Framework as a model, but separates the gateway from the NAS, and establishes RSGP as the protocol between the gateway and the NAS. This configuration is shown in Figure 10–4.

MESSAGES AND Q.931 MAPPINGS

The messages exchanged between the SG and the RAS are used to support call processing, and administration, operations, and maintenance (OAM) operations. The call-processing messages are based on

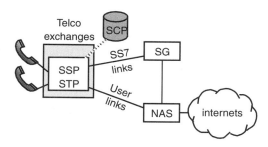

Figure 10–4   Reliable signaling gateway protocol (RSGP) configuration

Table 10–1   The RSGP messages

Message Name	Message Function
CONNECT	Confirm the SETUP message
CONNECT ACK	Confirm the CONNECT message
DISCONNECT	Disconnect the connection
RELEASE	Request the release of the connection
RELEASE CONFIRM	Confirm the RELEASE message
RESTART	Request to reset the call
RESTART ACK	Confirm the RESTART message
SETUP	Request to set up the connection
STATUS	Confirm the STATUS ENQUIRY message
STATUS ENQUIRY	Enquire about the status of a circuit
FACILITY	Provide more information about a call
ALERTING	Provide information about call progress
PROGRESS	Provide tones and announcements
NAS STATUS	Initialize NAS and SG interface
NAS STATUS ACK	Confirm the NAS STATUS message
CONTINUITY	Indicate outcome of circuit continuity check
CONTINUITY ACK	Confirm the CONTINUITY message
RESOURCE STATUS	Register interface and user port resources
RESOURCE STATUS ACK	Confirm the RESOURCE STATUS message
SERVICE	Change interface or channel status
SERVICE ACK	Confirm the SERVICE message

Q.931 and use this protocol's rules pertaining to the message contents (information elements and their coding). Other new messages are defined as well. All RSGP messages are listed in Table 10–1 with a brief description of their functions. The first thirteen messages in the table are derived from Q.931; the remainder are new RSGP messages.

Operations, Administration, and Maintenance (OAM) Procedures

The NAS and SG use the SERVICE message to configure the communications circuit (the T1/E1 interface) and the channels on the interface (DS0s) into the NAS. As implied in the previous statement, these links are based on the T1/E1 technology.[8] The RSGP defines how the NAS and SG must act upon receipt of the SERVICE message. The action is based on the information in the message. The message is coded to convey one of the following pieces of information:

- In Service: The interface is in service. The channel is available.
- Loop Back: The interface is in a loopback operation. The channel is in a loopback operation.
- Out of Service: The interface is inoperable. The channel is inoperable.
- Request Continuity Check: Applicable to a channel only.
- Graceful Shutdown: Interface and channel will tear down, but will not terminate established calls.

The actions that the NAS and SG perform upon the receipt of the SERVICE message vary, depending upon the message coding. For example, if the NAS receives the SERVICE message from the SG with the In Service bits set, and the interface and channel specified, the NAS will attempt to bring the T1/E1 circuit into service and mark the DS0 channel as available. If T1/E1 framing is achieved on the circuit, the NAS sends back a SERVICE message to the SG to inform it that the circuit and channel(s) are in service.

Examples of RSGP Operations

As we have done in previous chapters with the other VoIP protocols, I now provide some examples of the protocol flow between the SG and the RAS. I have selected key parts of RSGP for the examples and refer you to [HOLD98] for the explanation of the message contents, the coding rules for the messages, and the remainder of the protocol flows.

Figure 10–5 shows the message flow used for the NAS to register itself with the SG, and to provide interface and user port information to the SG. In order to show the message flow in a coherent way, Figure 10–5 is a redrawing of Figure 10–4. Here is a description of each event:

---

[8]No mention is made of SONET/SDH links, and RSGP uses the ISUP T1-based information elements for its work. If SONET/SDH is terminated into the NAS, additional capabilities must be added to RSGP to map T1 trunks and channels (DS0s) into SONET/SDH virtual tributaries/virtual containers. I expect the commercial implementations of the NAS and SG will support the mapping of RSGP T1-based information elements into SONET/SDH payloads.

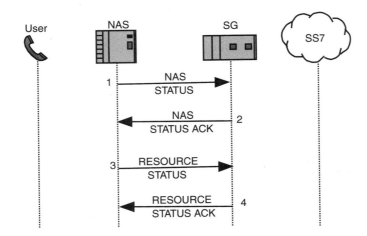

Figure 10–5 Registration procedures

- *Event 1:* The NAS sends an NAS STATUS message to the SG. This operation is used to initialize or reinitialize the RSGP operation. The message contains conventional fields, such as information element id, lengths, etc. and the NAS Status field. The field is coded to provide the following information: (a) the NAS is rebooting with a cold start, (b) the NAS is reestablishing connectivity to the SG with a warm start, (c) the NAS is in hot shutdown, is disconnecting, and terminating all calls, or (d) the NAS is in soft shutdown and will do a final shutdown when all existing calls are completed.

- *Event 2:* The SG acknowledges the NAS STATUS message.

- *Event 3:* The RAS sends the RESOURCE STATUS message to the SG. The key information elements in this message are interface status and resource. Interface status is coded to provide the following information: the interface is in (a) maintenance mode (loopback), (b) out of service (down), or (c) in service (up). The resource field provides information about the number of modems available at the RAS (the modem pool), or the number of HDLC-based logical channels available.

- *Event 4:* The SG acknowledges the RESOURCE STATUS message.

Once these operations are complete, and assuming that the RAS is in service, the RESOURCE STATUS message can be used to register more resources. The RAS is also ready to interwork with the SG in supporting customer calls. And for the customer call, Figure 10–6 is used. Here is a description of each event:

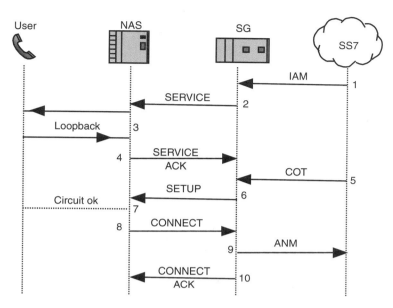

Figure 10–6   Call setup with continuity check

- *Event 1:* The SG receives an Initial Address Message (IAM) from SS7. A field in the message called Nature of Connection contains information about the circuit being setup (identified by the circuit identification code [CIC]). Information is coded to indicate if: (a) satellite circuits are in the connection, and if so, how many, (b) echo control devices are included, and (c) a continuity check (COT) is or is not needed. In this example, a COT is requested.
- *Event 2:* The SG forms a SERVICE message and sends it to the NAS. The key field in this message is Change Status. This field can be coded to provide the following information: (a) in service, (b) loopback, (c) out of service (d) request continuity check, and (e) graceful shutdown. For this example, field is coded to ask for a continuity check.
- *Event 3:* The NAS marks the circuit as busy and places it in a loopback mode.
- *Event 4:* The NAS then sends a SERVICE ACK message to the SG.
- *Event 5:* SS7 informs the SG that the continuity check was successful.

- *Event 6:* As a result of receiving the COT message in event 5, the SG sends a SETUP message to the NAS.
- *Event 7:* The NAS determines that the circuit is operational, and the circuit has been cut to the called party.
- *Event 8:* Therefore, it issues a CONNECT message to the SG.
- *Event 9:* As a result of receiving the Connect message for the NAS, the SG sends an Answer message (ANM) to SS7.
- *Event 10:* The CONNECT ACK message confirms the CONNECT message (this message is optional).

Figure 10–7 shows three more examples of RSGP operations. In Figure 10–7(a), The NAS has detected a failure of a T1/E1 line [loss of signal (LOS), a red alarm, etc.]. It informs the SG with the SERVICE message, and the SG acknowledges the message with a SERVICE ACK. In Figure 10–7(b), the SG is informed by SS7 that a T1/E1 circuit is to be taken out of commission. The example shows the user of the ISUP RELEASE (REL) message to accomplish this purpose, but other messages might be used, such as a FACILITY message. The SG informs the NAS with a SERVICE message and the NAS acknowledges the message with the SERVICE ACK. The last example in Figure 10–7(c) shows that the NAS is performing a graceful shutdown of a T1/E1 trunk. All established calls are not affected, and as these calls are completed, the associated DS0s are marked as out of service.

INTERWORKING H.323 AND SS7

In Chapter 9, we learned that H.323 (and the supporting protocols, H.225 and H.245) are used to support VoIP in local area networks. In addition, the H.323 Gatekeeper acts as Call Agent with a telephony network, and must therefore be able to correlate H.323 and ISUP message flows. [MA99] has developed the basic scheme for the interworking of H.323 and an SS7 Gateway. In this section, we examine the major features and the protocol flow of the H.323/SS7 Gateway operations. The interworking of H.323 and ISUP is fairly straightforward because the operations of the H Recommendations are similar to ISUP. For example, all of these signaling protocols use the bearer capability concept, so mapping the H.224 SETUP message to the ISUP IAM message is a relatively simple procedure.

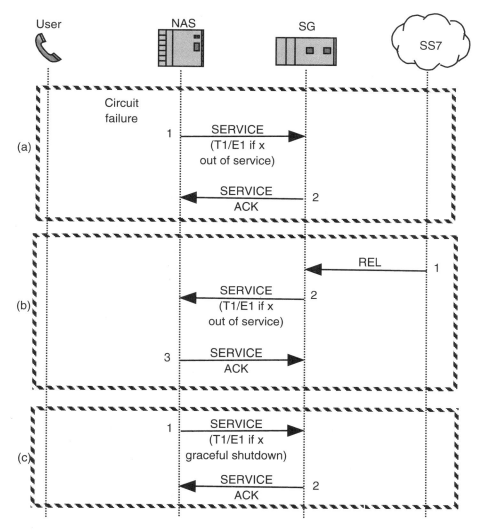

Figure 10–7 Other RSGP operations

Figure 10–8 shows the operations for the setting up of a call. Here is a description of each event.

- *Event 1:* The H.323 Gatekeeper issues a SETUP message to the Signaling Gateway.
- *Event 2:* The Signaling Gateway uses the information in the SETUP message to form the ISUP IAM message. It sends this

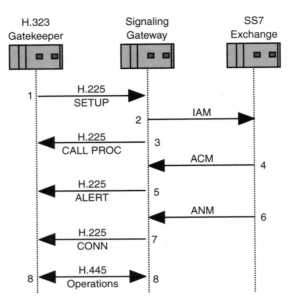

Figure 10–8   Call setup with H.323 protocols and ISUP

message to the next transit (and maybe final) telephony exchange (SS7 exchange in the figure).

- *Event 3:* The Signaling Gateway sends the CALL PROCEEDING message to the Gatekeeper.
- *Event 4:* The ISUP ACM message is sent by the transit exchange.
- *Event 5:* The receipt of the ACM message in event 5 precipitates the sending of the ALERT message by the Signaling Gateway to the Gatekeeper.
- *Event 6:* The transit exchange informs the Signaling Gateway that the called party has answered the call by sending the ANM message.
- *Event 7:* In turn, the Signaling Gateway sends the CONNECT message to the Gatekeeper.
- *Event 8:* Thereafter, the H.323 Gatekeeper and the Signaling Gateway enter into the H.445 operations to perform capability exchanges and logical channel setup.

It is possible for the Signaling Gateway to begin the H.445 operations immediately after receiving the H.225 SETUP message, since the message contains the TSAP address. So, it need not wait for the called party to respond. This approach will reduce the delay between the Gate-keeper and the Signaling Gateway after the ANM is received. The idea is shown in Figure 10–9.

The call set-up obviously can be made in the opposite direction, in which case the IAM from the SS7 exchange starts the set up operations between the Gatekeeper and the Signaling Gateway. And both sides of this operation may initiate call termination operations, refuse calls, and so on. I trust you have an idea of the interworking relationships between H.323 and SS7, but if you wish more details, I refer you to [MA99].

PROPOSAL FOR AN ADAPTATION LAYER

[MCGR98] proposes a scheme to use an adaptation layer between MTP-3 to provide an encapsulation/decapsulation function, and to map between MTP-3 point codes and IP addresses.

There is no interworking of IP and SS7 (that is mapping of functions, by header interpretation). The encapsulation/decapsulation operations imply a tunneling operation. There are no SCCP operations visible

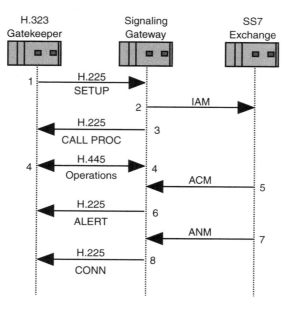

Figure 10–9   Initiating H.245 operations after receiving the SETUP message

in this approach. The idea is for the adaptation layer to emulate either MTP-3 or MTP-2 in the following scenarios:

- ISUP, TCAP, etc. over MTP-3 or over the adaptation layer that emulates MTP-3.
- MTP-3 over MTP-2 or over an adaptation layer that emulates MTP-2.

Figure 10–10 shows the layered structure for SS7 over IP. Two adaptation layers exist. The SUAL: Signaling UDP/IP Adaptation Layer (SUAL) implements UDP with additional enhancements for error checking, proper sequencing, and retransmissions; in other words, a scaled-down TCP. The Signaling TCP Connection/IP Adaptation Layer (SCAL) uses TCP, but is scaled-down for provide faster connection services. For both methods, the complete MTP-3 runs at each SS7 node (an SEP or STP as appropriate), and are designed to provide transparent transport for MTP users.

The idea is to implement an IP transport that will allow nodes without the full SS7 signaling resources to provide ISUP connections that interface with ISUP switches, and to have access to services that are part of the Intelligent Network (IN).

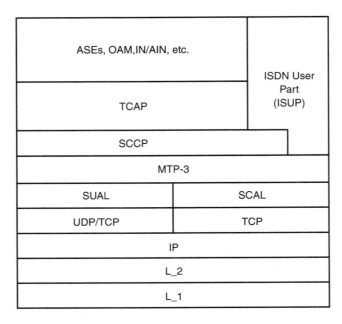

Figure 10–10   The IP/SS7 protocol stack [MCGR98]

The ideas in [MCGR98] are interesting, but as of this writing, they are not detailed enough to implement. The functions of the SUAL and SCAL need to be spelled out in more detail, so we shall have to wait to see if this draft is revised.

SUMMARY

SS7, IP, and H.323 must act as partners to support telephony traffic in packet networks. SS7 and H.323 are responsible for the signaling and connection management operations, and IP assumes its familiar role as the forwarding protocol for the voice traffic.

It would be a good idea for the reader to check the Internet for revisions to the specifications explained in this chapter. By the time this book is published, it is likely these drafts will have entered their final stages.

11

Other VoIP Supporting Protocols

H.323 and the MGCP are considered the principal systems to support VoIP, but as we have stated, many other protocols must operate with H.323 and the MGCP to support Internet telephony. This chapter provides an overview of them. Like the VoIP gateway specifications, some of these protocols are not fully standardized, and the reader should keep in mind that working drafts are likely to change.

An entire book or several books can be written on this subject, and a companion book in this series is being written about these protocols. Our goal in this chapter is to develop a general understanding of these supporting protocols.

IGMP AND MBONE

Multicasting (sending from one party to two or more parties) is of keen interest to internet telephony users and designers because it paves the road for conference calls, a fundamental part of doing business in many companies. The Internet has supported multicasting for a number of years with the Internet Group Management Protocol (IGMP).

This protocol defines the procedures for a user node (a host) to join a multicast group. Once the host has joined the group, it can receive any multicasting traffic sent within this group. For example, the multicast session may be a quarterly conference of a special interest group, or it may be a Rolling Stones concert.

One of the attractive features of IGMP is that it does not require a host to know in advance about all the multicasting groups in an internet. Instead, the routers are knowledgeable of multicast groups and send advertisements to the hosts about their multicasting groups. For example, if an Internet task force is meeting and its proceedings are to be made available to the public, a user machine will receive an advertisement from its router about the conference. In turn, the host can reply with a message stating whether it wishes to join the conference.

The multicasting backbone (MBONE) is another protocol that has been in operation for a number of years. MBONE is the "pioneer" system for Internet audio/video conferences. Originally, MBONE was used to multicast the various standards' groups meetings and its use has been expanded for activities such as viewing the space shuttle launches, video shows in general, and other activities.

MBONE relies on IP multicasting operations and IGMP to convey information. In addition, the term multicasting backbone does not mean that MBONE is actually a backbone network. MBONE is an application that runs on the Internet backbone.

The multicast traffic runs inside the data field of the IP datagram and relies on the conventional IP header for delivery of the traffic through an internet. This concept is called multicast tunnels in the sense that the multicast traffic is tunneled through an Internet by riding inside the IP datagram.

Figure 11–1 shows that multicasting traffic is destined to the hosts residing on the networks attached to routers B and C. The traffic emanates from a host attached to router A. The figure shows that the destination multicast IP address is 224.0.0.99. The figure also shows the unicast IP addresses of the sending host (172.16.1.3) and router B (172.16.1.1.), and router C (172.16.1.2).

Multicasting Addresses

Since IP multicast system is a one-to-many operation, the sender of the multicast traffic need only create one copy of the protocol data unit (PDU). This PDU is sent to a multicast server (for example a router) which is then responsible for creating as many copies as needed to send to the router's outgoing ports to reach the receiving nodes. This approach saves bandwidth at the sender since only one copy of the PDU is sent

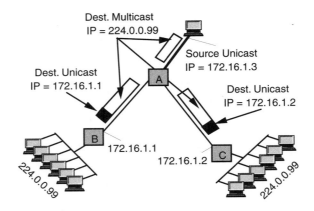

Figure 11–1   Multicasting tunnels

from the user. It also saves bandwidth at the receiver if multiple multi-cast recipients are attached to the same shared bus network.

IP multicasting is used in audio conferencing and video conferencing environments and is also seeing use for remote distance learning, meetings, and interactive chalk talks.

The format for the IP multicast address is shown in Figure 11–2. This address is also known as a class-D address and the first four digits of the address are set to 1110. The remaining 28 bits are set aside for the multicast address.

The IP address can take the values ranging from 224.0.0.0 to 239.255.255.255.

RSVP

As its name implies, the resource reservation protocol (RSVP) is used to reserve resources for a session in an Internet. This aspect of the Internet is quite different to the underlying design intent of the system, which as we learned earlier, was established to support only a best effort service, without regard to predefined requirements for the user application.

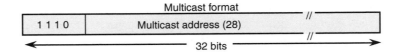

Figure 11–2   The multicast address

RSVP is intended to provide guaranteed performance by reserving the necessary resources at each machine that participates in supporting the flow of traffic (such as a video or audio conference). Remember that IP is a connectionless protocol which does not set up paths for the traffic flow, whereas RSVP is designed to establish these paths as well as to guarantee the bandwidth on the paths.

RSVP does not provide routing operations, but utilizes IPv4 or IPv6 as the transport mechanism in the same fashion as the Internet Control Message Protocol (ICMP) and the Internet Group Message Protocol (IGMP).

RSVP operates with unicast or multicast procedures and interworks with current and planned multicast protocols. Like IP, it relies on routing tables to determine routes for its messages. It utilizes IGMP to first join a multicast group and then executes procedures to reserve resources for the multicast group.

RSVP requires the receivers of the traffic to request QOS for the flow. The receiver host application must determine the QOS profile which is then passed to RSVP. After the analysis of the request, RSVP is used to send request messages to all the nodes that participate in the data flow.

Path Operations

RSVP operates with unicast or multicast procedures and interworks with current and planned multicast protocols. It utilizes IGMP to first join a multicast group and then executes procedures to reserve resources for the multicast group. RSVP requires the receivers of the traffic to request QOS for the flow. The receiver host application must determine the QOS profile which is then passed to RSVP. After the analysis of the request, RSVP is used to send request messages to all the nodes that participate in the data flow. As Figure 11–3 shows, the path message is used by a server (the flow sender) to set up a path for the session.

Reservation Operations

Figure 11–4 shows that the reservation messages are sent by the receivers of the flow, and they allow sender and intermediate machines (such as routers) to learn the receivers' requirements.

Reservation Messages

All RSVP messages consist of a common header followed by a body. The body contains a variable number of objects. Figure 11–5 shows the format of the RSVP common header.

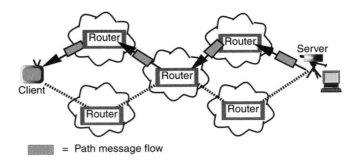

Figure 11–3   RSVP path messages

The fields in the common header are as follows:

- *Version:* Protocol version number. This is version 1.
- *Flags:* No flag bits are defined yet.
- *Message type:* Set to 1 = path, 2 = Resv, 3 = PathErr, 4 = ResvErr, 5 = PathTear, 6 = ResvTear, 7 = ResvConf
- *RSVP checksum:* The one's complement of the one's complement sum of the message, with the checksum field replaced by zero for the purpose of computing the checksum. An all-zero value means that no checksum was transmitted.
- *Send_TTL:* The IP TTL value with which the message was sent.
- *RSVP Length:* The total length of this RSVP message in bytes, including the common header and the variable-length objects that follow

Every RSVP object is coded in the message with one or more 32-bit words as shown in Figure 11–6.

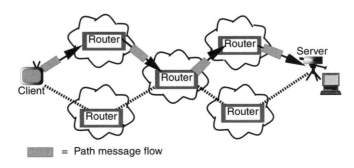

Figure 11–4   RSVP reservation messages

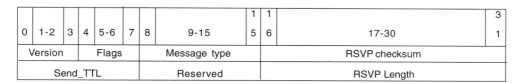

Figure 11–5   RSVP common header

The fields in this message are as follows:

- *Length:* The total length of the object field.
- *Class-Num:* Identifies the object class, discussed next.
- *C-Type:* Identifies the object type within the class-num, also discussed next.

RSVP Objects. The information in the RSVP messages are coded as objects, which contain the information exchanged between servers, clients, and nodes on the reserved path.

The following object classes must be supported in an RSVP implementation.

- *NULL:* This object has a Class-Num of zero, and its C-Type is ignored. A NULL object may appear anywhere in a sequence of objects, and its contents will be ignored by the receiver.
- *SESSION:* Contains the IP destination address, the IP protocol ID, and some form of generalized destination port, to define a specific session for the other objects that follow.
- *RSVP_HOP:* Carries the IP address of the RSVP-capable node that sent this message and a logical outgoing interface handle (LIH). RFC 2005 refers to a RSVP_HOP object as a PHOP (previous hop) object for downstream messages or as a NHOP (next hop) object for upstream objects.
- *TIME_VALUES:* Contains the value for the refresh period R used by the creator of the message.

*Class-Num and C-Type together total 16 bits, but each field can vary in length.

Figure 11–6   RSVP objects in the message

- *STYLE:* Defines the reservation style plus style-specific information that is not in FLOWSPEC or FILTER_SPEC objects.
- *FLOWSPEC:* Defines a subset of session data packets that should receive the desired QOS (specified by a FLOWSPEC object) in a Resv message.
- *SENDER_TEMPLATE:* Contains a sender IP address and perhaps some additional demultiplexing information to identify a sender.
- *SENDER_TSPEC:* Defines the traffic characteristics of a sender's data flow.
- *ADSPEC:* Carries OPWA data, in a Path message.
- *ERROR_SPEC:* Specifies an error in a PathErr, ResvErr, or a confirmation in a ResvConf message.
- *POLICY_DATA:* Carries information that will allow a local policy module to decide whether an associated reservation is administratively permitted. The use of POLICY_DATA objects is not fully specified at this time; a future document will fill this gap.
- *INTEGRITY:* Carries cryptographic data to authenticate the originating node and to verify the contents of this RSVP message.
- *SCOPE:* Carries an explicit list of sender hosts towards which the information in the message is to be forwarded.
- *RESV_CONFIRM:* Carries the IP address of a receiver that requested a confirmation.

Table 11–1 lists the RSVP objects and describes their purpose (in a general manner). The purpose of the objects is to describe the quality of service (QOS) needed by the conference nodes and to provide information on the operations that will support the session [THOM96].[1]

In the event of problems, RSVP provides for a number of diagnostics that are implemented with the error codes shown in Table 11–2.

A Summary of the RSVP Message Functions

We conclude this review of RSVP with a brief look at the functions of the RSVP messages. RFC 2205 contains the details, if you need them.

---

[1][THOM96]. Thomas, Stephen A. *IPng and TCP/IP Protocols.* New York: John Wiley & Sons, Inc, 1996.

Table 11–1   RSVP objects

#	Object	Type	Description
0	NULL		Ignored by recipient
1	SESSION	1	IPv4 session (destination of flow)
		2	IPv6 session (destination of flow)
3	RSVP_HOP	1	IPv4 previous or next hop address
		2	IPv6 previous or next hop address
4	INTEGRITY		Keyed MD5 authentication data
5	TIME_VALUES	1	Frequency of path or reservation refreshes
6	ERROR_SPEC	1	Error information from an IPv4 system
		2	Error information from an IPv6 system
7	SCOPE	1	List of IPv4 hosts to which reservation refresh messages apply
		2	List of IPv6 hosts to which reservation refresh messages apply
8	STYLE	1	Style of reservation
9	FLOWSPEC	1	Flow specification requiring controlled delay
		2	Flow specification: predictive quality of service
		3	Flow specification: guaranteed quality of service
		254	Flow specification: several unmerged flows
10	FILTER_SPEC	1	IPv4-based filter to apply to flow
		2	IPv6-based filter using source port values
		3	IPv6-based filter using flow label values
11	SENDER_TEMPLATE	1	IPv4-based description of flow that sender is generating
		2	IPv6-based description of flow that sender is generating
12	SENDER_TSPEC	1	Upper bound on traffic that sender will generate
13	ADSPEC		Sender's advertised information for flow
14	POLICY_DATA	1	Policy information for flow
		254	Several unmerged policy data objects
20	TAG	1	Collection of objects to be associated with a given name

Table 11–2   RSVP error codes

1	Admission failure, reservation could not be granted
2	Administrative rejection, reservation prohibited
3	No path information available for reservation
4	No sender for reservation
5	Ambiguous path
6	Ambiguous filter specification
7	Conflicting or unknown style
11	Missing required object
12	Unknown object class
13	Unknown object type
14	Object error
21	Traffic control error
22	RSVP system error

Path Messages.   Each sender host periodically sends a Path message for each data flow it originates. It contains a SENDER_TEMPLATE object defining the format of the data packets and a SENDER_TSPEC object specifying the traffic characteristics of the flow. Optionally, it contains an ADSPEC object carrying advertising data for the flow.

A Path message travels from a sender to receiver(s) along the same path(s) used by the data packets. The IP source address of a Path message must be an address of the sender it describes, and the destination address must be the DestAddress for the session. These addresses assure that the message will be correctly routed through a non-RSVP cloud.

Each RSVP-capable node along the path(s) captures a Path message and processes it to create path state for the sender defined by the SENDER_TEMPLATE and SESSION objects. Any POLICY_DATA, SENDER_TSPEC, and ADSPEC objects are also saved in the path state. If an error is encountered while processing a Path message, a PathErr message is sent to the originating sender of the Past message.

Periodically, the RSVP process at a node scans the path state to create new Path messages to forward towards the receiver(s). Each message contains a sender descriptor defining one sender, and carries the original sender's IP address as its IP source address. Path messages eventually reach the applications on all receivers; however, they are not looped back to a receiver running in the same application process as the sender.

Reservation (Resv). Resv messages carry reservation request hop-by-hop from receivers to senders, along the reverse paths of data flows for the session. The IP destination address of a Resv message is the unicast address of a previous hop node, obtained from the path state. The IP source address is an address of the node that sent the message.

The appearance of a RESV_CONFIRM object signals a request for a reservation confirmation and carries the IP address of the receiver to which the ResvConf should be sent. Any number of POLICY_DATA objects may appear.

Path Teardown Messages. Receipt of a PathTear (path teardown) message deletes a matching path state. Matching state must have match the SESSION, SENDER-TEMPLATE, and PHOP objects. In addition, a PathTear message for a multicast session can only match path state for the incoming interface on which the PathTear arrived. If there is no matching path state, a PathTear message should be discarded and not forwarded.

PathTear messages are initiated explicitly by senders or by path state timeout in any node, and they travel downstream towards all receivers.

A PathTear message must be routed exactly like the corresponding Path message. Therefore, its IP destination address must be the session DestAddress, and its IP source address must be the sender address from the path state being torn down.

Deletion of path state as the result of a PathTear message or a timeout must also adjust related reservation state as required to maintain consistency in the local node. The adjustment depends upon the reservation style.

Resv Teardown Messages. Receipt of a ResvTear (reservation teardown) message deletes a matching reservation state. Matching reservation state must match the SESSION, STYLE, and FILTER_SPEC objects. If there is no matching reservation state, a ResvTear message is discarded. A ResvTear message may tear down any subset of the filter specs in FF-style or SE-style reservation state.

ResvTear messages are initiated explicitly by receivers or by any node in which reservation state has timed out, and they travel upstream towards all matching senders. A ResvTear message must be routed like the corresponding Resv message, and its IP destination address will be the unicast address of a previous hop.

Path Error Messages. PathErr (path error) messages report errors in processing Path messages. They travel upstream towards senders and are routed hop-by-hop using the path state. At each hop, the IP destination address is the unicast address of a previous hop. PathErr messages do not modify the state of any node through which they pass; they are only reported to the sender application.

Resv Error Messages. ResvErr (reservation error) messages report errors in processing Resv messages, or they may report the spontaneous disruption of a reservation, e.g., by administrative preemption.

ResvErr messages travel downstream towards the appropriate receivers, routed hop-by-hop using the reservation state. At each hop, the I destination address is the unicast address of a next-hop node.

Confirmation Messages. ResvConf messages are sent to acknowledge reservation requests. A ResvConf message is sent as the result of the appearance of a RESV_CONFIRM object in a Resv message.

Rules for the Ports

An RSV session is normally defined by the triple: DestAddress, ProtocolId, DstPort. DstPort is a UDP/TCP destination port field. DstPort may be omitted (set to zero) if the ProtocolId specifies a protocol that does not have a destination port field in the format used by UDP and TCP.

RSVP allows any value for ProtocolId. However, end-system implementations of RSVP may know about certain values for this field, and in particular the values for UDP and TCP (17 and 6, respectively).

RTP

The real-time protocol (RTP) is designed for the support of real-time traffic; that is, traffic that needs to be sent and received in a very short time period. Two real-time traffic examples are (a) audio conversations between two people, and (b) playing individual video frames at the receiver as they are received from the transmitter.

RTP is also an encapsulation protocol in that the real-time traffic runs in the data field of the RTP packet, and the RTP header contains information about the type of traffic that RTP is transporting. (While RTP can perform this function, not all multiservice applications will use RTP.

Each IP telephony or video commercial product should be evaluated to determine the exact "protocol mix" in the offering).

RTP also has a time-stamp field in its header. It can be used to synchronize the traffic play-out to the receiving application.

Figures 11–7 and 11–8 show two major features of RTP in how it supports traffic from senders to receivers. First, in Figure 11–7 the RTP system is acting as a translator.

The RTP translator translates (encodes) from one payload syntax to a different syntax. This figure shows how the RTP translator operates. The user devices on the left side of the figure are set up to use a 512-kbit/s video stream for their video application. The user device on the right side of the figure uses a 384-kbit/s video stream. As another possibility, the transit network may not be able to support the 512 kbit/s rate. So, whether from the user station on the right or the network in the middle, the users cannot communicate with each other.

The RTP translator allows these user stations to interact with each other. The job of the translator is to accept the traffic of the stations on the left side of the figure, translate (encode) that traffic into a format that is (a) in consonance with the bandwidth limitations of the transit network, and/or (b) in consonance with the bandwidth limitations of the user station on the right side of the figure. The user's RTP packet shows that the user is the synchronization service.

Figure 11–8 shows an RTP server performing a mixer operation. Mixers combine multiple sources into one stream. Typically, mixers par-

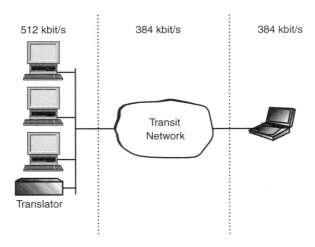

Figure 11–7   The RTP translator

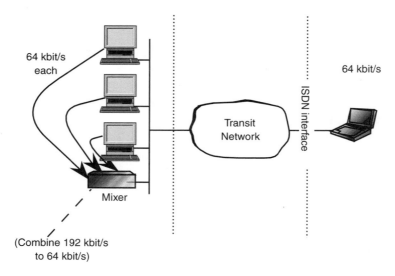

Figure 11–8   The RTP mixer

ticipate in audio operations and they do not decrease the quality of the signal to the recipients. They simply combine the signals into a consistent format. As stated earlier, the RTP mixer operation is particularly suited to audio conferences. As a general rule, it does not work well with video conferences because it is quite difficult to combine multiple video sources into one syntax.

RTP mixers do not translate each source payload into a different format. The original format is maintained, and the various source payloads are combined into one stream. The mixer is used for audio conferences, but not for video sessions, since mixing video streams is not yet a commercial reality. On the other hand, if the audio streams are uncomplicated pulse code modulation (PCM) traffic, it is possible to arithmetically sum the values of each source payload and combine them into a single stream.

The RTP Message

The designers of RTP were careful to keep all messages in common format which is shown in Figure 11–9. Before discussing the fields in the message, it should be noted that RTP does not have a well-known port (obviously it operates on a UDP port). Its default port is 5004, if an application does not have a port setup. The reason for not having a well-known port is that RTP will be used with several-to-many applications which themselves are identified with ports.

The message format for RTP is designed to support different types of payloads (operating in the application layer, L_7), such as the ITU-T G.722 audio standard, and the JPEG video standard. The RTP protocol data unit (PDU) is carried in the User Datagram Protocol (UDP) and Internet Protocol (IP) PDUs, with these protocols' headers as part of the complete data unit.

Since different applications' traffic may be carried by RTP, it does not have a well-known port, but port 5004 is designated as the default port if an application has not been assigned a port number.

This figure shows the format and contents of the RTP header. The fields are used in the following manner:

- *Version (v):* Version 2.
- *Padding (P):* Padding flag on, if padding bytes added to message.
- *Extension (E):* To indicate a header after RTP header (not used yet).
- *Contributor count (CC):* How many contributing source identifiers in message, which allows for 15 contributing sources.

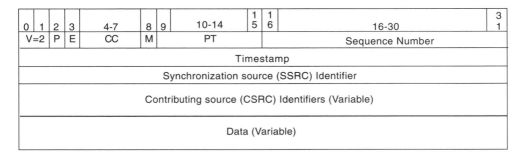

Where:

CC	Contributor count
E	Extension
M	Marker
P	Padding
PT	Payload type
V	Version

Figure 11–9   RTP message format

- *Marker (M):* Specific to application, typically used to set up demarcation boundaries in the data stream.
- *Payload type (PT):* Type of traffic in the data field (G.722 audio, GSM, etc.).
- *Sequence number (SN):* A number that increments by 1 for each RTP packet sent.
- *Source ID (Sync):* Original sender of the traffic (sets time stamp and SN).
- *Time-stamp:* Reflects the sampling instant of the first octet in the RTP data packet. The sampling instant must be derived from a clock that increments monotonically and linearly in time to allow synchronization and jitter calculations. The resolution of the clock must be sufficient for the desired synchronization accuracy and for measuring packet arrival jitter. If RTP packets are generated periodically, the nominal sampling instant as determined from the sampling clock is to be used, not a reading of the system clock. For example, for fixed-rate audio the time-stamp clock would likely increment by one for each sampling period. If an audio application reads blocks covering 160 sampling periods from the input device, the time-stamp would be increased by 160 for each such block, regardless of whether the block is transmitted in a packet or dropped as silent.
- *SSRC:* The SSRC field identifies the synchronization source. This identifier is chosen randomly, with the intent that no two synchronization sources within the same RTP session will have the same SSRC identifier.
- *CSRC list:* The CSRC list identifies the contributing sources for the payload contained in this packet. The number of identifiers is given by the CC field. If there are more than fifteen contributing sources, only fifteen may be identified. CSRC identifiers are inserted by mixers, using the SSRC identifiers of contributing sources.

The sync source ID is the identifier of the original transmitter of the RTP message, which is responsible in determining the values of the sequence number and the time-stamp in the message. This identifier is preserved by RTP translators, but an RTP mixer becomes the sync source and the other (original) sources become contributing sources, and are identified in the contributing source ID fields in the message.

The sequence number and time-stamp are used between the communicating parties to (a) make certain the traffic is in the proper sequential order, (b) if any traffic is missing/lost, and (c) synchronize the traffic flow.

Note that RTP does not define the contents of the application data field which of course is left to the application. Thus, RTP can carry various types of application traffic.

RTCP

After a reservation has been established through the use of RSVP, the traffic is then sent between machines with RTP. Next, the Real Time Control Protocol (RTCP) comes into the picture by providing the procedure for the machines to keep each other informed about (a) the quality of services they think they are providing (if they are service providers), and/or (b) the quality of services they are receiving (if they are service clients).

In concept, a server can adjust its quality-of-service operations depending on the feedback it receives from its clients. However, the manner in which these adjustments are made is not defined by RTCP.

The RTCP Packets. A productive way to analyze RTCP further is to examine the packet types that are used for these operations. Five packet types are used and are summarized in Table 11–3.

Periodically, the sender in the session sends sender reports to the receiver, which are coded as shown in Figure 11–10. The contents of the fields are as follows:

- *Version (v):* Version 2.
- *Padding (P):* Padding flag on, if padding bytes added.

Table 11–3   RTCP packet type

Number	Packet Type	Purpose
200	Sender report	Active senders send and receive statistics
201	Receiver report	Receivers only receive statistics
202	Source description	Source description items, including CNAME
203	Bye	End of participation
204	Application specific	—

0	1	2	3	4-6	7	8		9-14	1 5	1 6	16-30	3 1
V=2	P		RC					PT=SR=200			Length	
SSRC of sender												
NTP time-stamp, most significant word												
NTP time-stamp, most significant word												
RTP time-stamp												
Sender's packet count												
Sender's octet count												
SSRC_1 (SSRC of first source)												
Fraction lost								Cumulative number of packets lost				
Extended highest sequence number received												
Interarrival jitter												
Last SR (LSR)												
Delay since last SR (DLSR)												
SSRC_2 (SSRC of second source)												
. . .												
Application-specific extensions (Variable)												

Figure 11–10   RTP message format

- *Receiver block count (RC):* Indicates how many receiver blocks are contained in the message.
- *Packet type (PT):* Set to 200 for a sender report message.
- *Length:* Length of the sender report message.
- *SSRC:* Sync source ID of sender (correlates RTP and RTCP PDUs) of a source.
- *Network Time Protocol (NTP):* NTP time indicates the wallclock time when this report was sent, so that it may be used in combination with time-stamps returned in reception reports from other receivers to measure round trip propagation to those receivers. A sender that can keep track of elapsed time but has no notion of wallclock time may use the elapsed time since joining the session instead. A sender that has no notion of wallclock or elapsed time may set the NTP time-stamp to zero.
- *RTP Time-stamp:* Corresponds to the same time as the NTP time-stamp, but in the same units and with the same random offset as the RTP time-stamps in data packets. This correspondence may be

used for intra- and intermedia synchronization for sources whose NTP time-stamps are synchronized, and may be used by media-independent receivers to estimate the normal RTP clock frequency. This time-stamp is calculated from the corresponding NTP time-stamp using the relationship between the RTP time-stamp counter and real time as maintained by periodically checking the wallclock time at a sampling instant.

- *Sender's packet and byte count:* Used to inform the receivers of how many RTP packets (PDUs) and the number of bytes that the sender has sent.

The next set of fields is used by the sender to report on the RTP traffic that it is has received. By use of the sequence numbers in the RTP message header, the sender can report the percentage of PDUs lost (% lost), and total PDUs lost (Cumulative packets lost) since the last reporting period. Here is a description of each of these fields.

- *Source identifier (SSRC_n):* The SSRC identifier of the source to which the information in this reception report block pertains.
- *% lost:* The fraction of RTP data packets from source SSRC_n lost since the previous SR or RR packet was sent, expressed as a fixed point number. This fraction is defined to be the number of packets lost divided by the number of packets expected.
- *Cumulative packets lost:* The total number of RTP data packets from source SSRC_n that have been lost since the beginning of reception. This number is defined to be the number of packets expected less the number of packets actually received, where the number of packets received includes any which are late or duplicates. Thus packets that arrive late are not counted as lost, and the loss may be negative if there are duplicates.
- *Extended highest sequence number received:* The low 16 bits contain the highest sequence number received in an RTP data packet from source SSRC_n, and the most significant 16 bits extend that sequence number with the corresponding count of sequence number cycles.
- *Interarrival jitter:* An estimate of the statistical variance of the RTP data packet interarrival time, measured in time-stamp units and expressed as an unsigned integer. The interarrival jitter J is defined to be the mean deviation (smoothed absolute value) of the difference D in packet spacing at the receiver compared to the

sender for a pair of packets. Equations for jitter calculation are provided in the RTP documents and later sections in this chapter provide the H.225.0 equations.

- *Time of last sender report (LSR):* Middle 32 bits of the 64 bits in the NTP time-stamp received as part of the most recent RTP sender report packet from SSRC_n.
- *Delay since last sender report:* Expressed as 1/65536 seconds, the delay between receiving the last sender report from SSCC_n and sending this reception report.

In many circumstances, the participant in multiconferencing operations does not send traffic, so it does not generate sender reports. However, it can generate receiver reports. The contents of these reports are the same as the fields in the sender report.

Jitter Equation [CASZ97][2]

Interarrival jitter is the difference in relative transit time for two packets. It is the difference between the packet's RTP time-stamp and the receiver's clock at the time of arrival of the packet.

As shown in the equation below, this is equivalent to the difference in the "relative transit time" for two packets: the relative transit time is the difference between a packet's RTP time-stamp and the receiver's clock at the time of arrival, measured in the same units.

If Si is the RTP time-stamp from packet i, and Ri is the time of arrival in RTP time-stamp units for packet i, then for two packets i and j, D may be expressed as:

$$D(i,j) = (Rj - Ri) - (Sj - Si) = (Rj - Sj) - (Ri - Si)$$

The interval jitter is calculated continuously as each data packet i is received from source SSRC_n, using this difference D for that packet and the previous packet i-1 in order of arrival (not necessarily in sequence), according to the formula:

$$J = J + (\mid D (i-1,i) \mid -J)/16$$

---

[2][CASZ97] Annex A of H.225.0 and *Foundation of Digital Signal Processing and Data Analysis,* by J. A. Caszow, MacMillan, New York, 1997.

0	1	2	3	4-6	7	8	9-14	1 5	1 6	16-30	3 1
V=2				SC			PT			Length	
SSRC or CSRC for first source											
SDES Items (Variable)											
SSRC or CSRC of second source											
SDES Items (Variable)											
SSRC or CSRC of last source											
SCES Items (Variable)											

Figure 11–11   RTCP source description packet (SDES)

Source Description Packet (SDES).   RTCP allows a source to provide more information about itself. This operation takes place through the transmission of the RTCP source description packet (SDES), see Figure 11–11. These PDUs contain the sync or contributing source identifiers (SSRC or CCRC), and SDES items.

Table 11–4 shows the source description items that have been defined so far. As the table shows, the items simply provide more information about the source. How they are used is implementation-specific, and RFCs 1889 and 1996 provide additional information on this topic.

NETWORK TIME PROTOCOL (NTP)

The network time protocol (NTP), published in *Request for Comments* (RFC) 1119, is used for time-stamping operations.

Clocking information for a network is provided through the primary time server designated as a root. The time server obtains its clocking information from master sources. In the United States, this is usually one of three sources:

- *Fort Collins, Colorado:* Station WWV operated by the National Institute of Standards and Technology (NIST) uses high frequency (HF) frequencies
- *Kauai, Hawaii:* Station WWVH operated by NIST, also uses HF frequencies
- *Boulder, Colorado:* Station WWVB uses low frequency transmissions

Table 11–4   Source description items

CNAME	Unique and unambiguous name for the source
NAME	Real user name of the source
EMAIL	Email address
PHONE	Telephone number
LOC	Geographic location
TOOL	Name of application generating the stream
NOTE	Note about the source
PRIV	Private extensions
BYE	Goodbye RTP packet
APP	Application-defined RTCP packet

The primary and secondary time servers to calculate clock offsets and correct clocking inaccuracies. *Several control fields* are contained in the NTP message, which is beyond the scope of this discussion. The *sync distance* is an estimate of the round trip propagation delay to the primary clock, as seen by the originator of the NTP message. The *ID of the primary* clock contains the unique identifier of the primary time server. The next four fields contain time-stamp information. They contain the following information:

- *Time local clock updated:* The time that the originator of this message has had its local clock updated
- *Originate time-stamp:* The time that this message was originated
- *Receive time-stamp:* The time this message was received
- *Transmit time-stamp:* The time this message was transmitted after receiving it

All time-stamps are 64 bits in length with 32 bits reserved for a whole number and 32 bits for the fraction. Time-stamps are benchmarked from January 1, 1900. Does the 32-bit field provide enough space for growth? The answer is, most definitely. The value 2^{32} provides magnitudes well beyond what we foresee as needed in the future.

The last field is *Authenticator.* This is an optional field used for authentication purposes.

In addition to RFC 1119, the interested reader might wish to refer to RFCs 956 and 957.

Time uses port 37 and it can operate above UDP or the TCP. Be aware that the information retrieved and displayed to the user on a terminal is not very readable. For example, the value gives the number of seconds since January 1, 1900, midnight (GMT). Consequently, the date of January 1, 1980 GMT at midnight would be retrieved and displayed as 2,524,521,600. Of course, a simple program can be written which can translate this notation into a user friendly format.

SECURITY SERVICES

As the Internet has grown beyond its research and academic origins, it has become evident that privacy and security services to the data or audio user have been lacking. Fortunately, in the past few years, this situation has changed dramatically, and a wide range of security measures are now available. This part of the chapter provides a summary of some of the principal security protocols available. Several of these systems are used by H.323, MGCP, and IPS7 nodes, described in Chapters 9 and 10.

Secure IP Tunnels

The IPsec is being developed by the Internet Engineering Task Force (IETF) IPsec Working Group. The full set of specifications for IPsec are not finished as of this writing, but they are nearing completion. I will give you the latest information on the specifications, and I will provide references, as well as additional bibliography. In addition, this explanation of IPsec includes a specific approach from IBM on implementing the emerging RFCs. I refer you to [CHEN98][3] for an example of an organization's implementation of IPsec and related specifications.

To begin the explanation of IPsec, we first need to clarify the concept of an IP secure tunnel in the context of how it is used in IPsec, see Figure 11–12. Broadly speaking, a tunnel conveys the idea of the secure transport of traffic between two systems across a nonsecure network (an untrusted network), or a single link (in this example, the Internet is a nonsecure network).

The actual passing of traffic is an instantiation of the security policies existing between the sending and receiving systems. The security

---

[3][CHEN98] Cheng, P. C., Garay, J. A., Herzberg, A., Krawczyk H., "A Security Architecture for the Internet Protocol" *IBM System Journal,* Vol. 37, No. 1, 1998.

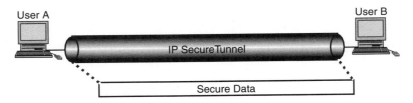

Figure 11–12   The IP secure tunnel

policy (also referred to as meta-characteristics) include the addresses of the endpoints, an encapsulation method (by which the traffic is encapsulated inside other protocol data units), the cryptographic algorithms, the parameters for the algorithms (which include the size of the key and the lifetime of the key).

An IP secure tunnel refers to *all* the procedures, including protocols, encryption methods, etc. that insures the safe passage of the traffic between the two systems. This set of capabilities is called a security association (SA). Be aware that a security association is not the tunnel itself, but an instantiation of the tunnel during a particular time, based on the SA.

We just learned that a security association defines a set of items (meta-characteristics) that is shared between two communicating entities. Its purpose is to protect the communications process between the parties.

An IPsec SA defines the following information as part of the security associations, and see Figure 11–13 for a graphical depiction of the ideas:

1. *Destination IP address*
2. *Security protocol* that is to be used, which defines if the traffic is to be provided with integrity as well as secrecy support. It also

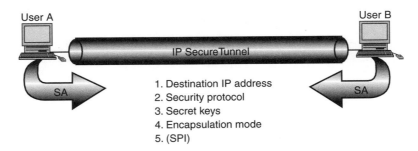

Figure 11–13   Security associations (SA) for IP secure tunnels

defines the key size, key lifetime, and cryptographic algorithms (the algorithms are called transforms in IPsec).

3. *Secret keys* to be used by the cryptographic transforms.

4. *Encapsulation mode* (discussed in more detail later) which defines how the encapsulation headers are created and which part of the user traffic is actually protected during the communicating process.

5. *Security parameter index (SPI)* is the identifier of the SA. It provides information to the receiving device to know how to process the incoming traffic.

Taken as a whole, the operations that are to be performed on the user traffic are defined by the security protocol, the cryptographic operations, and the encapsulation mode.

The specific SA is unidirectional, in that it defines the operations that occur in the transmission in one direction only. Notwithstanding, a secure tunnel can also be bidirectional. This means that a pair of SAs are used for the transport of traffic in both directions. The idea of a bidirectional process is to have the two SAs use the same meta-characteristics but employ different keys. This concept is known as a bidirectional SA.

SAs may also be grouped together (which is called an SA bundle) to provide a required security feature for the traffic. For example, one SA could be used to guarantee the secrecy of the traffic and another SA could be used to guarantee the integrity of the traffic. The rule with regard to the use of SA bundles is that the destination addresses of SAs must always be the same.

Firewalls

A firewall is a system that is used to enforce an access control policy within an organization or between organizations. A firewall is not just a machine but a collection of machines and software that institutes the access control policy (a security association).

In its simplest terms, the firewall allows or forbids traffic to pass from one side to the other of the firewall. Any authorized traffic that is allowed to pass through this firewall from one network-to-another or from one host-to-another host, must be defined by the security policy established in the access control plans of the organization. Another important attribute of the firewall is that it itself must be secure. It must also be immune to penetration.

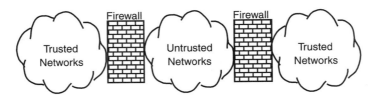

Figure 11–14   Firewalls

In its simplest terms, a firewall is a system that protects trusted networks from untrusted networks, see Figure 11–14. The trusted networks could be the internal networks of an organization and untrusted networks could perhaps be the Internet. However, the concept of trusted and untrusted systems depends on an organization. In some situations within an organization, trusted and untrusted networks could depend on the need to know and the need to protect the resources. Indeed, the concept of internal firewalls (internal to the company) and external firewalls (standing between an internal network and external networks) is an important consideration in building security mechanisms. In fact, internal firewalls are quite important because it is well known that internal hacking and security breaches are far more numerous than external hacking or external security breaches.

In summary, we can think of a firewall as a tool to an organization's security procedures, as a tool to its access control policies. It is used to accomplish the actual procedures and, therefore, it represents both the security policy and the implementation decisions of the organization.

RADIUS

In a large organization, security operations are a significant task. One of the concerns is the possible compromise of the organization's resources due to the dispersal of security measures throughout the system, resulting in a fragmented approach. To compound matters, employees, contractors, and customers need access to information, and these individuals dial-in to the organization's computers from practically anywhere. Authentication of these diverse sources must be accomplished in accordance with the organization's security policy. But how? Should there be an authentication system (a server) at each of the organization's sites? If so, how are these servers managed, how are their activities coordinated? Alternatively, should the organization deploy one centralized server to reduce the coordination efforts?

To aid an organization in establishing an integrated approach to security management, the Internet Network Working Group has published RFC 2138, the Remote Authentication Dial In User Service (Radius). This specification defines the procedures to implement an authentication server, containing a central data base that identifies the dial-in users, and the associated information to authenticate the users.

RADIUS also permits the server to consult with other servers, some may be RADIUS-based, and some may not. With this approach, the RADIUS server acts as proxy to the other server. It is however, a client/server model, and a client must initiate a request to a server, before the server can respond; that is RADIUS does not allow a server to send an unsolicited message to a client.

The specification also details how the user's specific operations can be supported, such as PPP, rlogin, telenet, etc.

Figure 11–15 shows the configuration for RADIUS. The end user communicates with the Network Access Server (NAS) through a dial-up link. In turn, the NAS is the client to the RADIUS server. The NAS and RADIUS server communicate with each other through a network, or a point-to-point link. As mentioned earlier, the RADIUS server may communicate with other servers, some may operate the RADIUS protocol, and some may not. Also, the idea is to have a central repository for the authentication information, shown in this figure as the data base icon.

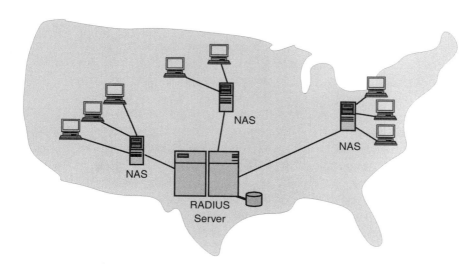

Figure 11–15   RADIUS set-up

The user is required to present authentication information to the NAS (hereafter called client), such as a user name and a password, or a PPP authentication packet. The client may then access RADIUS. If so, the client creates an Access Request message, and sends to the RADIUS node (hereafter called server). This message contains information about the user, this is called Attributes. The Attributes are defined by the RADIUS system manager, and therefore can vary. Examples of Attributes are the user's password, ID, destination port, client ID, etc. If sensitive information is contained in the Attributes field, it must be protected by the Message Digest Algorithm MD5.

The RADIUS-based request from the client must be a shared secret with the server, see Figure 11–16. Otherwise, the request is silently discarded. (nothing happens . . . no further processing). If the initial check is satisfactory, the server consults a database to authenticate the user. The database contains the information to validate the user; that is, a list of requirements.

If the authentication conditions are met, the server issues a challenge to the user in the form of an Access Challenge message. The client may relay this information to the user in the form of a prompt. Whatever the scenario may be between the user and the client, the client must resubmit the Access Request message. This message contains some different fields; the salient one for this example is an encrypted response to the challenge. The user is "challenged" by being presented with a random number, and tasked with encrypting it, and sending back the result of the encryption.

The server receives and examines this message. If all conditions are satisfied, the server returns an Access Accept message to the client. However, the RADIUS protocol goes much further than the support of authentication operations. The Access Accept message contains configuration information, such as PPP, Login User, etc. The idea is to use the RADIUS node to give the user all the information that is needed to support the user session with the network. For example, the configuration information can be an IP address for the session, compression services, maximum transmission unit size (MTU), etc.

The NAS client supports PAP and CHAP. The NAS client sends the PAP ID and password in the Access Request message in the User–Name and User-Password fields of the message. If CHAP is used, the NAS client generates a challenge and sends it to the user. In accordance with CHAP conventions, the user responds with the CHAP ID and CHAP user name. The NAS client then sends to the RADIUS server the Access Request message, containing the CHAP user name in the Access Request

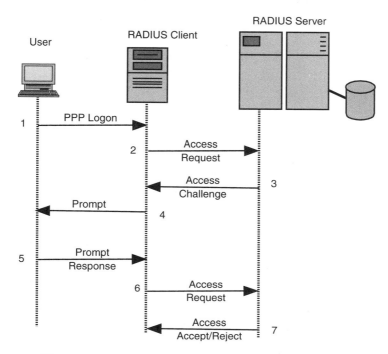

Figure 11–16   The RADIUS message exchange

message User Name, and the CHAP ID and CHAP response in the Access Request message CHAP-Password attribute.

DIAMETER

DIAMETER is used in VoIP Gatekeepers and Call Agents. It has been created to define common formats for security messages. It is considered by some to be a successor to RADIUS. The DIAMETER protocol defines these formats in a header, followed by objects. The objects are known as Attribute-Value-Pair (AVP). The Internet draft for DIAMETER is [CALH98a].[4]

Figure 11–17 shows the architecture for DIAMETER. It consists of a base protocol and the Resource Management and Accounting Manage-

---

[4][CALH98a] Calhoun, Pat R. DIAMETER Framework Document, Draft-calhoun-diameter-framework-01.txt.

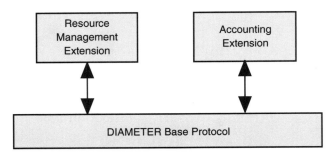

Figure11–17   DIAMETER architecture

ment extensions. The base protocol performs authentication and privacy services, version negotiation, feature discovery, and the overall coding and decoding of the messages, including those of the extensions. The base protocol permits a server to send unsolicited messages to a client.

Feature discovery is used to increase the efficiency of configuring clients and servers. The idea is to provide an easy means to locate a policy server (or servers) in a network, and use DIAMETER messages to retrieve information from the policy server.

DIAMETER supports interserver communications, for example between different domains, such as to different ISPs. For example, assume a person travels to another part of the world and does not wish to incur the long distance charges for dialing-in to the user's ISP. If a local ISP has an agreement with the user's home ISP, DIAMETER can be used to set up the needed configurations for the user to access the local ISP. This concept is called *Proxy Support.*

The *Resource Management* extension allows two nodes to share session information about internet users. For example, if a user needs reserved bandwidth, a designated server keeps track of the user's request and the resources associated with the session. Another example is simply keeping track of a user session to ensure that users are not giving their account number, and domain name to other users, thus permitting multiple logins with a single account.

The *Accounting* extension allows accounting records to be shared and exchanged between servers. In the example of the roaming user, two ISPs can use the Accounting extension to aid in their revenue sharing agreements (if any).

DIAMETER's procedures define a request/response protocol, and each message is identified as request or response. I will use DIAMETER's authentication procedures to show examples of DIAMETER messages, which are identified with command codes [CALH98b].[5] The messages are:

- *Domain-Discovery-Request:* Used to obtain contact information about a domain's home authentication server.
- *Domain-Discovery-Answer:* Sent in response to the request message.
- *AA-Request:* Used to request authentication and authorization for a user.
- *AA-Answer:* Used to indicate the authentication and /or authorization was successful.
- *AA-Challenge-Ind:* Used by a server to challenge another entity.

DIAMETER has other capabilities and services, and they are described in the Internet drafts. One other reference should prove useful if you wish more information; see [CALH98c].[6]

IPDC

The IP Device Control Protocol (IPDC) is an important component of the Media Gateway Control Protocol (MGCP), which is explained in Chapter 8. The protocol operates between the Media Gateway and the Media Gateway Controller, and is only implemented if these entities are separate from each other. The relationships of IPDC and MGCP are shown in Figure 11–18. IPDC resides at reference point N in the Call Model described in Chapter 9 (see Figure 9–1). The protocol defines the IP Signaling Transport (IPST) message set for the MGC to perform call and media control on the MG. Several Internet drafts are in various stages of development, and I refer you to [TAYL98][7] for the basic information on IPDC.

IPDC is based on DIAMETER, and uses many of its features. It uses the following messages for its operations:

- *Command-Unrecognized-Indication:* Used to indicate a message was received that is not understood.
- *Device-Reboot-Indication:* Send by a DIAMETER device to inform peer that the sender has rebooted.

---

[5][CALH98b]. Calhoun, Pat R., et al. DIAMETER User Authentication Extensions. Draft-calhoun-diameter-authent-04.txt.

[6][CALH98c]. Calhoun, Pat R., et al. DIAMETER Base Protocol. Draft-calhoun-diameter-03.txt.

[7][TAYL98]. Taylor, Tom. IPDC Protocol, Draft-ipdc-00.txt., July , 1998.

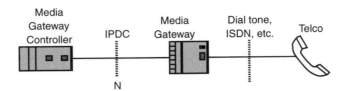

Figure 11–18   Placement of IPDC

- *Device-Watchdog-Indication:* Used to ping to peers as a keepalive mechanism.
- *Device-Feature-Query:* Used to query a peer about its supported extensions.
- *Device-Feature-Reply:* Sent in response to the query message.
- *Device-Config-Request:* Sent to peers under the administrative control of the sender to provide configuration information.
- *Device-Config-Answer:* Sent in response to the request message.

The IPDC defines a wide variety of AVPs, such as IP address, host name, version numbers, and various security values. Many of the AVPs deal with configuration parameters such as timers, buffers, transmission retry counts, and so on.

IPDC also defines a number of facilities for interworking the telco signaling operations with an IP network. In this regard, there are a lot of similar functions between IPDC and the IPS7 protocols discussed in Chapter 10. For example, IPDC defines several capabilities for interworking with SS7 and ISDN, and so do the IPS7 specifications.

IPDC defines two modes of signaling for the interworking function (IWF), shown in Figure 11–19. Native Mode Q.931 Signaling uses the ITU-T Q.931 messages to transport signaling information between the MGC and MG. The IWF resides in the MG, and terminates the external signaling protocol by mapping the Q.931 messages to the external signaling operations, and vice versa. The second mode is called Tunneled Mode Signaling, and translates into a simpler MG. With this mode, the MG does not process the Q.931 messages, but passes them to the MGC for processing.

To show how IPDC operates, we take one example from [BELL98],[8] shown in Figure 11–20. Here is a description of each event:

---

[8][BELL98]. Bell, Bob, IPDC Device Management Protocol, Draft-bell-ipdc-signaling-00.txt.

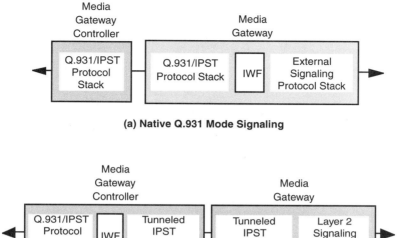

(a) Native Q.931 Mode Signaling

(b) Tunneled Mode Signaling

Figure 11–19   IPDC interworking functions

- *Event 1:* The MG receives a seizure signal from the telco device. Appendix A provides a tutorial on these signals.
- *Event 2:* The MG responds to the seizure signal with a return wink. At this point, the MG begins to monitor the links for dialed digits.
- *Event 3:* The MG collects a specific number of the dialed digits.
- *Event 4:* After the MG has collected enough information, it forms a Q.931 SETUP message, formatted as an AVP message, and sends it to the MGC.
- *Event 5:* The ALERTING message is returned to the MG, to inform the MG that the called party is being rung.
- *Event 6:* The called party answers, and the MGC sends the CON-NECT message to the MG.
- *Event 7:* The Seizure signal is returned to the telco device.
- *Event 8:* After all checks have been made (continuity checks, not shown here), the parties can talk to each other.
- *Event 9:* One party hangs up the telephone, causing the MGC to send a RELEASE message to the MG.
- *Events 10 and 11:* The link is released with the release seizure signals.

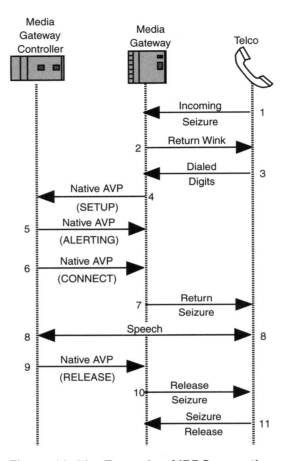

Figure 11–20   Example of IPDC operations

DIFFSERV

The Differentiated Services Model (DiffServ) is under development by the Internet DiffServ Working Group. I refer you to [CLAR97][9] for the details of the model.

The main ideas of DiffServ are to: (a) classify traffic at the boundaries of network, and (b) possibly condition this traffic at the boundaries.

---

[9][CLAR97].Clark, D. and Wroclawski, J. "An Approach to Service Allocation in the Internet," Draft-clark-diff-svc-alloc-00.txt.

The classification operation entails the assignment of the traffic to behavioral aggregates. These behavioral aggregates are a collection of packets with common characteristics, as far as how they are identified and treated by the network. The classification operation in this network classifies the packets based on the content of the packet headers.

The identified traffic is assigned a value (a differentiated services [DS] codepoint. For IPv4, the codepoint is in the TOS field; for Ipv6, the codepoint is in the traffic class octet.

After the packets have been classified at the boundary of the network, they are forwarded through the network based on the DS codepoint. The forwarding is performed on a per-hop basis; that is, the DS node alone decides how the forwarding is to be carried-out. This concept is called per-hop-behavior (PHB)

DiffServ uses the idea of a DS domain, as shown in Figure 11–21. It could be a collection of networks operating under an administration that could be a DS domain, say an ISP. It is responsible for meeting a service level agreement (SLA) between the user and the DS domain service provider.

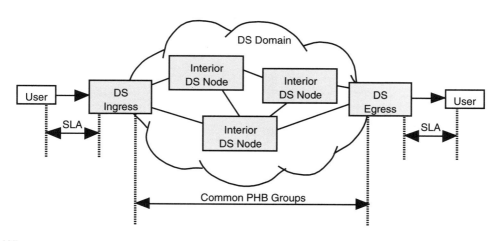

Where:
  DS   DiffServ
  PHB   Per-hop-behavior
  SLA   Service level agreement

Figure 11–21   The DS domain

The DS domain consists of a contiguous set of nodes that are DS-compliant, and agree to a common set of service provisioning policies. The DS domain also operates with a common per-hop-behavior (PHB) definitions (more than one PHB is allowed, and are called PHB groups). The PHB defines how a collection of packets with the same DS codepoint are treated.

The DS domain contains DS boundary nodes that are responsible for the classifying operations, and the possible conditioning of ingress traffic. I will have more to say about conditioning later; for this introduction, it consists of controlling the traffic to make sure it "behaves" according to the rules of the DS domain (and one hopes, the desires of the user).

Once past the ingress node, and inside the DS domain, the internal nodes forward packets based on the DS codepoint. Their job is to map the DS codepoint value to a supported PHB. Thus, there are DS boundary nodes and DS interior nodes. The DS boundary nodes connect the DS domain to other DS domains or noncompliant systems. There is no restriction on what type of machine executes the boundary or interior node operations. For instance, a host might play the role of a DS boundary node.

Regardless of what machine runs the DS boundary node functions, it must act as an ingress node and egress node for traffic flowing into and out of the DS domain. It is responsible for supporting traffic conditioning agreements (TCAs) with other domains. Traffic conditioning means the enforcement of rules dealing with traffic management and includes for major operations: (a) metering, (b) marking, (c) shaping, and (c) policing, see Figure 11–22.

Metering entails the measuring rate of a stream of traffic. Marking entails setting the DS codepoint. Shaping entails the emission of traffic (perhaps the delaying of it) to meet a defined traffic emission profile. Policing entails the discarding of packets (based on the state of the meter) to enforce a defined traffic profile.[10]

Multiple DS domains constitute a DS region. These regions are able to support differentiated services along paths in the domains that make up the DS region. One advantage to defining a DS region is that DiffServ allows the DS domains in the DS region to support different PHB groups. For example, a DS domain on a college campus may have different PHB groups than a DS domain in an ISP, yet these two "peering" domains must be able to interwork in a predictable and structured manner. They must define a peering SLA that establishes a TCA for the traffic that

---

[10]The term policing has a limited definition in DiffServ.

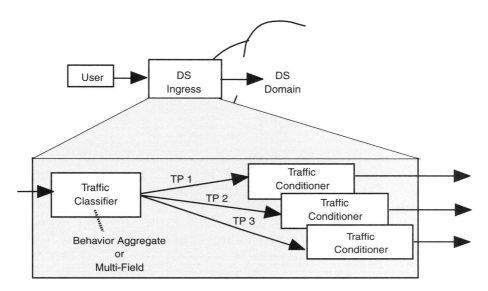

Figure 11–22   Traffic classifiers and traffic conditioners

flows between them. Of course, it might happen that these domains set up common PHB groups and codepoint mappings. That being the case, there would be no need for traffic conditioning between the two DS domains.

The DS node must provide traffic classification and traffic conditioning operations. The job of packet classification is to identify subsets of traffic that are to receive differentiated services by the DS domain. Classifiers operate in two modes: (a) the behavior aggregate classifier (BA) classifies packets only on the DS codepoint, (b) the multi-field classifier classifies packets by multiple fields in the packet, such as addresses, port numbers, and so on.

The classifiers provide the mechanism to guide the packets to a traffic conditioner for more processing. The traffic stream selected by the classifier is based on a specific set of traffic profiles, such as variable or constant bit rates, jitter, delay, etc.

The packets presented to a specific traffic conditioner may be in-profile, or out-of-profile. In-profile means the packets are "conformant" to the user-network SLA. Out-of-profile packets are outside an SLA, or due to network behavior, arrive at the traffic conditioner at a rate that requires the conditioner to condition them (delay their delivery, drop them, etc.).

As a general practice, classification and conditioning operations take place at the network boundaries. Nothing precludes the internal nodes from invoking these operations, but their classification and conditioning operations are more limited than the boundary nodes.

LABEL-SWAPPING PROTOCOLS

A separate book in this series is being devoted to label swapping, but we should mention it here because the technology offers a very fast, low delay switching service to IP datagrams, and fast, low delay is a vital part of reducing latency in VoIP traffic.

Several methods are employed to implement label swapping, also known as label switching or tag switching. Many of them are similar . . . variations on the same theme.

Some techniques use the concept of a flow, which is a sequence of user packets from one source machine or application to one or more machines or applications. For a "long" flow (many packets flowing between these entities), a router can cache information about the flow and circumvent the traditional IP-routing mechanisms (subnet masking, search on longest subnet mask, and so on) by storing the routing information in cache, thus achieving high throughput, and low delay.

One of the key aspects of high-speed forwarding systems is the use of a label or tag to identify the traffic. The assignment of the value to a packet varies, depending on the vendor's approach and/or the standard employed (an Internet RFC). The idea is to use a tag instead of the cumbersome IP address to make switching decisions.

SUMMARY

This chapter has provided a broad overview of some of the key supporting protocols to H.323, MGCP, and IPS7, discussed in Chapter 9 and 10. With the exception of a few RFCs, most of the VoIP specifications discussed in this chapter are working drafts, and should be treated accordingly.

12

Other Packet Voice Alternatives

V oIP is not the only way to transport voice traffic over non-telephony networks. Indeed, there are two alternatives discussed in this chapter that are efficient, fast, and can yield toll-quality signals at a reasonable cost. They are voice over Frame Relay (VoFR), and voice over ATM (VoATM).[1] A third alternative, voice over Ethernet, was explained in Chapter 9, as H.323 which runs on local area networks.

VOICE OVER FRAME RELAY (VoFR)

During the years of 1996 to 1998, the Frame Relay Forum added new features to Frame Relay, principally to support real-time traffic, such as voice. The following discussion provides a synopsis of these operations, and describes the three functions: (a) PVC fragmentation, (b) Service Multiplexing and (c) voice over Frame Relay (VoFR). We begin this discussion with an analysis of PVC fragmentation.

---

[1]This series includes three books on ATM. For more information on Frame Relay, I naturally recommend [BLAC98], Black, Uyless. *Frame Relay Networks*. New York: McGraw Hill Signature Edition, 1998.

PVC Fragmentation

The fragmentation operation was developed by the Frame Relay Forum to support delay-sensitive traffic such as voice connections. One approach is to multiplex the shorter frames onto the same physical interface that support longer frames. In other words, it is possible to interleave delay-sensitive traffic (in shorter frames) and non-delay sensitive traffic (in longer frames). Obviously, this feature allows the sharing of the link by both real-time and non-real-time traffic. The size of the fragments is implementation-specific and the fragment size can be configured based on the attributes of the line and interface as well as local clocking mechanisms, such as a channelized or an unchannelized interface. The idea is to allow each local interface to be responsible for fragmentation.

Fragmentation operations can be implemented at (a) the user network interface (UNI), (b) network to network interface (NNI), or (c) end-to-end. Figure 12–1 shows these three fragmentation models. The term DTE stands for data terminal equipment and it identifies the end user device. The term DCE stands for data circuit terminating equipment and it identifies a Frame Relay node, such as a router or multiplexer. The UNI fragmentation operation is local to an interface and can take advantage of transporting larger frames over the backbone network at the high bandwidths of the backbone links. The transmission of these longer frames is more efficient than the transport of a larger number of smaller fragments. In addition, in case a DTE does not implement fragmentation, this model allows the network to act as a proxy for this DTE.

Figure 12–2 shows the format for the fragmentation header for end-to-end fragmentation. The low-order bit of the first octet (octet 3) of the fragmentation header is set to 1 and the low-order bit of the Frame Relay header is set to 0 (octet 0). These bit settings are used to distinguish the headers from each other and for the receiver to be aware if it is receiving the proper header, and thus acts as a checkpoint that the fragmentation peers are configured properly. The contents of the header follows.

The first two octets consist of the conventional Frame Relay header. Octets 3–6 consist of the fragmentation header. Let's look at octet 5 first.

The beginning (B) bit is set to one for the first data fragment of the original frame. It is set to 0 for all other fragments of the frame. The ending (E) fragment bit is set to 1 for the last data fragment of the original data frame and it is set to 0 for all other data fragments. A data fragment can be both a beginning and ending fragment, therefore it can have both the B and E bits set to 1.

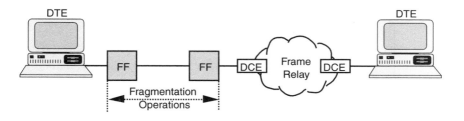

(a) At the UNI

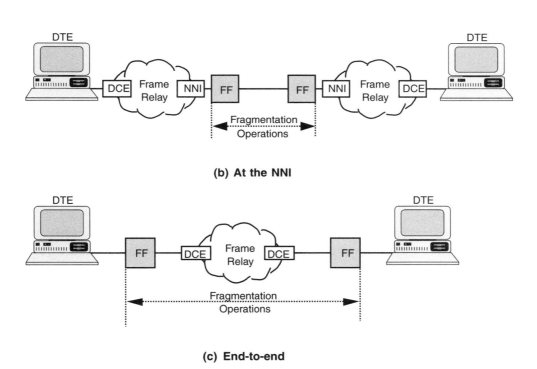

(b) At the NNI

(c) End-to-end

Figure 12–1   Fragmentation function (FF) operations

The control (C) bit is set to 0 and is not used in the current implementation agreement. It is reserved for future operations.

The sequence number (octets 5 and 6) is incremented for each data fragment transmitted on the link. A separate sequence number is maintained for each DLCI in the interfaces.

Bit 8	Bit 7	Bit 6	Bit 5	Bit 4	Bit 3	Bit 2	Bit 1	Octet
DLCI high six bits						C/R	0	1
DLCI low four bits				F	B	DE	1	2
0	0	0	0	0	0	1	1	3
1	0	1	1	0	0	0	1	4
B	E	C	Sequence number of high order 4 bits				R	5
Sequence number of low order 8 bits								6
Payload								5-n
Frame Check Sequence (FCS)								5-n+2

Figure 12–2   The fragmentation header

The end-to-end fragmentation also uses the multiprotocol encapsulation operation in accordance with Frame Relay Forum's specification FRF.3.1, titled "Multiprotocol Encapsulation Agreement." The unnumbered information (UI) octet (octet 3) is used for this process (0x03), and the network layer protocol ID (NLPID) value of 0xB1 has been assigned to identify the fragmentation header format (octet 4). The format for the DTE-to-DTE operation is shown in Figure 12–3.

Fragmentation Operations

The fragmentation procedures are based on RFC 1990, titled "The Point-to-Point Protocol (PPP) Multilink Protocol (MP)", August 1996. An example of fragmentation and reassembly operations is shown in Figure 12–3. The Q.922, optional PAD, and the NLPID fields are removed by the transmitter and placed in the first fragment. Each fragment must be transmitted in the same order as its relative position in its original frame, although fragments from multiple PVCs may be interleaved with each other across one interface. The receiving machine must keep track of the incoming sequence numbers and use the beginning and ending bits for proper reassembly of traffic. If lost fragments are detected and/or sequence numbers skipped, the receiver must discard all currently assembled fragments and fragments subsequently received for that PVC until it receives the first fragment of a new frame (that is to say a new beginning bit).

The data field of the original packet is broken up (fragmented) and the NLPID, B bit, E bit, and sequence number fields are all added to track the original packet. The B and E bits act as discussed in previous discussions. The sequence number is incremented for each data fragment to delineate the order of the transmission.

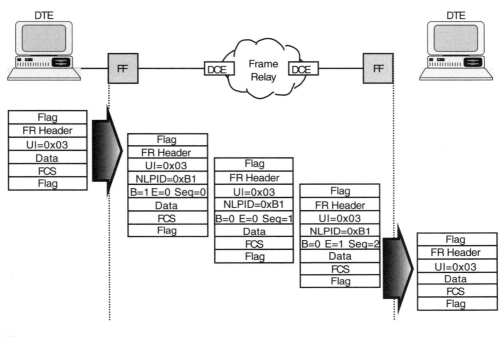

Where:
B, E	Beginning and ending bits
FCS	Frame check sequence
FR	Frame Relay
NLPID	Network level protocol ID
UI	Unnumbered information

Figure 12–3   Example of end-to-end fragmentation

SERVICE MULTIPLEXING

Due to the wide-scale use of Frame Relay, considerable effort has been made in expanding Frame Relay networks to support voice traffic. The Frame Relay Forum has published a specification for this process. It is titled, "Voice over Frame Relay Implementation Agreement—FRF.11".

The major components of this specification deal with analog-to-digital (A/D), digital-to-analog (D/A), voice compression operations, and the transmission of the digitized images in a Frame Relay frame. In addition to the transfer of the voice traffic, the frames can also convey data, and fax images, as well as the signaling needed to set up, manage, and tear down the voice or fax connection. Support is provided for dialed digits,

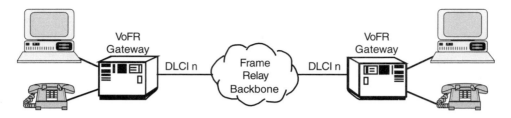

Figure 12–4   Service multiplexing

line seizures, and other needed signals used in telephony, such as the ABCD signaling bits.

One of the key components of voice over Frame Relay (VoFR) is called service multiplexing, which supports multiple voice and data channels on a single Frame Relay connection. This concept is shown in Figure 12–4. Multiple streams of user traffic (which are called subchannels) consisting of different voice and data transmission flows are multiplexed across one DLCI (DLCI n in this example). VoFR is responsible for delivering the frames to the receiving user in the order in which they were sent from the transmitting user.

Subchannels and the DLCIs

Figure 12–5 shows the relationships of the subchannels to the DLCIs. The user applications at A and B are multiplexed into one virtual circuit, identified with DLCI 5. The user application at C is multiplexed into another virtual circuit, identified with DLCI 9. It is the job of the VoFR gateway to assemble the subchannels to the Frame Relay frame. If two users are sending traffic that pertains to one overall traffic flow (for example, a conversation on the telephone that discusses the data exchanged and exhibited on a workstation screen), Frame Relay does not define how these two images are played out at the receiver's machines. This aspect of multiservice multiplexing is left to specific vendor implementations.

VoFR

All the operations discussed thus far in this chapter are supporting procedures to VoFR, although some of them can be used for other types of traffic. For speech, VoFR defines several specifications on the coding of the voice traffic. The reader can refer to the Annexes in FRF.11 for more

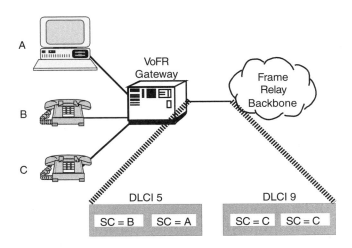

Figure 12–5   Subchannel (SC) concept

detail. For your convenience, the technologies that are supported are listed in Table 12–1. I have added an entry in the table to include another specification (ITU-T G.723 and Annexes) that will surely be used, but is not part of FRF.11 at this time. All organizations that belong to the International Media Teleconferencing Consortium (IMTC) have all selected G.723.1 for their basic coder.

Servicing the Dialed Digits

The telephone dialed digit payload contains the dialed digits entered by the calling party as well as several control parameters. The transmission occurs over an all-digital network and the telephone signals are dual tone multi-frequency (DTMF) signals. Because DTMF is not permitted in the VoFR specifications, binary representations are substituted for the analog signals.

In accordance with [FRF.1197],[2] a 20-ms window is used to encode the edge when a digit is turned on and off. This is the delta time, 0 to 19 ms, from the beginning of the current frame in ms. If there is no transition, the edge location will be set to 0 and the digit type of the previous windows will be repeated.

---

[2][FR.1197] "Voice over Frame Relay Implementation Agreement," Frame Relay Forum Document number FRF.11, 1997.

Table 12–1   Voice support in VoFR

Reference Document	Description
ITU G.729/ITU G.729 Annex A	Coding of Speech at 8 kbit/s using Conjugate Structure-Algebraic code Excited Linear Predictive (CS-ACELP) Coding, March 1996
ITU G.711	Pulse Code Modulation of Voice Frequencies, 1988
ITU G.726	40, 32, 24, 16 kbit/s Adaptive Differential Pulse Code Modulation (ADPCM), March 1996
ITU G.727	5-, 4-, 3-, and 2 bits Sample Embedded Adaptive Differential Pulse Code Modulation, November 1994
ITU G.764	Voice packetization—Packetized voice protocols, December 1990
ITU G.728	Coding of Speech at 16 kbit/s Using Low-Delay Code Excited Linear Prediction, November 1994
ITU G.723.1	Dual Rate Speech Coder for Multimedia Communications Transmitting at 5.3 & 6.3 kbit/s, March 1996
ITU G.723.1, Annex A	Silence Compression Scheme, March 1996
ITU G.723.1, Annex B	Alternative Specification Based on Floating Point Arithmetic, March 1996
ITU G.723.1, Annex C	Scaleable Channel Coding Scheme for Wireless Applications, March 1996

Figure 12–6 shows an example of how the dialed digits are placed into the dialed digit payload. When the VoFR transmitter detects a dialed digit from the calling party, it starts sending a dialed digit payload which is repeated every 20 ms. Each payload covers 60 ms of digit on/off edge information. Consequently, there is redundancy of edge information. Upon the VoFR receiver receiving the dialed digit payload, it generates the dialed digits according to the location of the on and off edges. After an off-edge and before an on-edge, silence is applied to the duration and digits are generated after an on-edge and before an off-edge.

For the next procedures, I quote directly from [FRF.1197].

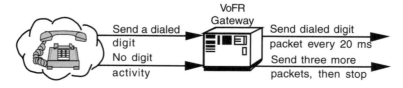

Figure 12–6   Procedure for the dialed digits

Procedure for Transmitting Dialed Digit Payloads.   When the transmitter detects a validated digit, it will start sending a dialed digit payload every 20 ms. Since each payload covers 60 ms of digit on/off edge information; there is redundancy of the edge information. The sequence number is incremented by one in each transmitted payload.

When the digit activity is off, the transmitter should continue to send three more dialed digit payloads for 60 ms.

Procedure for Interpreting Received Dialed Digit Payloads.   When the receiver gets a dialed digit payload, it will generate digits according to the location of the on and off edges. Silence will be applied to the duration after an off-edge and before an on-edge. Digits will be generated after an on-edge and before an off-edge.

If the sequence number is one greater than the last received sequence number, the receiver appends the current edge information to the previously received information.

If the sequence number is two greater than the last received sequence number, the receiver appends the recent and current edge information to the previously received information.

If the sequence number is three greater than the last received sequence number, the receiver appends the previous, recent and current edge information to the previously received information.

If the sequence number is more than three greater than the last received sequence number, the receiver appends the previous, recent and current edge information to the previously received information. It fills in the gap with the static values based on the previously received payload.

If a voice packet is received at anytime, an off-edge should be appended to the previously received digits on/off edge information.

As shown in Figure 12–7, if the signaling bits do not change for 500 ms the VoFR transmitter alters the frequency that it sends the signaling packets to one every 5 s. During this period of signaling inactivity, the se-

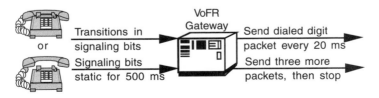

Figure 12–7   Procedures for processing the signaling bits

quence number is not incremented, which allows the receiver to discard this packet (or use the first value to set its current values).

Fax Transmission

Fax traffic is transported by VoFR using the same concepts employed for data, dial digits, or signaling traffic. The fax traffic is encapsulated into the Frame Relay sub-frame, and remains transparent to the Frame Relay network. The VoFR gateway is responsible for handling the fax-specific operations. Figure 12–8 shows an example of VoFR fax operations.

VoFR supports the world-wide standard for Group 3 facsimile systems, which is defined in ITU-T T.4 (1993). In addition to T.4, VoFR supports several ITU-T V Series modems, as well as the V.17 fax specification for 7.2, 9.6, 12.0, and 14.4 kbit/s transmission rates.

Since Frame Relay must convey fax and modem control signals between the user machines, the VoFR subframe for fax traffic is coded to identify operating parameters that are needed between the sending and receiving fax/modems. As examples, the subframe contains information on the modulation type used by the sending modem, the type of modem (V.17, V.33, etc.), the bit/s rate (14.4 kbit/s, etc.).

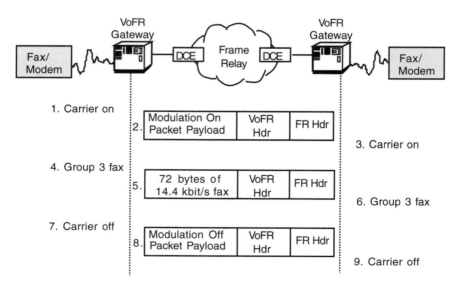

Figure 12–8 Example of VoFR support for fax transmissions

The fax/modem information elements are placed in octet 2c of the payload element of the subframe. This payload packet is called the modulation turn-on packet. This packet is sent when the VoFR gateway detects a frequency tone, at which time the VoFR sends at least three of these packets. The EI1 and EI2 bits are set to 1 and 0, respectively (they are header extension bits), and the sequence number remains at 0 during this handshake phase. The Relay Command field is set to 011 (modulation-on) to indicate that a carrier has been detected. The time-stamp is used to provide timing to the demodulator, and is coded in 1-ms units and must be accurate to +/− 5 ms. The timing assumes free-running clocks with no synchronization between them. The HDLC bit is used if an HDLC frame is used between the modems (bit = 1, HDLC is applied).

The modulation type is set to identify the type of modem that is sending this information. This information is conveyed in analog signals to the VoFR gateway, which converts the signals to 4-bit codes. For our example, the modulation type code for a 14.4 kbit/s V.17 fax/modem is 1011. A field in the frame is the frequency information element, and it is coded to indicate the sending modem's frequency tone.

The VoFR gateway continues to interpret the fax/modems analog signals and maps them into the Frame Relay subframes. After the handshake, it places the fax images into the subframes and sends them to the receiving VoFR gateway. At this machine, the data fields in the subframe are mapped back to analog signals for interpretation and processing at the receiving fax/modem.

VoFR Encapsulation

Table 12–1 lists the coder specifications that are supported by VoFR. I have selected G.723 because of its prevalent use in the industry and the fact that is it being supported as the preferred coder specification by the International Media Teleconferencing Consortium (IMTC). G.723 is described in more detail in Chapter 4.

The coder operates on frames of 240 samples each to support the 8000 sample-per-second input speech stream. Further operations (a highpass filter to remove the DC component) result in four subframes of 60 ms each. A variety of other operations occur, such as the computation of an LPC filter, and unquantized LCP filter coefficients, etc. resulting in a packetization time of 30 ms.

After the digitized frames are created by the coder, they are encapsulated into the VoFR voice information field, as shown in Figure 12–9. For MP-MLQ, the information field is 24 octets, and for ACELP, the in-

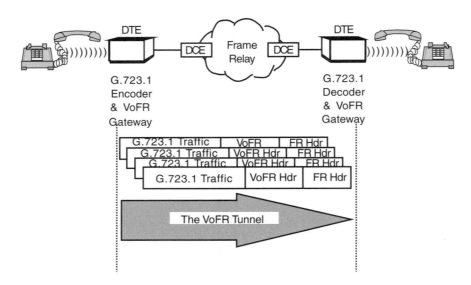

Figure 12–9   Transport of voice traffic

formation field is 20 octets. They are transported through the Frame Relay network and passed to the decoder. The decoder converts the digital images to the output voice signal, which is played out to the receiver.

VOICE OVER ATM (VoATM)

The ITU-T has issued a draft recommendation on the ATM Adaptation Layer type 2 (AAL 2). It is published in ITU-T I.363.2. The concept of AAL 2 is to provide a mechanism for sending small packets (such as voice, since AAL 2 targets packet telephony) over an ATM network in a manner that ensures small delay. AAL 2 supports the multiplexing of multiple connections into one cell, thus avoiding the unattractive aspect of sending cells through the network that are partially filled. The connections are called LLCs, for logical link connections.

AAL 2 supports the multiplexing of variable length packets, a service that is quite important in accommodating to variable bit-rate coders and silence compression. Indeed, a fixed-length requirement would mean only efficient accommodation to CBR applications, all using the same coders. This method, called *position-based multiplexing and delineation* is simply too rigid to service modern telephony requirements.

The ITU-T specification is still in the draft stages, but the following aspects are firm enough to warrant their description here, see Figure 12–10.

The fields in the 48 bytes are grouped into the start field, the CPS-packet header, the payload and the PAD. The functions of the fields are as follows (we examine the CPS-packet header first):

- The CID value identifies the AAL type 2 CPS user of the channel. The AAL type 2 channel is a bidirectional channel. The same value of channel identification shall be used for both directions.

  The value 0 is not used for channel identification because the all zero octet is used for the padding function. The values 1 ... 7 are reserved for management operations.

- The LI field is one less than the number of octets in the CPS-packet payload. The default maximum length of the CPS-packet payload is 45 octets; otherwise, the maximum length can be set to 64 octets.

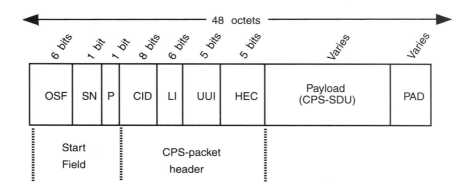

Note: CPS-packet header may exist more than once in ATM-SDU

OSF   Offset field
SN   Sequence number
P   Parity
CID   Channel ID
LI   Length indicator
UUI   User-to-user indication
HEC   Header error control
PAD   Padding bytes, if needed

Figure 12–10   The new AAL type 2

- The UUI field conveys information transparently between the CPS users and layer management to distinguish between the SSCS entities and management users of the CPS.

- HEC is used by the transmitter to calculate the remainder of the division (modulo 2), by the generator polynomial $x^5 + x^2 + 1$, of the product of x^5 and the contents of the first 19 bits of the CPS-PH. The coefficients of the remainder polynomial are inserted in the HEC field with the coefficient of the x^4 term in the most significant bit of the HEC field. The receiver uses the contents of the HEC field to detect errors in the CPS-PH.

- The OSF carries the binary value of the offset, measured in number of octets, between the end of the start field and the first start of a CPS-packet or, in the absence of a first start, to the start of the PAD field. The value 47 indicates that there is no start boundary in the CPS-PDU payload. Values greater than 47 are not allowed.

- The SN bit is used to number (modulo 2) the stream of CPS-PDUs.

- The P bit is used by the receiver to detect errors in the start field.

Figure 12–11 provides an example of how AAL 2 supports voice traffic. We assume a voice over ATM (VoATM) gateway accepts analog speech at the sender and digitizes it, thus creating G.729.A voice packets, which are presented to AAL 2. At the receiving VoATM gateway, this process is reversed.

The G.729.A recommendation is designed for low-bit rate audio coders and operates at 8 kbit/s. Each G.729.A frame is 10 octets in length. For this example the voice packet is encapsulated with the Real-Time Protocol (RTP), thus creating a 14 octet packet (the RTP header is 4 octets in length).

The offset field points to the start of the packet. This field is placed in the first octet of the 48-octet ATM-SDU. The RTP/G.729.A packet is appended with the LL2 packet header and these 17 octets are placed in the cell payload. The process simply loads the ATM-SDU with contiguous 17 octets until the 48 octets are filled. In this example, the third packet is placed in the last part of the first cell and the first part of the second cell. The offset field in the second cell points to the first CPS packet header, which is the fourth packet in this stream. The length of the packet is indicated in the packet header, therefore, and in this example, it is used to identify the remaining octets of the third packet residing in the second cell.

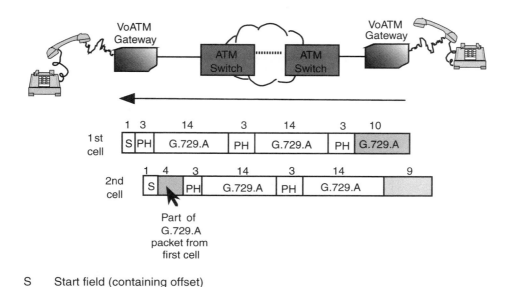

S   Start field (containing offset)
PH   Packet header

Figure 12–11   AAL 2 support of voice traffic

This example shows support of voice only, with fixed-length packets. AAL 2 can also support voice and data traffic by multiplexing these applications together, and identifying each traffic stream (fixed-length voice, and variable-length data) with a unique channel identifier (CID). The AAL 2 operations to handle these applications are like the example in this figure: The offset field identifies the packet boundaries, and those packets that cannot fit into one cell are segmented and the packet's remaining octets are placed in the next cell.

VoFR AND VoATM: PARTNERS WITH OR COMPETITORS TO VoIP?

The VoFR and VoATM approaches do not define the details needed to develop a full telephony supported system. Certainly, ATM furnishes the tools for carrying voice traffic through an ATM network and provides the means to negotiate the required level of service for this traffic. But it does not define the important procedures for interworking with the telephone user, for mapping the telephone signals into packets, etc. The same situation holds true for Frame Relay, although Frame Relay is a more complete packet voice specification than is ATM.

The emerging VoIP specifications will provide this level of detail, as described in several chapters in this book. The VoIP standards, even though not finished, will eventually be complete, and will provide sufficient detail for the designer to implement a complete standardized package.

What Resides in the User Workstation?

It is my view that Frame Relay and ATM will play a role in packet telephony, but the role will be one of supporting VoIP in Frame Relay and (especially) ATM backbone networks. Why? Because Frame Relay and ATM (with rare exceptions) do not reside in user PCs and workstations, and therefore, cannot compete with IP at the user workstation (at least at this stage of evolution of the industry). This point was made in Chapter 1 (see Figure 1–2).

However (and again at this stage of the game), ATM and Frame Relay can complement VoIP by acting as the high-speed transport backbone network for the VoIP traffic. With this approach, we can take advantage of the very fast label switching techniques of ATM (and secondarily, Frame Relay).

What Resides in the Backbone Network?

The focus to support a high-speed ATM-based backbone using label switching has been the subject of intense study and debate for the past several years. The interest stems from the fact that traditional software-based routing is too slow to handle the large traffic loads in the Internet or an internet. Even with enhanced techniques, such as a fast-table lookup for certain datagrams, the load on the router is often more than the router can handle. The result may be lost traffic, lost connections, and overall poor performance in the IP-based network. Label switching, in contrast to IP routing, is proving to be an effective solution to the problem.

Several methods are employed to implement label or tag switching. Many of them are similar ... variations on the same theme. One technique is called tag switching, and another is called multiprotocol label switching (MPLS).

Some techniques use the concept of a flow, which is a sequence of user packets from one source machine or application to one or more machines or applications. For a "long" flow (many packets flowing between these entities), a router can cache information about the flow. Thus, it circumvents the traditional IP routing mechanisms (subnet masking, search on longest subnet mask, and so on) by storing the routing information in cache, thus achieving high throughput, and low delay. Yet, even this situation is changing. Several manufacturers are in the process of designing high-speed routers that they claim will not need to use ATM as the switching fabric. I call this concept Layer 3 Switching.

LAYER-3 SWITCHING

A large community holds that the use of an underlying Frame Relay or ATM switching fabric is not efficient because it adds additional, superfluous logic and overhead to the system. This community is involved with the design of routers that operate directly on the IP address, and do not correlate the address to a label. This approach focuses on a multigigabit router (MGR), that uses Layer-3 switching techniques.

Figure 12–12 shows the overall architecture for the MGR. We will assume the packets enter the router from the left and exit to the right. The router contains multiple line cards (which support one or more interfaces), and forwarding engine cards, all connected to a switch. The arriving packet has its header removed and passed through the switch to the

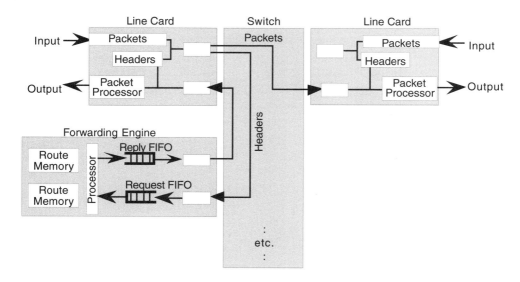

Figure 12–12   Layer 3 switching

forwarding engine card, while the other part of the packet is stored on the incoming line card. The forwarding engine examines the header, determines the routing for the packet, updates the header, and forwards it back to the incoming line card, with associated forwarding information. Then, this line card appends the revised header to the other part of the packet, and sends the reconstituted packet to the appropriate outgoing line card.

The MGR has a total capacity of 50 Gbit/s. Its packets-per-second rate (PPS) is cited at 32 MPPS. While there is variable delay in the router, it is quite small, and the vendors of these machines believe it will give the performance needed to support high-quality VoIP traffic in a public network.

SUMMARY

Very soon, the issues surrounding VoFR, VoATM, and VoIP will be decided by the marketplace. With the notable success of Frame Relay, and its presence in the marketplace, the technology will be a force for some time. If ATM continues its rapid (and recent) growth, it to will not be dislodged easily. For the foreseeable future, it is likely that these technologies will coexist. The deciding factors will be the acceptance of IP-based/packet-based protocols such as MGCP, H.323, IPS7, as well as Layer-3 Switching.

Appendix A
Telephony Signaling

Several discussions in this book are about the interworking of the telephone system with packet networks. This appendix provides the information you need to follow the telephony-IP internetworking discussions.

THE LOCAL LOOP

As depicted in Figure A–1, the line connecting a telephone to the telephone service provider—the central office (CO), consists of two wires. The connecting point between the CPE and CO is called the point of demarcation and is usually found in a box (the protection block or station block) on the outside of a house. The outside plant facilities include the wires and supporting hardware to the CO.

At the CO, the lines enter through a cable room (aerial lines) or a cable vault (buried lines). The lines are then spliced to tip cables and directed to the main distribution frame (MDF); each wire is attached to a connector at the MDF.[1] From the MDF, the wires are directed to other equipment such as a switch.

---

[1]Even though the MDF is at the CO, it is usually considered part of the outside plant and CO performance is usually measured between the MDFs.

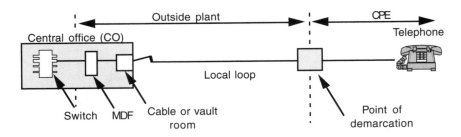

Where:
CPE   Customer premise equipment
MDF   Main distribution frame

Figure A–1   The telephone plant

The two wires on the twisted pair local loop are referred to as tip and ring. As Figure A–2 shows, the terms originated during the days of the manual telephone switchboards when the conventional telephone plug was used to make the connections through the switchboard. A third wire (if present) is sometimes called a sleeve, once again it was named for the switchboard plug. In a four-wire system the four leads are called T, R, T1, and R1.

THE OUTSIDE PLANT

Let us return to the subject of the telephone facility. Figure A–3 depicts several aspects of the subscriber loop. As shown in Figure A–3(a), the system consists of feeder plant, distribution plant, and the feeder-

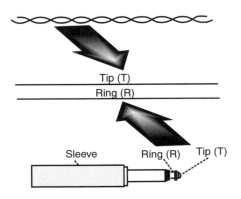

Figure A–2   Tip and ring (and their origins)

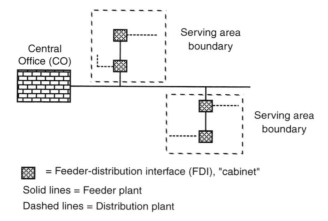

(a) Loop configuration of distribution plant

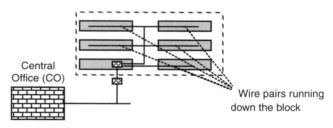

(b) Serving area in more detail

Figure A–3   The outside plant

distribution interface. The feeder plant consists of the large number of physical wires and digital repeaters. Usually, they are located based on geographical constraints and the customer locations. They often run parallel to roads and highways. The distribution plant consists of a smaller number of cables and connects to the customer's network interface (NI), which is usually located in a "box" attached to the customer's building. The serving area interface (interface plant) is the term used to describe the manual cross-connections between the feeder and distribution plants. This interface is designed to allow any feeder unit to be connected to any distribution pair.

The subscriber loop consists of sections of copper pairs (usually about 500 ft long). The sections are joined together with electrical joints, called splices at the telephone poles for aerial cables and at a manhole for underground cables. The cable pairs are bundled together in a cable binder group.

Figure A–3(b) shows the serving area boundary in more detail. This term describes the geographical division of the outside plant into discrete parts. All wires in a serving area are connected to a single serving area interface to the feeder plant, which simplifies ongoing maintenance and record keeping.

CONNECTING THE RESIDENCE

The feeder cables provide the links from the central office to the local subscriber area, and then the distribution cables carry on from there to the customer sites (as depicted in Figure A–4. Since the subscriber loop system is usually installed before all the customers are connected, there will be unused distribution cables. The common practice is to connect a twisted pair from a feeder cable to more than one distribution cable, and these unused distribution cables are called bridged taps.

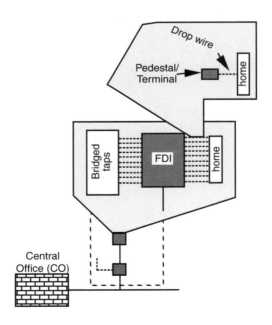

Where:
FDI   Feeder distribution interface

Figure A–4   Connecting the residence

Bridged taps must be set up within the loop plant rules to minimize adverse effects on the system, such as signal loss, radiation and spectrum distortions.

The connection points in the distribution cables are in pedestals for underground cables, and terminals for aerial cables. The connection into the customer site is called the drop wire. It is short and can (potentially) pick up other frequency radiations. It might also radiate signals to other devices.

TOLL OFFICES AND TRUNKS

Figure A–5 depicts several lines and types of equipment and types of "offices" found in the public network. Most of the terms in this figure are self-explanatory, but it should prove useful to amplify some of them:

- *Trunk:* A communication channel between two switching systems.
- *Tandem office:* A broad category of office that represents systems that connect trunks to trunks. Local tandem offices connect trunks within a metropolitan area. Toll offices connect trunks in the toll part of the network. With some exceptions, the end customer is not connected to a tandem.
- *Toll connecting trunk:* A trunk between an end office (local office) and a toll office.

SUBSCRIBER SYSTEMS

Subscriber-type systems are available that use the same operations as those systems that operate in the telephone network. These systems are also software programmable for voice and data circuits. The main difference is that one terminal is located in the central office while the other is in the field near or on the customer's location (see Figure A–6). They also may be referred to as a pair gain system, a digital loop carrier, or a subscriber loop carrier. Some of them can also extend a leased digital link to the customer premise for his/her own use.

Subscriber-type systems support a wide variety of applications by various operating companies. One of the more popular uses is providing service to developing areas for new subdivisions where an existing cable plant is insufficient. A system can provide the service immediately and

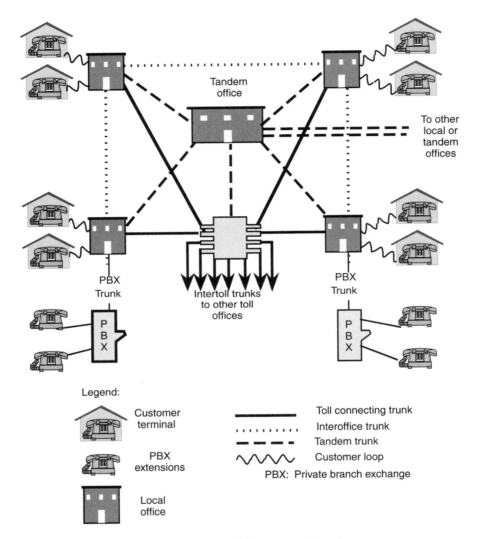

Tandem office

To other local or tandem offices

PBX Trunk

Intertoll trunks to other toll offices

PBX Trunk

Legend:

Customer terminal

PBX extensions

Local office

—————— Toll connecting trunk

· · · · · · · · · Interoffice trunk

– – – – – Tandem trunk

∿∿∿∿ Customer loop

PBX: Private branch exchange

Figure A–5   Offices and trunks

permanently, or it can be moved to another location (if growth in the area eventually justifies a central office). Regardless of whether the service is permanent or temporary, a subscriber system is easy to engineer and install on short notice. An example would be a new industrial park experiencing sudden and unexpected growth, resulting in demands for service exceeding available loop plant. The system can be installed and operating within a few weeks. Also, many companies use these systems to pro-

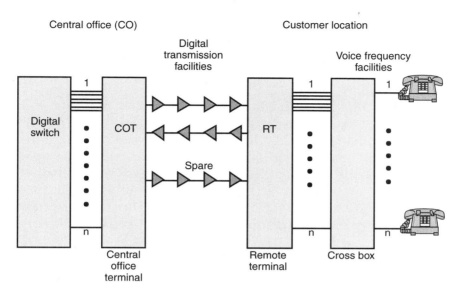

Figure A–6 Basic subscriber system arrangement

vide for temporary service to large functions such as business conventions or sporting events.

There are other reasons to justify the placement of a subscriber loop carrier in the loop plant. First, the copper pairs serving the subscribers will be much shorter, thus overcoming distance limitations in providing the newer services. Second, shortening the customer loop decreases the exposure to power-line interference with its resultant degradation and noise impact on these circuits. Third, electronics allow the future ability to provide new services quickly. The distance from the central office to the remote terminal is limited only by the copper span line performance. Today, most of these systems employ fiber optics, so there is very little distance limitation.

TELEPHONE SIGNALING BASICS

To keep matters simple, the telephone system was designed to perform signaling by onhook and offhook operations. The onhook operation means the telephone set is not being used, a term derived in the old days when the telephone handset was placed on a hook (later a cradle) when it was not being used. The offhook is just the opposite; the handset is being used—it is lifted from the telephone hook.

The offhook and onhook operations change the electrical state of the line between the terminal and the CO (or PBX). The signals listed in Table A–1 are onhook or offhook signals of various durations to convey different meanings, as summarized in the far right-hand column of the table.

Figure A–7 builds on the information provided in Table A–1 and shows the typical operations involved in the setting up of a call. One point should be made regarding the signaling between the originating office (CO) and the terminating office (CO). The example shows conventional onhook and offhook signaling, which has been the method used in the past. Newer systems replace this type of signaling with message-based operations. The same type of information is carried between the offices, but it is conveyed in a signaling protocol, that contains digital codes (fields) in the message. This "new" type of signaling is an example of Signaling System Number 7 (SS7), discussed in Appendix B.

Table A–1 Onhook and offhook signals

Name	Type	Direction — Originating	Terminating	Meaning
Connect	Offhook	——————————>		Request service & hold connection
Disconnect	Onhook	——————————>		Release connection
Answer	Offhook	——————————>		Terminating end has answered
Hangup	Onhook	<——————————		Message complete
Delay start	Offhook	<——————————		Terminating end not ready for digits
Wink start	Offhook	<——————————		Terminating end ready to receive digits
Start dialing	Onhook	<——————————		Terminating end ready for digits
Stop	Offhook	<——————————		Terminating end not ready for further digits
Go	Onhook	<——————————		Terminating end ready for further digits
Idle trunk	Onhook	<—————————>		
Busy trunk	Offhook	<—————————>		

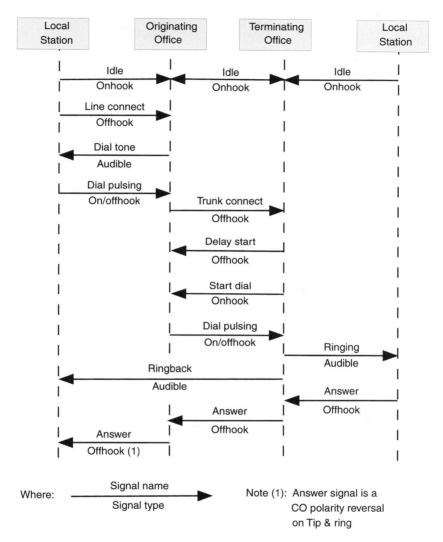

Figure A–7   Typical signaling in a connection operation

ACCESS-LINE SIGNALING

Access-line signaling can be implemented in a number of ways. The most common scheme used in the public telephone network is known as loop-start signaling. It is employed in the Bell Operating Companies' (BOC's) Message Telecommunications Service (MTS) for residence and business lines, the public telephone service, data/facsimile service and private branch exchange (PBX) or automatic call distributor (ACD) service (see Figure A–8).

Loop-start signaling requires that the network connect the "tip" connector to the positive end and the "ring" connector to the negative end of the power supply for an on-hook (idle) state. Stated another way, battery is on ring and ground is on tip. The voltage supply is usually 48 volts (V), but different line conditions may cause the voltage to vary from as low as 0 V to as high as 105 V.

The Bell system imposes stringent requirements on vendors' systems with regard to access line signaling. Nonetheless, within the confines of the standards, variations do exist. The variations are well-documented and well-understood and do not usually present a major problem to the end-user customer.

Most vendor's products establish a timer upon placing dial tone on the line until the detection of the first address signal. While implementations vary, if an address signal is not received between 5–40 s, the loop is connected either to an announcement and/or to a receiver-on-hook (ROH) tone and then to an open-circuit condition.

After all the address signals have been sent to the network, the calling party may hear call-progress tones and of course audible-ringing sig-

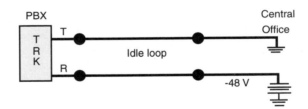

(a) Loop start: Battery always on ring and ground on tip

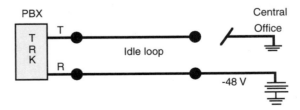

(b) Ground start: Battery always on ring and ground on/off on tip

Figure A–8   Loop start and ground start signaling

nals indicates a successful connection. At the calling end, the ringing signal is comprised of a 88-V, 20-Hz signal superimposed upon a 48-V nominal DC voltage. The ringing signal detector usually detects this signal, which is followed by about 4 s of silence.

Continuing with this discussion, because of this operation, a central office line may be seized up to 4 s before the seizure is detected by the user station. The possible outcome of this situation is that a person may attempt to establish a call during this period. This is not a big problem since the person who originates the call from that station is the person to whom the call is intended anyway. The reader may have experienced this situation when you pick up the phone and the party you want to call is already connected to you. It is not a poltergeist in action, there is really a practical explanation for it.

When the called party answers the call, the off-hook action removes the ringing signal and cuts through the talking path. This removal is called a tripping interval and usually lasts 200 ms. Although ringing can continue for longer intervals before it is tripped.

Of course, either party can end the call by going on-hook. This forces the telephone instrument to an idle state and no DC-loop current flows to the circuit. During this disconnect operation, the network does not send any type of signal to the called or calling terminal.

The ground start signaling for a two-way dial system is an old technology (introduced in the 1920s). It is used typically on two-way PBX central office trunks with direct outward dialing (DOD) and attendant-handled incoming call service. The ground-start line conductors transmit common battery-loop supervision, dual-tone multifrequency (DTMF) address signaling or loop dial pulses, alerting signals, and voiceband electrical energy.

Even though ground-start lines are an old technology, they may be used in place of loop-start lines because: (a) they provide a signal that can act as a start-dial signal (it is not necessary to detect dial tone in most situations), (b) they provide a positive indication of a new call, (c) they help prevent unauthorized calls, and (d) they indicate to the calling or called party the distant-end disconnect under normal operation.

Many examples could be provided with incoming calls, outgoing calls, disconnects, of course, ground start and loop start. Our approach here is to provide two examples to give you an understanding of the overall operations. Our examples will be (a) ground start trunk with an incoming call sequence, and (b) a loop start trunk with an outgoing call sequence.

Figure A–9 provides an example of an incoming call (that is, a call from the network to the subscriber) using ground start techniques. In Fig-

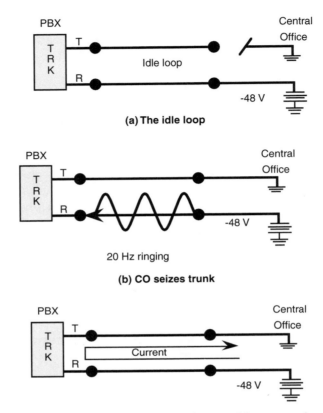

(a) The idle loop

(b) CO seizes trunk

(c) Call answered, loop resistance changes, CO removes ring

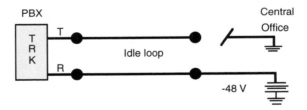

(d) Parties hang up, CO disconnects by removing ground on tip

Figure A–9   Ground start signaling example

ure A–9(a), the trunk is initially idle with battery on the ring with the tip open. This is called an idle state with the trunk in the high resistance.

In Figure A–9(b), the CO seizes the trunk by grounding the tip and superimposing the 20-Hz 86 VAC ringing on the ring lead and placing ground on tip. This operation leads to a trunk seizure state on the trunk.

The receiver sees a change of state and logic at the receiver reports the change of ground state which makes the trunk busy to all other calls. The ringing at the CO is superimposed on battery and the call is presented to the receiver.

If the receiver is a PBX, the call is presented to an attendant which would be a console loopkey. When the receiver answers, the loop is effectively closed, as shown in Figure A–9(c). The loop changes resistance with the current flowing across the ring and the tip (low resistance). This is an indication for the CO to remove ringing. Thereafter, the two-way voice path is established with battery on ring and ground on tip.

When a customer hangs up the handset, the CO disconnects by removing ground on tip. So, tip is open, battery is on ring, and the loop is once again in the idle state, as shown in Figure A–9(d).

The second example is a loop start trunk showing an outgoing call sequence (see Figure A–10). With loop start, the idle trunk exists with battery on ring and ground on tip (Figure A–10 [a]). When a call is to be processed, the PBX seizes the trunk by closing its connection from ring to tip. This changes the loop from high resistance to low resistance (Figure A–10 [b]). When the CO detects low resistance, it returns dial tone to the sender (Figure A–10 [c]).

Upon detecting dialtone, the sender begins outplusing the dialed digits (Figure A–10 [d]). The CO removes dialtone upon detecting the first pulse from the sender. The call is forwarded to the network when outplusing is complete. The network is then responsible for forwarding the call to the called party.

When the called party answers, the network returns an "offhook" signal back to the originating CO, this CO reverses the polarity on the tip and ring leads (Figure [e]). This reversal is detected by the calling end, and the call takes place.

OTHER SIGNALING EXAMPLES

Digital signaling systems must support (interwork with) the older analog signaling systems because analog is still the pervasive technology used in the local loop. The next part of this discussion shows two common operations.

These examples are not all-inclusive, but they represent common implementations. For the reader who needs information on each service option offered by the U.S. BOCs, I refer you to [Bellcore Document SR-TSV-002275, Issue 2, April 1994].

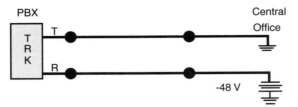

(a) High-resistance loop; battery on ring, ground on tip

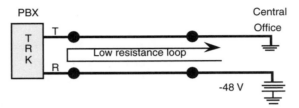

(b) High-resistance loop replaced with low-resistance loop

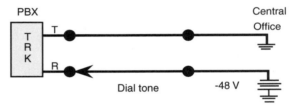

(c) CO detects low resistance and returns dialtone

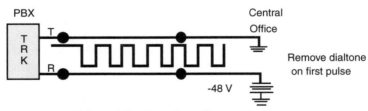

(d) Outpulsing from the calling end begins

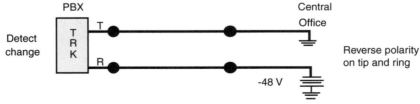

(e) Called party answers, CO reverses polarity

Figure A–10 Loop start signaling example

Example One: Feature Group B (FGB)

The BOCs classify several of their access arrangements with the title "Feature Group." This example is feature group B, which specifies an access agreement between an LEC end office (EO) and an interexchange carrier (IC) (see Figure A–11).

With this arrangement, the calls to the IC must use the initial address of: (I) + 950 + WXXX

Where: W = 0/1.

Figure A–11 is largely self-descriptive, but some rules for the signaling sequences shown in the figure should be helpful. For calls from EOs or an access tandem: (a) the carrier returns a wink signal with 4 s of trunk seizure, and (b) the carrier returns an off-hook signal within 5 s of completion of the address outpulsing. For calls originating from a carrier to an EO or access tandem: (a) the end office or access tandem returns the wink start signal within 8 s of trunk seizure; (b) the carrier starts

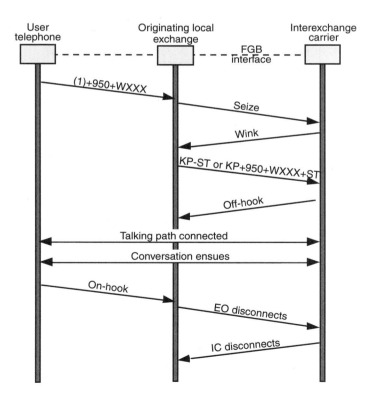

Figure A–11   Example of trunk-side access arrangement

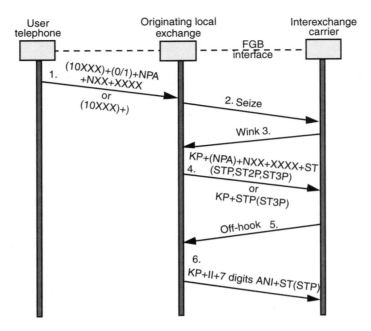

Figure A–12   Operator service signaling (OSS)

outpulsing the address with 3.5 s of the wink; and (c) the carrier completes sending the address sequence within 20 s.

Example Two: Operator Service Signaling (OSS)

OSS signaling is similar to one of the feature groups, but it has some characteristics that may be more familiar to the reader. Figure A–12 shows these operations, with six events.

In event 1, the customer dials 10XXX+(1)+7 or 10, or 10XXX+0+7 or 10. Upon receiving these signals, the EO (event 2) seizes an outgoing trunk. In event 3, the OS facility responds with a wink. Upon receiving the wink signal the EO outpulses in event 4 the called number after a delay of 40–200 ms. The outpulsing is KP + 7/10 digits + ST (STP, ST2P, ST3P), or KP+STP(ST3P)

In event 5, the OS facility will go off-hook (any time of the start of the ST pulse. Off-hook indicates its ability to receive ANI.

In event 6, the EO sends the ANI (after a delay of 40–200 ms). The signals are KP + 02 + ST (STP).

Appendix B

ISDN and SS7

During the past thirty years, the telephone system has been migrating to digital, message-based signaling. Two technologies have lead the way: (a) the Integrated Services Digital Network (ISDN) and (b) Signaling System Number 7 (SS7).

This appendix provides tutorials on these two technologies. There is also ISDN information in Chapter 5 (see Figure 5–5).

PLACEMENT OF ISDN AND SS7

It should be helpful during this introductory discussion to explain where these signaling technologies operate in relation to the customer premises equipment (CPE) and the network. Figure B–1 depicts the placement of ISDN and SS7.

The most common placement of ISDN and SS7 is to operate ISDN between the CPE (user) and the network node (such as a switch) and to run SS7 inside the network, as the trunking protocol between switches. While this placement is a common practice, it does not preclude running SS7 between the CPE and the network node.

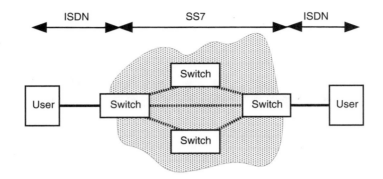

Figure B–1   System placement

ISDN is designed to operate at the boundaries of the network, but once again, no technical reason exists for not placing it inside the network. However, it is not done here because it conflicts with SS7 systems.

As we develop the analysis of ISDN and SS7, it will become evident that the two systems are designed to complement each other: ISDN at the user-network interface (UNI), and SS7 at the network node interface (NNI).

ISDN SIGNALING MESSAGES

Many of the VoIP Gateway operations entail the processing of ISDN signaling messages. These messages and their functions are defined in the ITU-T Q.931 Recommendation.

The ISDN Q.931 messages are used to manage ISDN connections on the B channels. These messages are also used (with modifications) by Frame Relay and ATM for setting up calls on demand at a UNI, and for provisioning services between networks at a NNI. Table B–1 lists these messages, and a short explanation is provided here about the functions of the more significant messages:

- *ALERTING:* This message is sent to indicate that the called user party has been "alerted" and the call is being processed. This message is sent in response to an incoming SETUP message, and it is sent in the backward direction (backwards from the called end to the calling end) after the called exchange has placed ringing signals on the line to the called party.

- *CALL PROCEEDING:* This message is sent to the call initiator to indicate that the call establishment procedures have been initiated. It also indicates that all information necessary to set up the connection has been received and that any other call establishment information will not be accepted. In ISDN-conformant implementations, the CALL PROCEEDING message is exchanged only at the originating end of the connection.

- *CONGESTION CONTROL:* This message is employed only on USER INFORMATION messages. As the name implies, it is used to govern the flow of USER INFORMATION messages. In most implementations, congestion control is not used or, if it is used, it is rarely invoked.

- *CONNECT:* When the called party picks up the telephone and goes off-hook, this action precipitates the invocation of this message. The message is sent in the backward direction (from the called party to the calling party) to signal the call acceptance by the called party.

- *CONNECT ACKNOWLEDGE:* This message is sent in response to the CONNECT message. It's invocation means that the parties have been awarded the call.

- *DISCONNECT:* This message is sent when either party (calling or called) hangs up the telephone (goes on-hook). It is a trigger to the network that the end-to-end connection is to be cleared and the resources reserved for the connection are to be made available for another call.

- *INFORMATION:* As the name implies, this message is sent by either the user or the network to provide more information about a connection. For example, the message may be invoked by an exchange if it wishes to provide additional information about a connection to another exchange.

- *NOTIFY:* This message is not often used, but is available for the user or the network to provide information regarding a connection. The NOTIFY message contains a field called the notification indicator, which is described in the next section of this chapter.

- *PROGRESS:* The progress message is part of the call establishment procedure although it is not invoked in a typical implementation. However, it is available to indicate the progress of a call and it ms invoked in situations where interworking is required or where the exchanges need to provide information about in-band information. This information is provided through a field in the message called the progress indicator which is described in the next section.

- *RELEASE:* This message is invoked in response to the reception of a DISCONNECT message. It is sent by the network or the user to notify its recipient that the equipment has disconnected the circuit that had been reserved for the connection. In essence, it tells the receiver that it should also release the circuit. The RELEASE message is designed also to free and make available the call reference numbers (and the associated resources) associated with the call.

- *RELEASE COMPLETE:* As the name implies, this message is sent in response to the RELEASE message and it indicates by its invocation that the sender has released the circuit, the call reference and, of course, the resources associated with the connection. The combination of the RELEASE and RELEASE COMPLETE messages means that the circuit has been completely cleared and made available for other calls, and that the call reference is no longer valid.

- *RESUME:* This message is used for a relatively simple operation, which is to request that the network resume a suspended call. The arrangements for resuming a suspended call vary between network providers, but the idea is to allow users to change their minds (within a brief period of time) upon hanging up.

- *RESUME ACKNOWLEDGE:* This message is sent by the network in response to the RESUME message. It indicates the completion of a request to RESUME a suspended call.

- *RESUME REJECT:* This message is sent by the network to indicate that it cannot fulfill the request to resume a suspended call.

- *SETUP:* The setup message contains more information elements than any of the other Q.931 messages. It is used to begin the call setup procedure. The SETUP message is always issued by the calling user to the network at the originating end and by the network to the called user at the terminating end.

- *SETUP ACKNOWLEDGE:* This message is sent in response to the SETUP message to indicate that the SETUP message has been received correctly. It is used to indicate that call establishment has been initiated. It may also indicate that additional information may be required to complete the call. For the latter case, the recipient of the SETUP ACKNOWLEDGE is required to send the additional information which is coded in an INFORMATION message.

- *STATUS:* This message is sent in response to a STATUS IN-QUIRY message. It may also be sent in the event of certain error conditions that occur at a network node.
- *STATUS ENQUIRY:* This message is sent by either the user or the network to inquire about the status of an ongoing operation, such as a call in progress. Both the STATUS and STAUS EN-QUIRY messages are intended to be flexible enough to allow the implementor latitude in their implementation. The only information element in these messages is the display information element described later in this chapter.

ISDN permits calls to be suspended. The reason for the suspensions are not defined in the specifications. Whatever the reasons, Q.931 provides for three messages to support these operations. They are as follows:

- *SUSPEND, SUSPEND ACKNOWLEDGE, and SUSPEND RE-JECT:* The SUSPEND message is sent from the user to request that the network suspend the call. The direction of the message is important in that the network is not allowed to send this message; so, call suspension can only be initiated by the user. SUSPEND ACKNOWLEDGE is an acknowledgment by the network of the reception of the SUSPEND message; it also indicates the completion of the call suspension. SUSPEND REJECT is an acknowledgment by the network of the reception of the SUSPEND message, but it indicates that the network did not suspend the call.
- *USER INFORMATION:* This message is slightly different from the INFORMATION message described earlier, in that it contains different parameters than the INFORMATION message. The major aspect is the existence of the user-user field which does not reside in the INFORMATION message. As the next section will explain, the user-user field is passed transparently by ISDN to ISDSN users.
- *FACILITY:* This message is used by either the user or the network to provide additional information about a call. Examples are key-pad facility and display information, described in the next section.
- *RESTART:* This message is sent by the user or the next work to request a restart of a connection. It returns the identified channel to an idle state.
- *RESTART ACKNOWLEDGE:* This message acknowledges the RESTART message.

Table B–1   ISDN layer-3 messages

(Note: use of these messages varies across vendors and national boundaries)

Call Establishment
  ALERTING
  CALL PROCEEDING
  CONNECT
  CONNECT ACKNOWLEDGE
  PROGRESS
  SETUP
  SETUP ACKNOWLEDGE

Call Disestablishment
  DISCONNNECT
  RELEASE
  RELEASE COMPLETE
  RESTART
  RESTART ACKNOWLEDGE

Call Information Phase
  RESUME
  RESUME ACKNOWLEDGE
  RESUME REJECT
  SUSPEND
  SUSPEND ACKNOWLEDGE
  SUSPEND REJECT
  USER INFORMATION

Miscellaneous
  CANCEL
  CANCEL ACKNOWLEDGE
  CANCEL REJECT
  CONGESTION CONTROL
  FACILITY
  FACILITY ACKNOWLEDGE
  FACILITY REJECT
  INFORMATION
  REGISTER
  REGISTER ACKNOWLEDGE
  REGISTER REJECT
  STATUS
  STATUS INQUIRY

Q.931 Example

Figure B–2 provides an example of how a call is set up with the Q.931 messages. The two persons involved in this connection are using conventional telephone handsets that are attached to ISDN terminals, shown in this figure as the calling terminal and the called terminal. The exchange termination's (ET) are located at the central offices.

The calling party goes off-hook and dials the telephone number of the called party. This information is used by the calling terminal to create an ISDN SETUP message, which is sent across the ISDN line to the

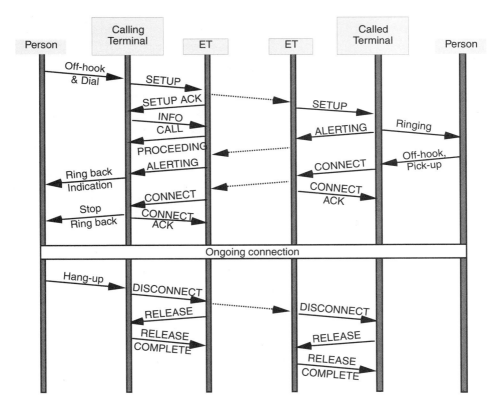

Where:

BC Bearer capability
CDN Called party number
CGN calling party number
CSE Cause code

Figure B–2 ISDN signaling example (note: use of INFO varies)

local ET. This ET acknowledges the message with the SETUP ACK message, and initiates actions to set up a circuit to the next ET, which is shown in the figure with the dashed arrow. The SETUP ACK, and INFORMATION messages are optional, and were described in the previous section. The local ET sends a CALL PROCEEDING message to the calling terminal to indicate that the call is being processed.

At the called end, the SETUP message is forwarded to the called terminal by the terminating ET. This terminal examines the contents of the message to determine who is being called and what services are being requested. It checks the called party's line to see if it is idle, and if so, places the ringing signal on the line. When the ringing signal is placed on the line, the called terminal transmits an ALERTING message in the backward direction, which is passed all the way to the calling terminal. This message indicates to the calling terminal that the called party has been signaled, which allows a ring back signal to be placed on the line to the calling party.

When the called party answers the call, the called terminal sends a CONNECT message in the backward direction, which is passed to the calling terminal. Upon receiving this message, ring back is removed from the line, and the connection is cut-through to the calling party. The CONNECT messages are acknowledged with CONNECT ACK messages.

The on-hook action initiates the ISDN connection termination operations. The DISCONNECT messages are used to indicate that the connection is to be terminated. The RELEASE and RELEASE COMPLETE messages follow the DISCONNECT messages.

MAJOR FUNCTIONS OF SS7

SS7 defines the procedures for the set-up, ongoing management, and clearing of a call between telephone users. It performs these functions by exchanging telephone control messages between the SS7 components that support the end-users' connection.

THE SS7 TOPOLOGY

Figure B–3 depicts a typical SS7 topology. The subscriber lines are connected to the SS7 network through the Service Switching Points (SSPs). The SSPs receive the signals from the CPE and perform call processing on behalf of the user. SSPs are implemented at end offices or access tandem devices. They serve as the source and destination for SS7 messages. In so doing, SSP initiates SS7 messages either to another SSP or to a signaling transfer point (STP).

The STP is tasked with the translation of the SS7 messages and the routing of those messages between network nodes and databases. The STPs are switches that relay messages between SSPs, STPs, and service control points (SCPs). Their principal functions are similar to the layer-3 operations of the OSI Model.

The SCPs contain software and databases for the management of the call. For example, 800 services and routing are provided by the SCP. They receive traffic (typically requests for information) from SSPs via STPs and return responses (via STPs) based on the query.

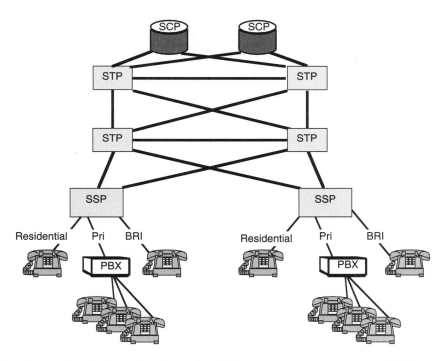

Note: Another node called the signaling point (SP) may exist between user and SSP

Where:

BRI   Basic rate interface
PBX   Private branch exchange
PRI   Primary rate interface
SCP   Service control point
SSP   Service switching point
STP   Signaling transfer point

Figure B–3   Typical SS7 topology

Although the figure shows the SS7 components as discrete entities, they are often implemented in an integrated fashion by a vendor's equipment. For example, a central office can be configured with a SSP, a STP, and a SCP or any combination of these elements. These SS7 components are explained in more detail later in this section.

The SSP

The service-switching point (SSP) is the local exchange to the subscriber and the interface to the telephone network. It can be configured as a voice switch, an SS7 switch, or a computer connected to switch.

The SSP creates SS7 signal units at the sending SSP and translates them at the receiving SSP. Therefore, it converts voice signaling into the SS7 signal units, and vice versa. It also supports database access queries for 800/900 numbers

The SSP uses the dialed telephone numbers to access a routing table to determine a final exchange and the outgoing trunk to reach this exchange. The SS7 connection request message is then sent to the final exchange.

The STP

The signal transfer point (STP) is a router for the SS7 network. It relays messages through the network but it does not originate them. It is usually an adjunct to a voice switch, and does not usually stand alone as a separate machine.

The STP is installed as a national STP, an international STP, or a gateway STP. Even though SS7 is an international standard, countries may vary in how some of the features and options are implemented. The STP provides the conversions of the messages that flow between dissimilar systems. For example, in the U.S. the STP provides conversions between ANSI SS7 and ITU-T SS7.

STPs also offer screening services, such as security checks on incoming and/or outgoing messages. The STP can also screen messages to make certain they are acceptable (conformant) to the specific network.

Other STP functions include the acquisition and storage of traffic and usage statistics for OAM and billing. If necessary, the STP provides an originating SCP with the address of the destination SCP

The SCP

The service control point (SCP) acts as the interface into the telephone company databases. These databases contain information on the subscriber, 800/900 numbers, calling cards, fraud data, etc. The SCP is usually linked to computer/databases through X.25. The SCP address is a point code, and the address of the database is a subsystem number (addresses are explained shortly).

Bellcore provides guidance on SCP databases, but BOCs vary in how they use them. The most common databases used are:

- Business Services Database (BSDB):
- Call Management Service Database (CMSDB):
- Line Information Database (LIDB):
- Home Location Register (HLR):
- Visitor Location Register (VLR):

THE SS7 LAYERS

Figure B–4 provides a more detailed description of the SS7 layers, and will serve as an introduction to subsequent material on these levels. MTP level 1 performs the functions of a traditional OSI physical layer. It generates and receives the signals on the physical channel.

MTP level 2 relates closely to the OSI layer 2. It is a conventional data link level and is responsible for the delivery of traffic on each link between SS7 nodes. The traffic in the upper layers of SS7 are encapsulated into MTP 2 "signal units" (this term is used instead of the conventional HDLC "frame"), and sent onto the channel to the receiving node. This node checks for errors that may have occurred during transmission and takes remedial action (discussed later).

MTP level 3 performs OSI layer-3 functions, notably, the routing of messages between machine and between components within a machine. It performs load sharing operations across multiple links, and reconfiguration operations in the event of node or link failure.

SCCP corresponds to several of the operations associated with OSI layer 3 (and although not generally discussed in literature, OSI layer 4, as well). Some of its principal jobs are: (a) supporting the MTP levels with global addressing, (b) providing connectionless or connection-oriented services, and (c) providing sequencing and flow-control operations.

The transaction capabilities application part (TCAP) corresponds to several of the functions of the OSI layer 7. It uses the remote operations service element (ROSE). As such, it performs connectionless, remote procedure calls on behalf of an "application" running on top of it.

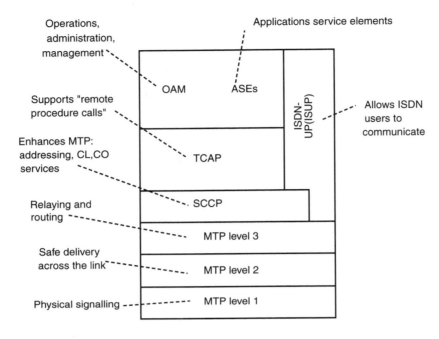

Where:
    ISUP   ISDN user part
    MTP   Message transfer part
    SCCP   Signaling connection control point
    TCAP   Transaction capabilities application part

Figure B–4   The SS7 layers

Finally, the ISDN user part (ISDN-UP or ISUP) provides the services needed to support applications running in an ISDN environment.

SS7 POINT CODES

SS7 nodes are identified with an address and each node must have a unique address. The SS7 addresses are called point codes (PCs) (see Figure B–5). The point code is a hierarchical address consisting of a network identifier, a network cluster and a network cluster member. The network identifier, as its name implies, identifies a unique network (123 in this example). The network cluster identifies a cluster of nodes which belong to a network (1 or 2 in this example). Typically, a cluster of signaling

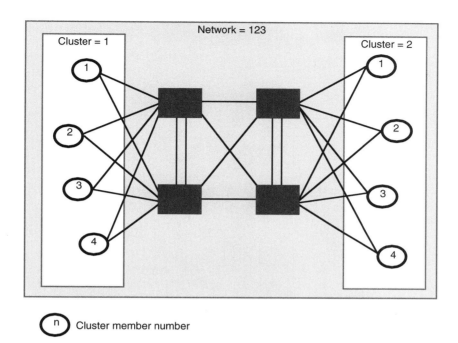

Cluster member number

Figure B–5   SS7 numbering plan with point codes

nodes consists of a group that home-in on a mated pair of STPs. They can be addressed as a group. The network cluster member code identifies a single node operating within a cluster (1, 2, 3, or 4 in this example).

The structure of the point code fields is different in U.S., ITU-T, and other national specifications. Each country may implement its own point code structure, but is expected to support an ITU-T structure at the international gateway between two countries.

In addition to the point code (PC) used by MTP for routing to a node in the network, SS7 also utilizes a subsystem number (SSN). This number does not pertain to a node but to entities within a node, such as an application or some other software entity. As examples, it could identify enhanced 800 (E800) services running in a node or an automated calling card service (ACCS) module operating in the node.

SS7 also supports the global title (GT) identifier. Perhaps the best way to view GT is that it is mapped to an SS7 network address of PC + SSN.

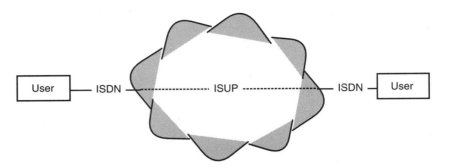

Figure B–6   ISDN user part (ISUP)

ISUP

This book has discussed SS7 and ISDN as separate subjects. Indeed, they are separate, and they perform different operations in a transport and signaling network architecture. However, SS7 and ISDN are "partners" in that ISDN assumes SS7 will set up the connections within a network and SS7 assumes ISDN will set up connections at network boundaries (outside the network). Therefore, we can view ISDN as a user network interface (UNI) operating between the user device and the network node, and we can view SS7 as a network node interface (NNI) operating between the nodes within the network. Of course, nothing precludes using SS7 as an internetworking interface allowing two networks to communicate with each other.

The ISDN user part (ISUP) is used to coordinate the activities of ISDN and SS7. In effect ISUP "bridges" the two ISDN UNIs across the SS7 network. Figure B–6 shows this relationship.

The ISUP Messages

Table B–2 shows the names of the major ISUP messages, their abbreviations, and their functions. The table is self-explanatory.

EXAMPLE OF ISDN AND SS7 SIGNALING

In this section, we piece together some of the information explained earlier by providing an example of how the SS7 signaling procedures and call set-up occur. This example also shows the relationship of ISDN and SS7 connections.

Table B–2   ISUP call processing messages

Message	Name	Function
ACM	Address Complete Message	Indicates all information necessary to complete a call has been received
ANM	ANswer message	Indicates called party has answered (used also for billing start in toll calls)
CPG	Call ProGress	Indicates an event of significance to the originator has occurred (backwards direction only)
IAM	Initial Address Message	Invitation to establish a call
PAM	Pass Along Message	Used as "mailing envelope" to pass other messages
RLC	ReLease Complete	Indicates circuit has been placed in an idle state
RLS	ReLease	Indicates circuit is being released for reasons given (see cause value)

As depicted in Figure B–7, a call set-up begins when a telephone or PBX (in this example) send an ISDN Setup message, which is used to create the SS7 initial address message (IAM). This message is sent to an exchange. The IAM contains all the information required to set-up and route the call. All codes and digits required for the call routing through the national (and international) network will be sent in this message. Other signals may also be sent in certain situations. For example, the end of pulsing (ST) signal is sent to indicate the final digit has been sent of the digits in the national or international numbers. Also, since the SS7 network does not pass over the speech path, it must provide facilities to provide a continuity check of the speech circuit to be used. It also makes cross office checks to ensure the reliability of the connection through the various digital exchanges.

A call is processed by the outgoing exchange analyzing the address signals in the message. Based on these address messages, an appropriate outgoing circuit is seized and an initial address message (IAM) is forwarded to the next exchange.

This exchange analyzes the address message to determine: (a) the circuit to be seized; (b) routing through another country, if necessary; (c) the nature of the circuit (terrestrial or satellite); (d) if echo control is needed; (e) the calling parties category; and, (f) the need for continuity

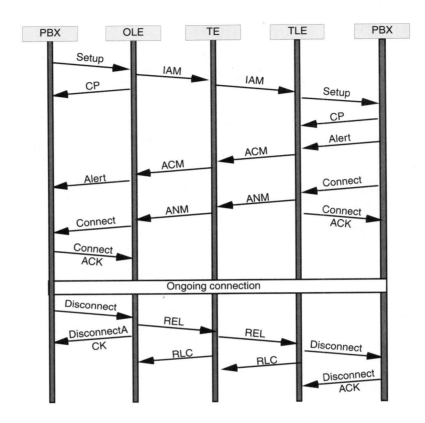

Where:
    ACM   Address complete message
    ANM   Answer message
    CP   Call proceeding
    IAM   Initial address message
    OLE   Originating local exchange
    PBX   Private branch exchange
    RLC   Release complete
    TE   Transit exchange
    TLE   Terminating local exchange

Figure B–7   Example of an ISDN/SS7 call

checks. The exchanges will disable any echo suppressors (if necessary) at this time.

If all the checks are completed successfully, the network begins the call establishment (when enough address signals are received to determine routing). The address messages are analyzed to determine if all the required signals have been received, at which time the speech path setup is completed. The destination exchange provides a ringing tone back to the originator, and upon the receiving telephone user answering the call, the answer signals are returned by the originating exchange to the user.

At the receiving end, the SS7 IAM is mapped back to the ISDN Setup message and sent to the terminating PBX. Notice the Call Proceeding messages that are sent in response to the Setup messages.

Once the terminating end answers the call, an ISDN Connect message is sent to the network, which maps this message into an SS7 answer message (ANM), which is then mapped into an ISDN Connect message and given to the originating caller.

Eventually one of the subscribers hangs up, which activates an ISDN Disconnect message, and in turn, the messages shown in the bottom part of this figure. After a certain period of waiting, if no other signals emanate from the end-user, additional supervisory signals are exchanged between the two exchanges to make the circuit available for new traffic.

Appendix C

Tutorial on the V.34 and V.90 Modems

Welcome to the world of intelligent modems. Just a few short years ago, modems were rather prosaic instruments, and did little else but transport digital bits across the analog link. Today's modems are quite different from their predecessors, as we will see in this examination of V.34 and V.90. I have included V.34 in this discussion because the newer V.90 modem in the fall-back mode uses the V.34 operations on the analog side of the modem. V.90 also uses V.34 modulation in the upstream direction (from user modem to the network).

V.34

To begin this analysis, Table C–1 is an extraction of several tables in the V.34 Recommendation. (We will be using the 2400 and 3200 symbol rates, and high-carrier throughout this discussion).

The symbol rate is $S = (a/c) \times 2400 \pm 0.01\%$ two-dimensional (2D) symbols per second. Therefore, using Table C–1, the symbol rate of 3200 is derived by $(4/3) \times 2400 = 3200$.

The carrier frequency is $C = (d/e) \times S$. Therefore, using Table C–1 once again, a carrier frequency of 1800 is derived by $(3/4) \times 2400 = 1800$. A carrier frequency of 1920 is derived by $(3/5) \times 3200 = 1920$.

Table C–1   Symbol rates and carrier frequencies

(Note: Partial examples, see V.34 for complete tables)

Symbol Rate, S	a	c	----High Carrier---- Frequency	d	e	Framing Parameter J	P
2400	1	1	1800	3	4	7	12
3200	4	3	1920	3	5	7	16

	SWP, b.			
	----S = 2400--		----S = 3200---	
	----P = 12------		----P = 16------	
Signaling Rate	b	SWP	b	SWP
2400	8	FFF	–	–
28800	–	–	72	FFFF

V.34 alternates between sending b-1 and b bits per mapping frame based on a switching pattern SWP (of period P in the table). The result is that the transmission of a fractional number of bits per mapping frame is N/P. The value of b is the smallest integer not less than N/P.

SWP consists of 12- to 16-bit binary numbers. V.34 contains information on all combinations of signaling rate and symbol rate. For our examples of S = 2400 and 3200, the second table gives some partial examples of b, SWP. The value of SWP is shown as a hex value.

As with all V Series modems, V.34 uses a subset of the V.24 interchange circuits. Table C–2 provides a summary of these circuits. V.24 is a "superset" recommendation and all the V Series modems utilize a subset of the V.24 interchange circuits.

The Four Phases

V.34 executes four phases before it begins sending user data (in superframes). Some of these procedures are defined in V.8. This section examines each phase. For purposes of clarity, We describe some of the V.8 and V.34 terms with a general description that you should be able to follow without having to read (at least, initially) the V.8 and V.34 recommendations. Table C–3 defines the V.8 and V.34 signals that are used in this discussion. Table C–3 does not show the bit structure for each signal. The reader should study V.8 and V.34 if this level of detail is needed. The signals in the table are listed according to the order of their invocation by the V.34 modem.

Table C–2   The V.34 Use of V.24 Interchange Circuits

Interchange Circuit	Description
102	Signal ground or common return
103	Transmitted data
104	Received data
105	Request to send
106	Ready for sending
107	Data set ready
108/1 or 108/2	Data terminal ready
109	Data channel received line signal detector
113	Transmitter signal element timing (DTE source)[1]
114	Transmitter signal element timing (DCE source)[2]
115	Receiver signal element timing (DCE source)[2]
125	Calling indicator
133	Ready for receiving[3]
140	Loopback/maintenance
141	Local loopback
142	Test indicator
118	Transmitted secondary channel data[4]
119	Received secondary channel data[4]
120	Transmit secondary channel line signal[4,5]
121	Secondary channel ready[4,5]
122	Secondary channel received line signal detector[4,5,6]

[1]When the modem is not operating in a synchronous mode at the interface, any signals on this circuit shall be disregarded. Many DTEs operating in an asynchronous mode do not have a generator connected to this circuit

[2]When the modem is not operating in a synchronous mode at the interface, this circuit shall be clamped to the OFF condition. Many DTEs operating in an asynchronous mode do not terminate this circuit.

[3]Operation of circuit 133 shall be in accordance with 7.3.1/V.42

[4]This circuit is provided where the optional secondary channel is implemented without a separate interface.

[5]This circuit need only be provided where required by the application.

[6]This circuit is in the ON condition if circuit 109 is in the ON condition and the optional secondary channel is enabled.

Table C–6 Key V.8 and V.34 Signals and Their Use

Notation	Name	Function
CI	Function indicator signal	Indicates a session
ANSam	Modified answer tone	Response to a CI signal
Te		A silent period, which begins with the termination of the call signal or after detection of ANSam. Can be used for echo canceller disabling, if necessary
CM	Call menu signal	Initiates modulation-mode selection[1,2,3]
JM	Joint menu signal	Response to the CM signal[1,2,3]
CJ	CM terminator	Acknowledges JM signal and terminates CM signal
INFO	Information sequence	Exchanges modem capabilities, results of line probing, and data mode modulation parameters[4]
A, A	2400 Hz tone	Transmitted by answer modem, with A and A representing 180° phase reversals of 2400 Hz tone
B, B	1200 Hz tone	Transmitted by call modem, with B and B representing a 180° phase reversal of the 1200 Hz tone
L1, L2	Line probing signals	Used to analyze channel characteristics
S, S	——	S and S sent as part of quarter-super constellation rotation
MD	Manufacturer-defined signal	Used to train a vendor-specific echo canceller
PR	——	Used to train equalizer
TRN	——	A sequence of symbols chosen from 4- or 16-point 2D constellation
J	——	Indicates 4- or 16-point constellation size used by remote modem
J'	——	Terminates the J sequence
MP, MP'	Modulator parameter sequences	Contains parameters to negotiate: signaling rate, trellis code choice, auxiliary channel enable, amount of constellation shaping
E	——	Signals end of MP
B1	——	Sent at the end of start-up

[1]Part of the signal is used to indicate the V Series modulation modes: (a) V.34 half-duplex or duplex, (b) V.32/V.32 bis, (c) V.22/V.22 bis, (d) V.17, (e) V.29 half duplex, (f) V.27 ter, (g) V.26 ter, (h) V.26 bis, (i) V.23 half duplex or duplex, and (j) V.21. For CM, it indicates the suggested signaling mode; for JM, it indicates the lowest signaling mode
[2]Part of the signal is used to indicate the use of LAPM (V.42)
[3]Part of the signal is used to indicate the use of cellular access
[4]Two sets of INFO messages are used (where a = answer modem and c = call modem): INFO0a, INFO0c and INFO1a and INFO1c

As stated earlier, the V.34 modem executes four phases of operations before it is ready for data transfer. These phases are listed here and described in more detail in this section.

- Phase 1   Network interaction (see Figure C–1)
- Phase 2   Probing/ranging (see Figure C–2)
- Phase 3   Equalizer and echo canceller training (see Figure C–3)
- Phase 4   Final training (see Figure C–4)

The information is Table C–3 should be used during this analysis. Additionally, the next four provide a general depiction of the four phases. Be aware that these figures (a) do not show exact timing relationships and (b) do not show the overlapping of the signals on the duplex channel. They do show typical (but not all) sequences. This other information can be found in Section 11 of V.34.

Phase 1: Network Interaction. Figure C–1 shows the signal exchange for phase 1, network interaction. The call modem conditions its receiver to accept ANSam and then transmits CI to the answer modem. The answer modem, after it is connected to the line, remains silent for 200 ms and then transmits ANSam to the call modem, and conditions its receiver to detect CM.

When the call modem receives ANSam, it remains silent for the period Te, and conditions its receiver to detect JM and sends CM to set up the categories to be used during this session (see footnotes of the previous table).

The answer modem receives CM, and since CM indicates the V.34 operations, the modem sends JM and conditions its receiver to detect CJ.

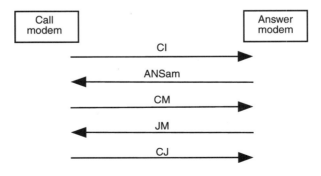

Figure C–1   Phase 1: Network Interaction

At the call modem, after it has sent CJ, it remains silent for 75 ± 5 ms and enters phase 2. At the answer modem, after receiving CJ, it remains silent for 75 ± 5 ms and enters phase 2.

Phase 2: Probing and Ranging.   Phase 2 is concerned with channel probing and ranging, (see Figure C–2). These operations begin with the

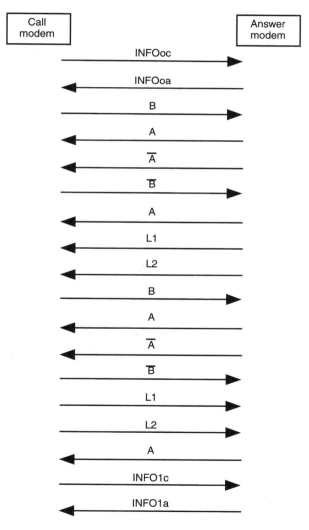

Figure C–2   Probing and Ranging

exchange of INFO0c and INFO0a, which contain the following negotiated parameters: (a) symbol rate, (b) the use of a high or low carrier, (c) maximum allowed symbol rate in the transmit and receive directions, and (d) transmit clock source.

Next, the receivers are conditioned to each other. Then, round trip delay is calculated between the two machines by the alternate sending and receiving of Tone A and Tone B. A an B are 2400- and 1200-Hz tones, respectively, while A and B are 180°-phase reversals, respectively.

The next part of phase 2 deals with sending and receiving of L1 and L2, which are line-probing signals. They are used by the two modems to analyze the characteristics of the channel. Both L1 and L2 are a defined set of tones that enable the receiver to measure channel distortion and noise.

The final part of phase 2 deals with the exchange of INFO1c and INFO1a (see footnote 4 in the previous table). These signals provide the following functions: (a) permissible power levels for the session and minimum power reduction that can be accepted; (b) length of MD (for phase 3); and (c) final symbol rate selection as a result of the previous probing.

Phase 3: Equalizer and Echo Canceller Training. Phase 3 is concerned with training both modem's equalizers and echo cancellers, (see Figure C–3). The answer modem begins these procedures by sending S and S. Signal S is sent by alternating between point 0 of the quarter-superconstellation and the same point rotated counter-clockwise by 90°. Signal S is sent by alternating between point 0 rotated by 180°, and point 0 counter-clockwise by 270°.

Next MD is sent, following (once again) by S and S, and then PR is transmitted, which is used to train the receiver's equalizer. The answer modem completes its phase 3 by sending TRN and J. It can be seen that the call modem's phase-3 procedures are identical to the answer modem.

Phase 4: Final Training. After the two modems have moved from phase 3 to phase 4 by exchanging J, J' and S, S, both modems send TRN signals (discussed earlier) (see Figure C–4). Next, MP and MP' are exchanged, which contains parameters used to negotiate a variety of options explained in the previous table. The E signals end the MP sequence, and the B1 signals end this phase and the overall start-up procedure.

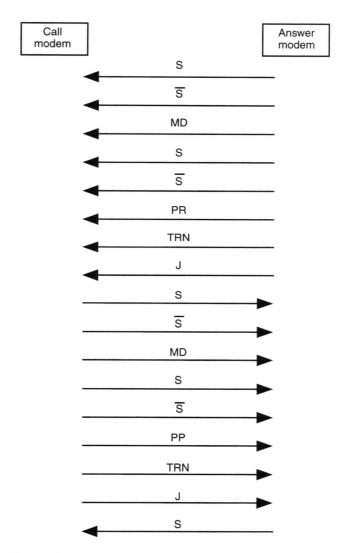

Figure C–3   Equalizer and Echo Canceller Training

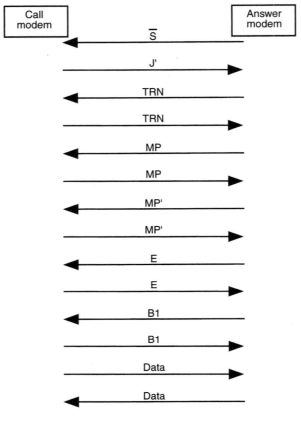

Figure C–4   Final Training

V.90

I have included V.34 is this discussion because the newer V.90 modem in the fall-back mode uses the V.34 operations on the analog side of the modem. V.90 also uses V.34 modulation in the upstream direction (from user modem to the network).

The V.90 modem, also known as the 56 kbit/s modem, has become the dominant modem technology in the industry. It has the following characteristic:

- Operates in full duplex on telephone lines (local loops).
- Echo cancellation used for separating channels.

- Uses pulse code modulation (PCM) in the downstream direction (from network to user modem) at a symbol rate of 8000.
- Downstream data rates range from 28 kbit/s to 56 kbits/s in incriments of 8000/6 bit/s.

V.34 modulation is employed in the upstream direction, ranging from 4.8 kbit/s to 28.8 kbit/s, in increments of 2.4 kbit/s.

- Optional upstream rates for 31.2 kbit/s and 33.6 kbit/s.
- Adaptive signaling rate capabilities to permit the modem to operate at the maximum data rate, depending on the quality of the channel.

The V.90 Modem Pair

The V.90 operates as a modem pair. The analog part of the pair is for the upstream channel, and the digital part is for the downstream channel. As stated, the analog part is based on V.34. Let us focus on the digital part.

The ITU-T G.711 Recommendation: The Basis for the Digital Modem

The key to understanding the V.90 digital modem is to know about the G.711 specification. The experienced reader can skip to the next section. For the newcomer I provide a brief tutorial on G.711 PCM.

Several methods are used to change an analog signal into a representative string of digital binary images. Even though these methods entail many processes, they are generally described in three steps: *sampling*, *quantizing*, and *encoding*.

The devices performing the digitizing process are called channel banks or primary multiplexers. They have two basic functions: (1) converting analog signals to digital signals (and vice versa at the other end); and (2) combining (multiplexing) the digital signals into a single time division multiplexed (TDM) data stream (and demultiplexing them at the other end).

Analog-to-digital conversion is based on Nyquist sampling theory, which states that if a signal is sampled instantaneously at regular intervals and at a rate at least twice the highest frequency in the channel, the samples will contain sufficient information to allow an accurate reconstruction of the signal.

The accepted sampling rate in the industry is 8000 samples per second. Based on Nyquist sampling theory, this rate allows the accurate reproduction of a kHz channel, which is used as the bandwidth for a voice-grade channel. The 8000 samples are more than sufficient to capture the signals in a telephone line if certain techniques (discussed shortly) are used.

With pulse amplitude modulation (PAM), the pulse carrier amplitude is varied with the value of the analog waveform. The pulses are fixed with respect to duration and position. PAM is classified as a modulation technique because each instantaneous sample of the wave is used to modulate the amplitude of the sampling pulse

The 8 kHz sampling rate result in a sample pulse train of signals with a 125 microseconds (µsec.) time period between the pulses (1 second/8000 = .000125). Each pulse occupies 5.2 µsec. of this time period. Consequently, it is possible to interleave sampled pulses from other signals within the 125 µsec. period

One of the problems with the conversion of an analog signal to a digital representation is the fact that digital signals are discrete in their nature. That is to say, they are coded as either a binary 1 or a binary 0. In contrast, the analog signal is non-discrete and varies continuously, displaying various levels of amplitude.

As a consequence of the nature of discrete and non-discrete signals, it is impossible to accurately capture with digital samples the complete characteristics of the analog waveform.

The process of asseiging values to the analog wave form is known as quantizing (which simply means assigning a value to something). Quantizing introduces errors into the conversation process, but their negative effects can be mitigated, as we will see shortly.

The problem discussed in the previous figure is partially solved by varying the amplitude space between the quantizing values. As this figure shows, the quantizing scales are closer together for the measurement of the higher-amplitude signals.

By "compressing" the quantizing scales to more accurately capture the lower-amplitude signals, another goal has been achieved. Lower-amplitude signals are less discernible to the human ear than the higher-amplitude signals. Therefore, it is desirable to take special actions to represent them more accurately. This goal is accomplished by the use of the varying quantizing levels.

The A/D process uses a compression technique, called companding, to compensate for errors in the assignment of values to each sample. (This assignment process is called companding.) Errors occur because the sampled signal may not correlate exactly to a quantizing value.

The distortion in the quantization is a function of the differences between the quantized steps. Ideally, one would like to use many quantizing steps in order to reduce the quantizing "noise." Studies show that 2048 uniform quantizing step provide sufficient "granularity" to represent the voice signal accurately. However, 2048 steps requires an 11-bit code (2^{11}), which translates to 88000 bit/s (8000×11). Since the voice signals in a telephone system can span 30 dB of variation, it makes sense to vary the distribution of the quantization steps. The variable quantizing levels reduce the quantizing noise.

The nonlinear companding is implemented in a step-wise linear process. For the μ-law, the m = 255 is used and the companding value is coded by a set of eight straight-line segments that cut across the compression curve (actually eight for negative segments and eight for positive segments; since the two center segments are collinear, they are considered one).

With this approach, each segment is double the amplitude range of its preceding segment and each segment is also one-half the slope of the preceding segment. In this manner, the segments representing the low range of PAM signals are more accurately encoded than the segments pertaining to the high range of PAM signals.

The A-law functions similarly to the μ-law characteristics. Eight positive and eight negative segments exist as in the u law characteristics, but it is described as the 13-segment law.

The code of μ 255 PCM consists of: (a) a one bit polarity where 0 = positive sample value and 1 = negative sample value; (2) a three bit segment identifier(s); and (3) a four bit quantizing step identifier.

How V.90 Exploits the G.711 Operations

V.90 uses G.711 signals for the downstream channel. The key is the Uchord, a data unit that makes up a Ucode. The Ucodes are grouped into eight Ucords. For example, Ucord1 contains Ucodes 0-15, and Ucord8 contains Ucodes 112-127.

The Ucode describes the μ-law and the A-law PCM codewords. V.90 defines the codes in a table, and Table C–4 shows several Ucodes.

The idea of the V.90 digital modem is that the values do not represent the conventional analog signal. Rather, the values are symbols. The modem generates 128 of the G.711 levels in order to send at 56 kbit/s. The proof for this rate is beyond this general discussion, but using the well-known equation of:

Table C–4   Examples of V.90 PCM Codewords

Ucode	μ-law PCM	μ-law linear	A-law PCM	A-law linear
0	FF	0	D5	8
63	C0	1884	EA	2016
127	80	32124	AA	32256

$$\text{Bit/s} = R_s \log_2 N_s$$
$$\text{Bit/s/} R_s = \log_2 N_s$$
$$2^{\text{bit/s/Rs}} = N_s$$

Where: R_s = symbol rate, and N_s = number of symbols

The 128 value is obtained as:

$$2^{56,000/8,000} = N_s$$
$$N_s = 2^7$$
$$N_s = 128$$

The V.90 encoder creates data frames. Each data frame has a six-symbol organization. Each symbol in the data frame is called a data frame interval and is identified by a time index of i=0 through 5.

The actual data rate is determined during the training or rate negotiation procedures. During this time, mapping parameters are established as follows:

- Six PCM code sets, one for each data frame interval 0-5, where data frame interval i has M_i members.
- K, the number of modulus encoder input data bits per data frame.
- S_r, the number of PCM code sign bit per data frame used as redundancy for spectral shaping.
- S, the number of spectral shaper input data bits per data frame, where $S + S_r = 6$.

Based on these functions, V.90 defines the data rates achieved by different combinations of K and S during the data mode, and during Phase 4, and the rate renegotiation procedures.

In some situations, the V.90 cannot achieve the 56 kbit/s rate due to a poor quality line. Therefore, fewer levels are used. For example, a 48 kbit/s data rate requires only 2^6 levels.

For the reader who is familiar with bandwidth theory, V.90 is not violating Shannon's Law. Furthermore, by treating the quantization levels as symbols in conventional modem symbol space (combinations of QAM [quadrature amplitude modulation] amplitude and phase), many of the conventional modem techniques can be employed, such as forward error correction.

Why Not Use a 64 kbit/s Rate?

Due to FCC restrictions, the nature of codec design (DC offset problems, nonlinear distortion), difficulty of accurately determining a quantization point, etc., the achievable data rate is 56 kibt/s

Abbreviations

AAL 2   ATM Adaptation Layer type 2

ACCS   automated calling card service

ACELP   Algebraic-Code-Excited Linear-Prediction

ACKs   TCP acknowledgments

ACM   Address Complete Message

Abs   analysis-by-synthesis

ACD   automatic call distributor

A/D   analog-to-digital

ADPCM   Adaptive differential pulse code modulation

ADSL   Asymmetric Digital Subscriber Line

AIN   Intelligent Network

ANM   Answer message

API   Application Programming Interface

ASIC   application-specific itegrated circuits

ASN.1   Abstract Syntax Notation.1

ASP   Access Signal Protocol

AI   artificial intelligence

ATM   Asynchronous Transfer Mode

ATU-R   ADSL transmission unit, remote side

AVP   Attribute-Value-Pair

BA   Behavior Aggregate classifier

BC   Bearer capability

BCR   Business Communication Review

B-ISDN   broadband ISDN

BOC   Bell Operating Company

BRI   basic rate interface

BSDB   Business Service Database

CAP   Competitive access provider

C bit   cost bit

CBR   constant bit rate

CC   Contributor node

CC   contributor count

CDN   called party number

CELP   Code excited predictive linear coding

CICs   Circuit Identification Code

CID   Channel ID

CGN   calling party number

CIX   Commercial Internet Exchange

CLNP   Connectionless Network Protocol

CMSDB   Call Management Service Database

CO   central office
CO   terminating office
COT   continuity test
CP   call proceeding
CPE   Customer premises equipment
CPG   Call Progress
CPU   capacity of computers
CS   circuit switch
CS-1   Capability Set 1
CSB   circuit-switch bypass
D/A   digital-to-analog
D bit   delay bit
DCS   digital cross connect
DiffServ   Differentiated Services
DM   memory location
DNS   Domain Name System
DOD   direct outward dialing
DS   DiffServ
DSL   Digital Subscriber Line
DSU   data service unit
DSP   digital signal processor
DTE   Data Terminal Equipment
DTMF   dual-tone multi-frequency
E   extension
E800   enhanced 800
E-COM   electronic commerce
EFT   electronic funds transfer
EO   end office
ESP   Enhanced Service Provider
ET   exchange termination
FCC   Federal Communications Commission
FCS   frame check sequence
FDDI   Fiber distributed data interface
FEC   forward error correction
FFT   Fast Fourier Transform
FIN   finish message
FIR   Finite Impulse Response
FIX   Federal Internet Exchange
FM   Frequency modulation
FPGA   field-programmable gate arrays
FTP   File Transfer Protocol
GCC   Generic Conference Control

GCF   Gatekeeper Confirmation
GRQ   Gatekeeper Request
GSTN   General Switched Telephone Network
GT   Global title
HEC   Header error control
HDSL   High bit-rate Digital Subscriber Line
HF   High Frequency
HFC   Hybrid Fiber Coax
HLR   Home Location Register
IAM   Initial Address Message
ICMP   Internet Control Message Protocol
IDC   International Data Corporation
IDLC   Integrated Digital Loop Carrier System
IDSL   ISDN Digital Subscriber Line
IETF   Internet Engineering Task Force
IGMP   Internet Group Message Protocol
IMTC   International Media Teleconferencing Consortium
IN   intelligent Network
IP   packet-based protocols
IPDC   Internet Protocol Device Control
IPST   IP Signaling Transport
IR   intermediate rate
IRR   information request response
ISDN   Integrated Services Digital Network
ISDN-UP or ISUP   ISDN User Part
ISO   International Standards Organization
ISP   Internet Service Provider
ISUP   ISDN User Part
IWF   interworking function
IXC   interchange carrier
LAN   Local Area Network
LAPB   Link Access Procedure, Balanced
LAPM   Link Access Procedure for Modems

LD-CELP   Low delay CELP
LEC   Local Exchange Carrier
LI   length indicator
LIDB   Line Information Database
LPC   Linear prediction coding
LSR   last sender report
M   marker
MAC   multiple and accumulate operation
MAE   Mertropolitan Area Exchange
MAN   Metropolitan Area Network
MBONE   Multicasting backbone
MC   multipoint controller
MC   media gateway controller
MCS   Multipoint Communication Service
MCU   Multipoint Control Unit
MDF   Main distribution frame
MELP   Mixed-Excitation LPC
MG   Media gateway
MGC   Media Gateway Controller
MGCP   Media Gateway Control Protocol
MIME   Multipurpose Internet Mail Extension
MIP   millions of instructions per second
MPEG   Motion Pictures Expert Group
MOS   Mean Opinion Score
MP   Multilink Protocol
MP   Multipoint Processor
MP-MLQ   Multipulse Maximum Likelihood Quantization
MPLS   Multiprotocol Label Switching
MTP   Message Transfer Port
MTS   Message Telecommunications Service
MTU   Maximum Transmission Unit
NA   not applicable
NAP   Network Access Point
NAS   Network Access Server
NCP   Network Control Protocol
NI   network interface

NIST   National Institute of Standards and Technology
NNI   network to network interface
NNI   network node interface
NSF   National Science Foundation
NTP   Network Time Protocol
OAM   operations, administration, and maintenance
OLE   Originating local exchange
OSF   offset field
OSI   Open Systems Interconnection
OSS   Operator Service Signaling
P   parity
P   padding
PAD   Padding bytes
PBX   private branch exchange
PC   personal computer
PC   point codes
PCM   pulse code modulation
PDN   public data network
PDU   protocol data unit
PHB   per-hop-behavior
PM   memory location
POP   point of presence
POTS   plain old telephone service
PPP   Point-to-Point Protocol
PPS   packets-per-second rate
PRI   primary rate interface
PS   Packet Switch
PSTS   Public Switched Telephone System
PSVQ   predictive split vector quantizer
PT   Payload type
PTT   Postal, Telephone, and Telegraph
QAM   quadrature amplitude modulation
64-QAM   64-State QAM scheme
QCIF   Quarter Common Intermiadiate Format
QOS   Quality-of-Service
QPSK   quadrature phase-shift keyed
RA1   rate adapter 1
RA2   rate adapter 2

RAS   Registration, Admissions, and Status

RBOC   Regional Bell Operating Companies

RCF   Registration Confirmation

RDT   remote digital terminal

RDSL or RADSL   Rate Adaptive ADSL

REL   Release message

RFC   Request for Comments

RLC   ReLease Complete

RLS   Release

ROH   receiver-on-hook

ROM   read-only-memory

ROSE   Remote Operations Service Element

RPC   remote procedure call

RRQ   Registration Request

RRJ   Registration Reject

RSPG   Reliable Signaling Gateway Protocol

RST   reset message

RSVP   Resource Reservation Protocol

RT   Routing Tables

RTCP   Real-Time Control Protocol

RTP   Real-Time Protocol

RTSP   Real-Time Streaming Protocol

RTT   round trip time

S   splitter

SA   Signaling Agent

SA   Security Association

SABM   Set Asynchronous Balanced Mode

SAP   Session Announcement Protocol

SCAL   Signaling TCP Connection/IP Adaptation Layer

SCN   Switched Circuit Networks

SCP   Service Control Point

SDES   Source Description Packet

SDSL   Symmetical Digital Subscriber Line

SG   Signaling Gateway

SG&A   Sales, general, and administrative

SGMP   Simple Gateway Control Protocol

SIP   Session Initiation Protocol

SLA   Service level agreement

SLIP   Serial Link IP

SMTP   Simple Mail Transfer Protocol

SN   Sequence Number

SNA   Systems Network Architecture

SNMP   Simple Network Management Protocol

SNMP2   Simple Network Management Protocol , Version 2

SONET   Synchronous Optical Network

SPI   Security Parameter Index

SS7   Signaling System Number 7

SSP   Service Switching Point

SSN   subsystem number

SSP   Service Switching Point

ST   signaling tone

STDM   statistical TDM

STP   Signaling Transfer Point

TA   terminal adaptater

T bit   throughput bit

TASI   Time-Assigned Speech Interpolation

TCA   Traffic Conditioning Agreement

TCAP   transaction capabilities application part

TCP   Transmission Control Protocol

TDM   time division multiplexing

TE   Transit exchange

TE   terminal equipment

TFTP   Trivial File Transfer Protocol

TLE   Terminating local exchange

TOS   Type of Service

TSAP   Transport Service Access Point

TTL   time-to-live

UA   unnumbered acknowledgment

UCF   Unregister Confirm

UI   Unnumbered information

UDP   user datagram protocol

UNI   User Network Interface

URI   Unregistered Reject

URI   Uniform Resource Identifier
URQ   Unregistered Request
UUI   User-to-user indication
V   version
VBR   Variable Bit Rate
VDSL   Very-high-bit Subscriber Line
VLR   Visitor Location Register
VoATM   voice over ATM

VoFR   voice over Frame Relay
VoIP   voice over IP
VQ   Vector quantization
WAN   Wide Area Network
WDM   wave division multiplexing
XDSL   X Digital Subscriber Line
XID   exchange ID

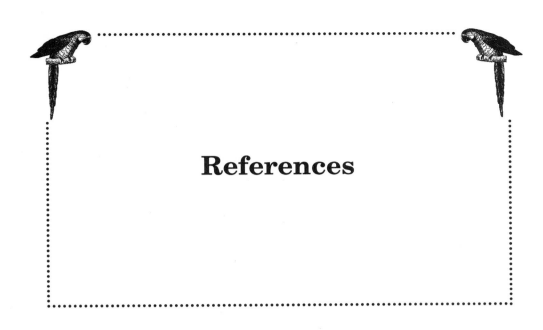

References

[STUC98] Stuck, Bart and Weingarten, Michael, "Can Carriers Make Money on IP Telephony?", *Business Communications Review*, August, 1998.

[SCHM98]. Schmelling, Sarah and Vittore, Vince. "Evolution or Revolution," *Telephony*, November 16, 1998.

[LUCA98]. Lucas, Jerry, "IP Myth vs. Reality," *Telestrategies*, September/October, 1998.

[POLE98]. Poleretsky, Zoltan. "Customer Interaction in an Electronic Commerce World," *Business Communications Review* (BCR), Nortel Supplement, January, 1999.

[RAPP98]. Rappaport, David M. "The Next Wave in Do-It-Yourself Customer Service." *Business Communications Review* (BCR), June, 1998.

[RADI94] Radhika R. Roy. "Networking constraints in Multimedia Conferencing and the Role of ATM Networks," *AT&T Technical Journal*, July/August, 1994.

[BORE97]. Borella, M. S. "Analysis of End-to-End Internet Packet Loss: Dependence and Asymmetry," *IEEE Network,* Reprint, 1997).

[PAXS97]. Paxson, Vern. IEEE/ACM Transactions on Communications, "End-to-End Routing Behavior in the Internet." Vol. 5, No. 5, October 1997.

[STEV98]. Stevens, W. Richard. *TCP/IP Illustrated*, Addison-Wesley, 1997. Mr. Steven's figure in his book (page 112) does not contain the error-check operation, which I have added in this figure.

[KRAP98] Krapf, Eric. "DSPs: Powering the Packet-Voice Revolution," *Business Communications Review's Voice 2000.* Oct. 1998.

[LAPS97]. Lapsley, Phil. *DSP Processor Fundamentals*, IEEE Press, 1997.

[CRAN97]. Crandall, Richard E. "The Challenge of Large Numbers," *Scientific American*, February, 1997.

[EYRE98] Jennifer Eyre and Jeff Bier, "DSP Processors Hit the Main Stream," *Computer*, August 1998.

[STEV98] Stevens, Jeff. "DSPs in Communications," *IEEE Spectrum*, September 1998.

[MINO98] Minoli, Daniel. *Delivering Voice over IP Networks*, John Wiley & Sons, 1998.

[WEST96] Westall, F. A., Johnston, R. D., Lewis, A. V., "Speech Technology for Telecommunications," *BT Journal*, Vol. 14, No. 1, January, 1996.

[WONG96] Wong, W. T. K., Mack, R. M., Cheetham, B. M. G., Sun, X. Q., "Low Rate Speech Coding for Telecommunications," *BT Journal*, Vol. 14., No. 1, January, 1996.

[COX98]. Cox, R. V., Hassle, B. G., Lacuna, A., Shahraray, B., and Rabiner, L., "On the Applications of Multimedia Processing to Communications," *Proceedings of the IEEE,* Vol. 86, No. 5, May 1998.

[RUDK97] Rudkin, S., Grace, A., and Whybray, M. W. "Real-Time Applications on the Internet," *BT Journal,* Vol. 15, No. 2, April 1997.

[BATE99] Bates, Bud. *Data Communications: A Business View.* Published by TCIC International, Phoenix AZ, 1999.

[GORA98]. Goralski, Walter. *ADSL and DSL Technologies*, McGraw-Hill, New York, 1998.

[WEXL98] Wexler, Joanie. "56k Modems: A Bandwidth Bird in the Hand," *Business Communications Review*, October, 1998.

[HEND96] Henderson, P. Michael. "56kbps Data Transmission Across the PSTN," A paper published by Rockwell Semiconductor Systems. No date given.

[MIER99] Mier, Edwin, E. "Voice-Over-IP: Better and Better," *Business Communications Review*, January, 1999.

[MIER98] Mier, Edwin, E. "Voice-Over-IP: Sounding Better," *Business Communications Review*, February, 1998.

[MIER99a] Mier, Edwin, E. "VoIP Gateways-Tradeoffs Affecting Voice Quality," *Business Communications Review Voice 2000*, January, 1999.

[KOST98] Kostas, T. J., Borella, M. S., Sidhu, I., Shuster, G. M., Grabiec, J., and Mahler, J. of a 3Com, paper "Real-Time Voice Over Packet Switched Networks, *IEEE Network,* January, February 1998.

[VAND98] Vandenameele, Jozef. "Requirements for the Reference Point ('N') between Media Gateway Controller and Media Gateway," *Draft-vandenameele-tiphon-arch-gway-decomp-00.txt*, November 1988.

[ARAN98] Arango, Mauricio, Huitema, Christian. Simple Gateway Control Protocol (SGCP), Internet Engineering Task Force draft-huitema-sgcp-va-o2.txt.

[ARAN98a] Arango, Mauricio, Dugan, Andrew, Elliott, Isacc, Huitema, Christian, Pickett, Scott. Media Gateway Control Protocol (MGCP). Internet Engineering Task Force draft-huitema-MGCP-v0r1–01.txt

[TAYL98] Taylor, P. Tom, Calhoun, Pat R., Rubens, Allan C. IPDC Base Protocol. Internet Engineering Task Force. Draft-taylor-Ipdc-99.txt.

[HUIT98a] Huitema, Christina , Andreasen, Flemming, Arango, Mauricio, "Media Gateway Control Protocol (MGCP) Call Flows." Draft-huitema-mgcp-flows-00.txt, November 11, 1998.l.

[GREE98] Greene, Nancy. SS7-Internet Internetworking-Architectural Framework. Draft-green-ss7-arch-frame-01.txt., 1998.

[DALI98]. Dalias, R. Bay Networks SS7-Internet Gateway Architecture. Draft-ong-ss7-internet-gateway-01.txt., 1998.

[HOLD98]. Holdrege, Matt. Reliable Signaling Gateway Protocol (RSGP). Draft-ong-rsgp-ss7-info-00.txt., 1998.

[MATO99]. Matousek, J. and Ong, L. Bay Networks SS7-Internet Access Signaling Protocol. draft-long-ss7-signal-00.txt., 1998

[MA99]. Ma, Gene. H.323 Signaling and SS7 ISUP Gateway: Procedure Interworking. Draft-ma-h323-isup-gateway-00.txt., 1999.

[MCGR98] McGrew, Michael. Transport SS7 Signaling, Over IP. Internet Draft draft-mc-grew-tss7s-00.txt.,1998.

[THOM96]. Thomas, Stephen A. *IPng and TCP/IP Protocols.* New York: John Wiley & Sons, Inc, 1996.

[CASZ97] Annex A of H.225.0 and *Foundation of Digital Signal Processing and Data Analysis,* by J. A. Caszow, MacMillan, New York, 1997.

[CHEN98] Cheng, P. C., Garay, J. A., Herzberg, A., Krawczyk H., "A Security Architecture for the Internet Protocol" *IBM System Journal,* Vol. 37, No. 1, 1998.

[CALH98a] Calhoun, Pat R. DIAMETER Framework Document, Draft-calhoun-diameter-framework-01.txt.

[CALH98b]. Calhoun, Pat R., et al. DIAMETER User Authentication Extensions. Draft-calhoun-diameter-authent-04.txt.

[CALH98c]. Calhoun, Pat R., et al. DIAMETER Base Protocol. Draft-calhoun-diameter-03.txt.

[TAYL98]. Taylor, Tom. IPDC Protocol, Draft-ipdc-00.txt., July , 1998.

[BELL98]. Bell, Bob, IPDC Device Management Protocol, Draft-bell-ipdc-signaling-00.txt.

[CLAR97].Clark, D. and Wroclawski, J. "An Approach to Service Allocation in the Internet," Draft-clark-diff-svc-alloc-00.txt.

[FR.1197] "Voice over Frame Relay Implementation Agreement," Frame Relay Forum Document number FRF.11, 1997.

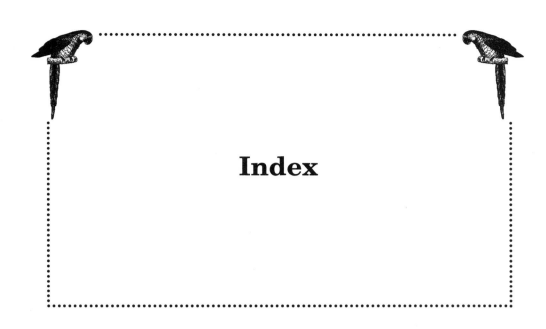

Index

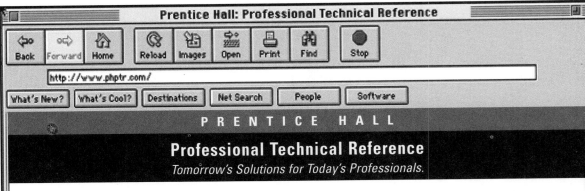

PRENTICE HALL

Professional Technical Reference
Tomorrow's Solutions for Today's Professionals.

Keep Up-to-Date with

PH PTR Online!

We strive to stay on the cutting-edge of what's happening in professional computer science and engineering. Here's a bit of what you'll find when you stop by **www.phptr.com**:

@ **Special interest areas** offering our latest books, book series, software, features of the month, related links and other useful information to help you get the job done.

Deals, deals, deals! Come to our promotions section for the latest bargains offered to you exclusively from our retailers.

$ **Need to find a bookstore?** Chances are, there's a bookseller near you that carries a broad selection of PTR titles. Locate a Magnet bookstore near you at www.phptr.com.

! **What's New at PH PTR?** We don't just publish books for the professional community, we're a part of it. Check out our convention schedule, join an author chat, get the latest reviews and press releases on topics of interest to you.

✉ **Subscribe Today!** **Join PH PTR's monthly email newsletter!**

Want to be kept up-to-date on your area of interest? Choose a targeted category on our website, and we'll keep you informed of the latest PH PTR products, author events, reviews and conferences in your interest area.

Visit our mailroom to subscribe today! **http://www.phptr.com/mail_lists**